ACCEPTABLE COSTS:

PLANTING THE CHURCH IN DAHOMEY
1946 TO 1975

by

Colin S. McDougall
and
Edna M. McDougall

Wipf & Stock
PUBLISHERS
Eugene, Oregon

Wipf and Stock Publishers
199 W 8th Ave, Suite 3
Eugene, OR 97401

Acceptable Costs
Planting the Church in Dahomey, 1946 to 1975
By McDougall, Colin S. and McDougall, Edna M.
Copyright©2005 by McDougall, Colin S.
ISBN: 1-59752-134-5
Publication date 3/31/2005

Dedicated to the memory and service of Stewart (1910 - 1966) and Edna (1914 - 2004) McDougall

Table of Contents

Foreword

Introduction

Part III: Building The Church

Part IV: Perspective: Thirty Years Later

Foreword

Jesus Christ taught His disciples to count the cost of discipleship. Disciples in the 21st Century also need this lesson. It costs to serve Him. It costs to reach out to men and women with physical and material help. It costs to carry Christ's message of salvation.

The book of Acts tells us that the early disciples "hazarded their lives for the gospel's sake." This book reminds us vividly that we follow the same precarious path. Here is the story of what it cost to plant the church of Jesus Christ amongst various tribes in the country of Benin. It tells of death; death by drowning; death by car accident; death by train wreck and the heroic action of a missionary to save others; death by serious disease—all truly dedicated missionaries. The loss of each, at the time, seemed to be a serious blow and caused many to wonder at God's ways.

Why do missionaries take such risk? Shouldn't they pull back in the face of lethal disease and other physical dangers? These are legitimate questions with no easy answer. With Judas, we are tempted to ask, "Why this waste?"

The stories recorded here show us that these workers did not risk their lives capriciously. When each of the recorded incidents took place, the missionaries were in their places, convinced that they were doing what God wanted them to do. They knew what risks there were to them as humans. They also knew that if God called them home in the midst of it all, it would be in His will, which to them was more important than life itself.

These missionaries entered into risk because God, who is the ultimate sender and administrator of Missions, sent them into it. The Christian life is like being in a hurricane. Those who lie down may not even understand the nature of the storm. Those who stand are battered by the tempest. We do not understand now all the details of this invisible war in which we are engaged. We do feel its effects.

As long as the battle rages, there will be those who will give themselves to it and those who will die in so doing. These are the ones who remember that Jesus taught His disciples that "no one, having put his hand to the plow, and looking back, is fit for the kingdom of God."

The title of this book shows the heart attitude of those who paid so dearly to bring the Gospel to Benin. Ultimately, it was worth it all and the costs were acceptable. This is seen at the end of the book in the *Union of Evangelical Churches of Benin* (UEEB), this denomination representing the various tribes whose stories are recorded here. The vision of Stewart and Edna McDougall and all the other missionaries whose stories are recorded here has been realized. The church stands in spite of all the heart-ache and hardship.

You hold in your hand a record of the partial fulfillment of a direct prophecy of our Lord Himself. Shortly before His transfiguration, Jesus revealed a new truth to His disciples. He told them He would build His church, and nothing would hinder it. He also told them He would do it through them. He gave them the authority and the responsibility to do the task. The church of Jesus Christ today is being built through people like Peter, James and Paul, but also through the likes of these stalwart missionaries. I trust that reading this part of history will challenge all of us to renewed effort and sacrifice. It will be worth it all when we see Him. The sacrifice is acceptable.

Ian M. Hay, D. Miss.

SIM International Director Emeritus

Introduction

When I was a small boy and a house guest would recount their adventures, my mother's response was often, "You ought to write a book!" It seemed to her that one ought not keep lessons learned from a rich experience to oneself. She felt obligated somehow to make the story of the history of the church plant in Dahomey/Benin a matter of public record. The writing for posterity would give meaning and perspective to future generations.

Edna started her research and collection of data when she returned to the U.S. in 1966 and it absorbed her thoughts for almost forty years. Her greatest goal was to present the church in Benin with an eye witness account of its history. She spent many months at different intervals searching and making copies in the SIM archives in Toronto and in Charlotte and solicited many friends and family over the years to assist her. Dr. Jean Soutar worked with her on her notation. Her daughter, Janet, spent countless hours trying to collate her files and record her writing on the computer. Her grandson, Colin Jr. and his wife Becca, were a great help. They interviewed Grandma Edna and wrote out her memories of events which make up most of Part II. She could tell the stories but had great difficulty writing them down.

She suffered her first stroke in March, 1997, and subsequently had to be moved to the SIM Retirement Center in Sebring, Florida, to be sure of appropriate care. She now had all her time to devote to the project but found that her mind was now unable to do the work. I assured her that if she did the research and provided a written account of her thoughts and recollections, I would complete the writing and publishing of the book. After her funeral in May, 2004, I brought home six full boxes of documents, letters, copies of articles and random notes in her hand-writing along with several smaller boxes full of pictures. It has absorbed my energies and cost much more than time as I read through my parents' love letters, letters to my parents I wrote when I was eight or ten years old, hundreds of letters to and from my parents and seemingly endless quarterly station reports required of missionaries.

I generally used her recollections as a starting point but quickly discovered that her memory was faulty, so I relied primarily on the official station reports and official correspondence to and from mission leaders for detail and their passports for precise dating. Missionary letters often were not dated so collateral evidence was needed to be able to rely on them for important information.

I am indebted to Dr. Howard Dowdell for his suggestion that the book be presented as a case study to be available for schools of mission and agencies. That required much rewriting and planning but proved to be an important dimension of the book.

My deepest appreciation goes to Pastor Gabriel Doko who left his extremely busy schedule and a sick wife to come to North Carolina for a month to assist in getting the geography, spellings and picture identifications accurate. Dr. Ian M. Hay, General Director Emeritus of SIM, kindly offered suggestions through difficult places in the writing and has added his "Foreword" for the book. He was also the founding chairman of Eternal Truth Ministries of North Carolina and remains a valued friend. My sister, Janet, has guided and facilitated the whole process from setting up and maintaining Mother's files to making all the software cooperate, helping with research and arranging all the graphics. My wife, Jinny, has patiently and persistently suffered the thankless and stressful job of proof-reading. Finally, I must express my sincere appreciation to all the retired missionaries who kindly took my phone calls and answered my e-mails with corrections, information, suggestions and helpful pictures.

The book was written with four significant audiences in mind: 1) the church in Benin for which such a high cost was paid; 2) the families who paid the high personal costs; 3) those engaged in discussing and planning future church planting endeavors; 4) my family. Perhaps you, the reader, don't fit in any of those categories but, just as I have been reading many letters not intended for me personally with great profit, I trust you also will benefit from reading what was intended for others.

Colin S. McDougall

Robbinsville, North Carolina

December, 2004

List of Abbreviations

BIOLA   Originally, the Bible Institute of Los Angeles, renamed BIOLA College and became Biola University in 1981.

DS   Designation in SIM for District Superintendent, later called "field leader."

ECWA   SIM related church in Nigeria.

EFMA/IFMA: International Associations of mission agencies.

ELWA   SIM radio station located in Liberia.

EMS   Evangelical Mission Society: the missions arm of ECWA.

FWA   French West Africa.

MK   Missionary Kid.

RC   Roman Catholic missions.

SIL   Summer Institute of Linguistics, training arm of Wycliffe Bible Translators.

SIM   Originally Sudan Interior Mission, now SIM International.

UEEB   SIM related churches in Benin.

WEC   World Evangelization Crusade.

WCC   World Council of Churches also referred to as ICCC.

Part I:

In the Fullness of Time

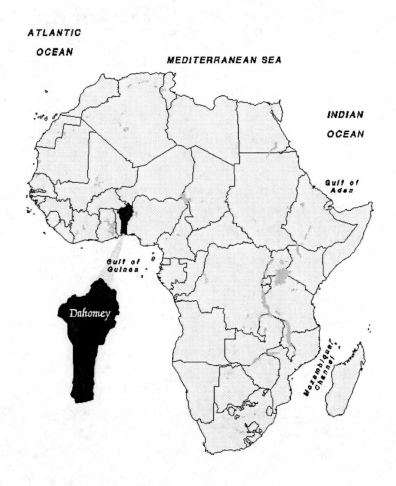

Historical Reference Points for the Early Mission Work in Dahomey

I. Political History

1904:	Dahomey declared colony of France under the federation of French West Africa.
1940-1944:	France occupied by Germany changing relationship and administration of the colonies to France.
1944:	Conference of Brazzaville ended French colonialism and formed the French Union.
May 8, 1945:	World War II ended.
1958:	Dahomey proclaimed a republic.
1960:	Dahomey gained independence and three presidents: Maga, Apithy & Ahomadegbe.
1972:	Military coup led by Matthieu Kérékou: formed a Marxist-Leninist government.
1975:	Dahomey changed its name to Benin.

II. Mission History

A. S.I.M. Leadership: General Directors.

1893-1942	Rowland V. Bingham.
1944-1957	Guy W. Playfair (Field Dir. 1917-44).
1957-1962	Albert D. Helser.
1962-1975	Raymond J. Davis.
1975-1993	Ian M. Hay.

B. Federation of Protestant Missions.

C. Planning and Planting.

1914:	Bingham's expression of concern for Dahomey.
1929:	E. F. Rice's travel and expression of concern.

1934:	Playfair's expression of concern.
1931-1944:	Kapp's persistent efforts from Niger.
1944:	Playfair urges Osborne to scout the country and make recommendations.
1944:	Trip and report of trip through Dahomey to field council by Osborne and Strong.
1945:	Kapp applied for permission to open mission work.
May, 1946:	Kapp visited governor of Dahomey.
October, 1946:	Permission granted to open mission stations at Kandi and Nikki. Morrows move to Kandi.
March, 1947:	McDougalls move to Nikki.
August, 1948:	Linguist Dr. Welmers in Nikki to assist in a Bariba grammar.
January, 1949:	Stewart McDougall challenged the assembly of the annual Yoruba Church conference at Egbe, Nigeria, to send missionaries to Dahomey and three trained pastors responded.
1949:	Parakou opened by J.B. Williams.
1950:	Djougou opened by Ed Morrow.
1951:	Sinendé opened by Earl Playfairs.
1952:	Dompago opened by Roland Pickering.
1952:	Tchaourou opened by Orville Thamers.
1952:	N'dali opened by Nigerian missionary Elisha Olu.
February, 1953:	Dogon Yaro evangelistic outreach among Fulanis began.
1954:	Ségbana opened by Bob Blaschke.

1956:	Tchatchou church built and Nigerian missionary pastor Amos Ayorinde began ministry.
1959:	Simpéru opened by Oswald Zobrists.
1960:	Bembèrèkè opened by Dr. and Mrs. Dreisbach.
1961:	Dogon Yaro and family began ministry in Tchatchou and opened the Fulani Bible School.
July 3, 1961:	Bembèrèkè hospital dedication included President Maga.
1962:	Major crises in the Parakou and Djougou churches.
February, 1966:	Yves Perrier evangelistic campaign in Cotonou. Death by drowning of Stewart McDougall and Gus Fredlund.
1967:	Guest House in Cotonou opened by Orville Thamers.
May 30,1967:	Biafran War of secession began in Nigeria.
January 15, 1970:	Biafran War ended.
October, 1974:	Death of Rowland Pickering in auto accident.
November, 1974:	Death of Alan Gibbs in train accident.
1975:	Tchatchou occupied by S.I.M. missionaries, the Radlingmayrs.
May 23, 1975:	Founding of the UEEB (Union of Evangelical Churches in Benin) with Pastor Gabriel Doko as its first President.

Chapter 1: Mission Accepted

The founder of the Sudan Interior Mission, Dr. Bingham, a man of great vision, heard the call of the unreached peoples of Dahomey before the First World War. Over the years he spoke of the urgency of sending missionaries to them. He referred to this need in his book <u>Seven Sevens of Years</u> (1943). In a letter addressed to French West Africa Field Director, David Osborne in November, 1929, pioneer missionary, E. F. Rice (stationed at Zinder, Niger) wrote:

> Now what you say about Dahomey interests me. You know I passed through Dahomey on my way down. I came through Gaya, Kandi and Parakou . . . Sairé (Savé) and Cotonou through to Porto Novo and then to Lagos.
> After one leaves Kandi going South the population increases in number. After Parakou the people seem to be Yorubas. There is (sic) no missionaries at Savé but there is one about 40 miles south of Savé. . . .
> I really think Dahomey a great field to occupy.

Many were aware and some were deeply concerned for the need but nothing seemed to happen. Refusals and delays were the story of S.I.M.'s work in French Territory. Mr. Playfair (then West Africa Field Director) recorded the mood of those times when he wrote in the December 1934 <u>Sudan Witness</u>:

> We have been disappointed in our plans for going forward in French Territory. It seems that favour has been shown to the Roman Catholics and we had a refusal of our application for a site at Dogon Dutsi [Niger], in the Mauri tribe. We have been restricted in our labours among the Touareg people also and we ask for prayer that there may be a more favourable attitude to our mission work so that we may be able to enter the Maori tribe of 65,000, that we may be allowed to open Diapaga [Haute Volta], about 150 miles east of Fada n'Gourma [Haute Volta] in the Gourma tribe, and that we may secure greater liberty in reaching the Touareg people. We are also keeping before us the hope of

entering Taouha [Niger], the largest town in the colony, directly North of Sokoto.

A 1935 Sudan Witness editorial explains further that "The refusal of a site at Dogan Dutsi in the Maouri tribe has been confirmed and that door is definitely closed to us as a Mission for the present. The R.C.'s, however, have been given a place and a building."

One of Mr. Playfair's first actions as General Director was to urge a trip to explore the possibilities of opening a work in Dahomey. Such a trip was made early in 1944, a year after the death of Dr. Bingham. Missionaries David Osborne and Bill Strong made an extended tour of French West Africa which included Northern Dahomey. Mr Osborne described the experiences this way in the Sudan Witness of July 1944:

> Soon after passing the border into Dahomey we crossed a fairly large river reputed to be the watering place of crocodiles, hippos, elephants, etc. Of smaller wild game such as gazelle there seemed to be no end.
>
> For hours we passed through country peopled by the Berba tribe numbering about 17,000. . . . Soon we entered the territory of another tribe of about 56,000. These are Sombas and a very warlike people. All the men carry bows and poisoned arrows when away from home, and it seems they use them freely, not only on wild animals, but on each other.
>
> Soon we began to climb the Atakora Mountains which rise to a height of nearly 2,000 feet...climbing steadily into these beautiful, wooded hills by a well formed and graded road, we rejoiced in the glories of God's fair creation. It seemed as though we were suddenly transported into another world. It would be difficult to find any place more beautiful than these hills in any part of Nigeria.
>
> Near the summit is Natitangou, the administrative centre, where reside several Frenchmen. It is also a large market centre and for that reason, thousands of Sombas were gathered from surrounding towns and villages. Here, too, is a well established Roman Catholic Mission.
>
> From Natitangou our course lay due east. Soon we descended to the plains. This country is also thickly populated by another tribe, called by the French the

Baribas. They call themselves Bargou people and their original tribal center is Nikki. They cover a wide area extending far to the south of where we traveled, but it would seem that there are about 150,000 in this district. They are pagans living and farming in much the same style as the Hausas. It is evident Islam is already having a strong influence on them.

We passed on up to Kandi and from there to Gaya, where we ferried across the Niger. For the whole area of Northern Dahomey at least four stations are needed, and needed at once. Three new languages would have to be learned to adequately give the gospel to the people.

The door is open wide. Never have we known the French officials to show a more sympathetic and friendly attitude towards us and our work. God has wonderfully answered the many prayers sent up over a period of at least ten years for the creating of this very attitude and the opening of these very doors.

Osborne's rejoicing over their findings and the wide open door reflected a lifting of his long-carried burden.

In 1953 Newton Kapp reviewed these early times in the January edition of the Sudan Witness.

The work in FWA [French West Africa] is almost 30 years old and for a long time it faced a real obstacle in that we were unwanted by the authorities. For in FWA our workers were often misunderstood, particularly since few knew much French and through adverse propaganda they were treated as spies. Because of this by 1940 we had been able to open only three stations.

From 1931 to 1945 there was little occupying of new lands. Each time we applied for a station it was refused, political or religious reasons being claimed for their opposition. In 1940 Maradi was opened and at the same time the government seriously considered allowing us to start a leper work in the Niger. The war hindered this realization.

Indeed World War II was the hindering factor in the forties, almost totally occupying government officials and influencing all decisions. The collapse of France came in June of 1940. During 1940-44 France was in the hands of the Germans and the colonies were very involved in the war effort. Encyclopedia Britannica reports, ". . . It was only from the

colonies and with their resources that General Charles de
Gaulle and his associates could continue the fight."

The ending of the war at midnight of May 8, 1945
cleared away many of the problems confronting S.I.M.'s
entrance. Alert to the situation, Newton Kapp applied to the
governor of Dahomey for permission to open work in the North.
He then followed it up with a visit to the governor in May,
1946.

In the meantime, Stewart McDougall's call had been
clear. He was teaching at Igbaja Bible School in Nigeria at the
time. On his trips to Ilorin as S.I.M. District Superintendent,
he often had business with the British District Officer. On one
particular occasion the District Officer described a recent trip
he had made to Dahomey and the desperate situation of the
people there. As Stewart returned home to Igbaja, he kept
turning over and over in his mind thoughts of the Dahomey
peoples, their neighbors just across the border, and of their
need for the Gospel.

Together Stewart and Edna prayed about the
missionary responsibility of the Yoruba believers who had the
Gospel for more than forty years and now had well founded
churches. Stewart envisioned the Yoruba Church sending
young men to these unreached people. He started emphasizing
in the classroom the clear command of our Lord to take the
gospel to those who had never heard. Some students caught
the vision and joined the McDougalls in prayerful concern as
they lifted up their eyes and looked beyond the border.

Stewart was strongly impressed that he should lead the
way, so he made request to the Field Council in May, 1945, for
permission to go to Dahomey after their upcoming furlough
(December, 1945–January, 1947). God's leading was clearly
seen in the timing of their request, for Mr. Osborne had
completed his exploratory trip and his report on the wide open
door was before the Council also. The Council approved the

McDougalls' request and they began planning for their new assignment. After their furlough, their plan was to proceed to Dahomey and open a station in Nikki twelve miles across the Nigerian border.

While the McDougalls were on furlough in the U.S. and Canada acquainting their churches with their move from Nigeria to Dahomey, they asked special prayer for key men to be prepared and come forward to help them find their way into the hearts of the people.

During this year progress was being made in the mission's application to enter the country but permission from the French colonial government had not yet come. In October of 1946, as Newton Kapp prepared to leave on his visitation tour of the western stations, he decided to extend his trip to include Dahomey (January 1947 report). He and his party, including Ed Morrow, started their journey of 2000 miles on the afternoon of October 4. They stopped by the post office in Maradi, Niger, to pick up a registered letter. The letter contained the long awaited permits to open stations in Nikki and Kandi. After waiting and watching the mails for over nine months, the letter arrived on this day! Encouraged by this affirmation from the Lord they started their trip with gratitude and praise. On the 12th day they reached Kandi and Mr. Morrow rejoiced to be in the land of his prayers. The administrator welcomed them and the work began. Further south in Nikki the missionaries reported a "royal reception".

These positive reports of warm welcomes and cordial receptions reflected the changes in government attitudes resulting from the outcome of the war in Europe. There was a new political system based on the decisions reached at the Conference of Brazzaville in 1944. These decisions ended colonialism and resulted in the formation of the French Union which included the Republic and all overseas territories. Each colony of French West Africa became a territory and each territory a member of the Federation of FWA.

Dahomey now had a share in her own government. There was a council which elected its own executive. However their movements were closely monitored and heavily supervised. There was a resident French Commandant in all larger towns and the military was still very much in evidence.

The McDougalls entered Nikki in March of 1947 by way of Ilorin and Kaiama. Even as far north as Nikki this climate of change and adjustment prevailed. Some changes that caught their attention included the increase of Muslim influence and the movement of the youth to the cities looking for jobs which resulted in the breaking of former patterns of ancestral life and customs. Communist propaganda also caused disquiet along with a thirst for independence, status and affluence. They heard rumbles from the city centers in the South, but, for the moment, these influences were only mildly felt in the North.

The McDougalls' orientation into this new country and their understanding of the times was greatly aided by the S.I.M. being a part of the Federation of Protestant Missions in FWA. The three mission agencies in Dahomey were Methodists, Assemblies of God and S.I.M. The Federation was headquartered in Dakar, Senegal, and representatives from each mission attended their periodic meetings. All plans for mission advance required the approval of the Federation and agreement of all members. Geographical boundaries were set which determined all mission movements for the purpose of witness and church planting.

Dr. Keller (Methodist Mission) was the head of the Federation in 1950 and, at the meeting of delegates that year, explained that his work was to build bridges between the Protestant missions and the government administrations. The service he rendered brought him into constant contact with officials and ceremonies where he had opportunity for unofficial conversations. So it was very reassuring when he said, "I meet everywhere in administrative spheres much good will, and the desire to help missionary activities to be integrated into the general social work of the colony."

He also had counsel especially directed to American missionaries concerning conduct in the country in light of the times. There was a spirit of mistrust abroad and he advised candidly how to walk carefully and avoid suspicion and pointed out areas of sensitivity.

The missionaries welcomed his wise counsel since it was their desire as well to walk circumspectly and not hinder the impact of the message they came to bring.

Dr. Keller and his successor, Mr. Benignus, visited in the McDougall home from time to time blessing the work with their sincere interest. They kept mission leaders abreast of the shifts and changes in government procedures and attitudes. Their gracious and encouraging attitudes helped to create a spirit of openness and acceptance for the McDougalls and their entry into Dahomey.

Stewart and Edna returned to their previous home in the Yoruba district to gather some belongings and say their good-byes. They were sent on their way with many expressions of sadness and promises of continued prayer and support from the Yoruba church family. So with encouragement, much prayer and support, they made the difficult arrangements for transport and left for Dahomey.

The journey from Nigeria to Dahomey in March, 1947, was wrenching for the McDougalls since they were leaving the people they loved and a work they had enjoyed for ten years. They took only a few things since they were going into French territory and a totally unknown situation. Besides, the road was uncertain and Stewart had agreed, in negotiating with the lorry driver, that he was responsible only to take them as far as possible.

They were accompanied by their two youngest children, Murray (3½ years old) and Janet (22 months), so it was a tremendous relief to be able to get all the way through to Nikki.

Nikki was the government center of a large subdivision and the tribal center for the Bariba people. It had a population of 50,000 people who were made up of many different ethnic groups. The majority of these were Baribas and most of the others understood Bariba and could be evangelized using this language. The people were considered animist but in most villages one could find a mosque and a small group of professing Muslims. The Baribas, who were professing Muslims, were not fanatical and were mostly open to the gospel.

The French Commandant in Nikki was most gracious in his reception and invited the family to move into the government guest house. Soon after, an old man trained in cooking by the French was eager to work for the missionaries. He knew where to find the food provisions they needed and how to prepare it. His offer was welcome since Edna's years of experience in Nigeria hadn't included cooking over an open fire or baking in a mud oven. This man, appropriately called "Koukou", became a friend and stayed with the family wherever they lived in Dahomey for nearly twenty years.

The land designated for the missionaries to occupy was uncleared so Stewart's priority was obvious. There were no building crews to hire, no lumber supply, no cement, no tools—just a pioneer missionary family on their own. They were operating under the direction of S.I.M.'s French West Africa office and whenever any missionary asked why this or that, the response was always, "This is how it is for pioneers."

Both Stewart and Edna were conversant in Yoruba and Stewart had some French, but Bariba was an unwritten language and a tremendous challenge. The language had to be their first ministry priority. Yoruba-speaking Baribas helped them communicate. One interpreted for Stewart as he visited in the villages and preached in the market places and another acted as informant in their attempts to unravel the language. The building and language activities occupied them almost completely over a long period of time.

At first the Baribas did not know what to make of these strange folk. They had been quite accustomed to the French military making their demands and some wondered if they were military folk. Yoruba traders had come in from Nigeria and settled there so some decided they had come to Dahomey for commercial reasons. The missionaries' greatest daily challenge was finding acceptance for themselves and the message they brought. The best way proved to be simply doing each day whatever making a home for themselves demanded. Whatever it was, they had an audience—always.

Soon after their arrival, Gus Fredlund, a missionary experienced in working in French territory, joined them for a couple of months and assisted Stewart in becoming acquainted with government offices and regulations, learning the postal system and where to obtain supplies. Mostly, however, Stewart's time was occupied with the men who were clearing the land and preparing for building.

There were no materials available for building so Stewart had to make many trips to Ilorin in Nigeria. They had no vehicle, so he rode his bicycle the seventy dangerous miles through what the Africans called "lion country". Sometimes he would catch a lorry part of the way. From Nigeria he brought in a Yoruba building crew as well as a crew of sawyers to cut the lumber. All cement and supplies had to be imported from Nigeria and the missionaries were grateful to be allowed to bring them in.

Their first project was a mud-brick, two-room house much like the local people had with no foundation, no windows,

no doors–just mats. They put this building up quickly so the
family could move onto the land and not wear out their
welcome at the government residence. The Bariba chief of
N'dari and town leaders came daily to watch the progress.
Baba N'dari spoke Yoruba and often joined Stewart and Edna
in observing the work. One day as they were visiting, the chief
suddenly jumped up yelling when one of the Yoruba building
crew struck a Bariba laborer. He cried, "Our fathers used to eat
your fathers," revealing the depth of feeling between the tribes
and another brick in the wall that needed to be broken down.
Baba became a dear friend of the family and called for the
missionaries when he was dying, assuring them that he would
see them in heaven one day.

God, in His wise directing of their affairs, held up their
baggage for months and months; neither did He provide a
vehicle; and funds were delayed to build their house. As a
consequence, they lived very, very close to the people. Edna
planted a large garden, blessed of God with an abundant crop,
which she shared with their neighbors. In return, their
neighbors brought her eggs and produce from their farms.

Edna visited in their homes and the women soon started
visiting her. The women's lives were busy so she visited with
them at the dye pots, under the tree where they made shea
butter from the nuts, or on the large rocks where they dried the
peppers and okra.

By the time the missionary house was completed, the
people felt very possessive of the family and would bring folk to
"come see our house." When the loads finally arrived, the
people all rejoiced with them and especially admired the wood
stove with its oven, the virtues of which Koukou untiringly
demonstrated to curious and chattering audiences. Soon the
McDougalls received a pick-up truck sent out by a church in
Oregon. As anticipated, all their friends needed a ride
somewhere to show off "our truck".

At the end of March, 1949, the McDougall family was restored when their two older sons, Colin and Donald, who had been in school at the Gowans Home for Missionaries' Children in Canada, were able to join them. The Baribas understood their joy and welcomed the boys, calling them by their given tribal names. The family felt settled and had a sense of belonging.

Pioneer missionary, Tommy Titcombe, who had taken the gospel to the Yoruba people in 1908, visited the family in Nikki soon after they were settled there. He was their dear friend and Stewart's mentor whose wise counsel was always treasured. When he said, "Stewart, I do not know why you insist on 'planting' when you could be 'reaping'", they seriously reevaluated their move but reaffirmed the rightness of their decision. God had strongly affirmed them through the joyous response of their prayer warrior, Miss Frances Boyce, children's editor for the <u>Christian Herald</u> in London. Miss Boyce had taught Stewart as a child in Canada and had followed him with special interest through the years. Her generous gift had provided much of his transportation money in 1934. When he visited her in London en route to Nigeria he wrote: "I never saw anyone in all my life keep up the pace Miss Boyce does, and she expects everyone else to do likewise. In her day I don't believe one minute is wasted. Her whole life and substance is being spent for Missions. She hasn't much money to give so she goes to different missions and does typing and all such work. With her it is surely a case of 'spend and be spent.'"

In responding to Stewart's going to Dahomey Miss Boyce had explained that she began asking God to send someone to Dahomey in 1914 after she had read an article by an explorer who had traveled through there describing the need. It seemed to her very fitting that the Holy Spirit should now, thirty-five years later, send a man she had taught when he was a child and later supported as a missionary with both her prayers and finances. Surely the Lord of the harvest had been brooding over Dahomey for many years and was putting His team together. It was good to be part of it. All doubts about God's leading were put to rest.

Prior to coming to Nikki in 1947, the McDougalls had spent a year in the U.S. and Canada acquainting supporting churches of their move from Nigeria to Dahomey. They joined in a company of prayer for a continued open door, ready acceptance by the people and a special request for key men to be prepared and come forward to help them find their way into the hearts of the people.

This pioneer field with unwritten languages was not just a great challenge, it was overwhelming. The study of linguistics was still developing, and the missionaries' short course at BIOLA had only been an introduction–just enough to reveal their inadequacy. They were very aware of what was required due to their contacts with the Wycliffe movement through the Church of the Open Door in Los Angeles. Dr. Eugene Nida encouraged them to go ahead, make a start and call for help when needed.

Chapter 2: Politics and Strategies

S.I.M. was part of the Federation of Protestant Missions of French West Africa. This organization was very helpful in the pioneer missionaries' orientation into life in the colony. The Bureau of the Federation was at Dakar; leaders from each Protestant Mission attended their periodic meetings and the "delegué" visited Nikki station from time to time. His visits were most welcome and encouraging to the McDougalls.

Dr. Keller was the "delegué" in 1950 and his words about his purpose as well as the information on political issues reveals the climate of these times. Excerpts from a paper entitled "Note about the political organization of the 'Union Française'" follow.

> In the beginning and at the base of the new political system on the Union Française, is the Conférence of Brazzaville (1944). This Conference was partly an answer to those who after the Atlantic Pact reproached France for keeping her colonies in tutelage. There was also the fact that promises had been made to populations who had been engaged in the war effort during the occupation of France, promises which they wanted to keep; the recommendations of the Conference of Brazzaville agreed with the predominant tendencies of the French colonization and confirmed the liberal mentality of the French.
>
> The Conference of Brazzaville has declared openly that the end of French colonization is the liberty of individuals but not autonomy. They want to give each man, whatever may be his origin, the same liberty and the same rights as to metropolitan French, to make them become responsible members of the Union Française, but they exclude the possibility of disaggregating the whole: 'the end of the civilization work of France in its colonies removes every idea of autonomy, of evolution out of the French block; the eventual and even remote constitution of Self-Government in the colonies is to be removed.' So says the preamble of the recommendations of the conference.

Yet, since the Conference of Brazzaville, the situation has changed in some way and a more supple attitude has been adopted, in which two tendencies–assimilation and federalism–are manifested. In fact, if the concrete attitude is rather an assimilating one, the doctrine is not fixed and the Constitution has not taken a definitive position in the matter: the two tendencies subsist: A. O. F. is a 'Territoire d'Outre-Mer" and for this reason rather turned towards Assimilation, but following the evolution of populations, it may become an "État Associé", and in this case the federalistic tendency will predominate.

It is important to understand the actual attitude of French Administration towards the Africans. Its aim is to establish democracy, but a democracy in connection with France; every inhabitant of the 'Territoires d'Outre-Mer' shall be able to become a citizen of the 'Union Française'.

He explained how the government of France planned to govern the colonies, some ambivalence inherent in their policies and the objections of other governments to the insistence of the French government to hold onto its colonies. He explained the role of the federation and its role as liaison between the missionaries and the colonial officials. Behind his description of the colonial French bureaucracy was the old world view of the relationship between missionaries and colonial expansion. France, Spain, Portugal, etc. had encouraged missionary advance into new territories in Africa, North America and South America as the spearhead of pacification and colonization followed up by military presence and colonial administration. The competition for colonies had dominated European politics for two centuries. It was no wonder that French colonials would be suspect of American missionaries wanting entry into its colonies when it felt most vulnerable.

Then in a separate paper he spoke from his heart:

. . . But the main work of the 'délégué' is probably to build bridges, to help to a better comprehension of the purposes and means between the Protestant Missions and the Administration. . . .

We must mention that in spite of their gratitude for the Marshall help, some people are afraid of an economical and even political influence of the United States. On this point, there is a great sensitiveness and you must know it. They have decided to give freedom to Africans but not a whole independence, and they do not want them to be dazzled by the American wealth and perhaps to have the idea of parting from France.

This explains the reason why you are especially watched; by your being and way of living, you bring in some way America with you, and this arouses suspicions. These are facts; we can do nothing against them; they come from the principles of French policy and from the spirit of mistrust existing in the world of today. We must consider them. Unfortunately, this state of spirit causes a psychosis which is used and increased by those who want to be prejudicial to Protestant Missions, or by narrow-minded people. Here is the source of an always reviving propaganda according to which American Missions do a work of economic spying, give the U.S.A. consulate information about the subsoil of French West Africa. . . . Again and again we have to protest and to show that the reports on this matter arriving at Dakar have no basis nor reliability.

I cannot insist enough in asking you to be careful and not to give cause for suspicion. Sometimes you are not cautious. . . .

Excuse me if I am talking about disagreeable things. I believe it is my duty to let you know what others think about you. You understand well that I am not taking the side of French interests; I only speak as a missionary, but a missionary working in a French territory. Those who come and want to work effectively in a French country must remember this French evolution. Americans must remember that whatever they do and are is important because of the might of their nation.

Dr. Keller made it clear that just being Americans created distrust in their motives no matter how pure they may be or how circumspect their behavior might be. He reminded them that, although France was grateful for the American liberation, it was nervous about what American intentions might be regarding its colonies. He reminded them that they would need to get their permits, visas, etc. through French officials which meant leaving all contacts with governments up to the federation. His warning was that Americans must not try to develop their own direct colonial channels if they hoped to succeed in their missionary endeavors.

Because the S.I.M. missionaries to Dahomey were novices to French policy, because they wanted their efforts to succeed, and because they trusted the experience of their seniors in these matters, they accepted these observations as governing their planning and decisions. It took many years for the S.I.M. missionaries to discover that the federation itself was a function of colonial rule, set up on colonial principles, i.e. the Methodists have a certain territory, the Assemblies of God another territory and S.I.M. whatever is not already claimed. It would take Dahomey's independence to finally bury the system.

Chapter 3: S.I.M. Entry Strategy

For an enterprise to be successful, it must have a coherent statement of strategic objectives and the processes by which those objectives will be realized. The following is such a statement which formed the structure for determining priorities and allocating funds and personnel in Dahomey. It is obviously modeled or copied from another source, probably a similar statement from the McDougalls' work in Nigeria, however, the document is not dated. It was in a file of early correspondence but it is unclear if the strategies preceded entry into Dahomey or were written shortly after the opening of the field. Whatever the source, they were closely followed.

A. **Establish a presence.** This will require care in coordinating with other agencies through the Federation of Protestant Missions of French West Africa. It will also require much care in meeting all the regulations of the colonial authority and tribal custom. The Catholic missions have historically had a monopoly in French territories and, one must assume, will have inside information on all formal government applications for building and expansion. The mission permissions, finances, supplies and personnel to occupy must be attended to before official application is made to avoid a concerted opposition to the building phase or a peremptory intervention to a proposed ministry.

B. **Translation and literacy.** Without the Word and access to the Word, the building of a mature church body is impossible. That being the ultimate objective, translation of the scripture and training of tribals to read must be the highest, most urgent priority. Even

though it may slow the process of completing a translation, these two objectives should be pursued together.

C.   **Evangelism.** This is our goal and high calling and,
although the other two above indicated priorities must
take strategic precedence, every means must be sought
and implemented to communicate the gospel of the
grace of God whereby men's eternal destiny may be
assured. Pursuit of the precedent strategic priorities
must not be allowed to preclude, negate or obscure the
goal of evangelism of the lost.

D.   **Medical work.** Attention to the obvious physical
ailments of the tribal population is essential to
acceptance of the missionary's presence and spiritual
objectives. General community health issues like clean
water and epidemics may be assumed to be the responsibility of the colonial authority, however, personal
concern for individuals, especially those of the household of faith, is necessary to the exercise of Christian
grace as well as the credibility of the gospel we bring.

E.   **Education.** The only means of assuring the continuity
and maturity of the indigenous church is through an
educated leadership. Attention must therefore be given
to literacy, primary, secondary and Bible School training. Book stores and reading rooms must also be
provided.

<u>S.I.M. Continuation Strategy (1958)</u>

The strategy report delivered by Stewart McDougall to the missionaries' field conference in November, 1958, demonstrates a notable shift in emphasis to the process of nationalization of all institutions and areas of ministry.

In obedience to our Lord's Commission, we are to preach and live the Gospel, so as to bring the lost to a knowledge of Jesus Christ, and to make disciples of those who receive and follow Him, so as to establish an "indigenous" church.
These churches should:

(1) be able to handle their own affairs.
(2) know the Word of God.
(3) have the Word of God for themselves (in their own language).

To accomplish this aim for any work, the missionary should:

a. Learn the language, also the customs of the people as much as possible, and familiarize himself with the area.
b. Give out the Gospel message when able.
c. Translate the Word.

When there is only one missionary on the station:
a. First learn the language, customs, etc.
Begin some translation, even if there are no Christians, so that Christians will have something on which to feed, as well as to provide the missionary with a message.
b. Teach and train new converts, which includes their learning to read, right from the start–not waiting for any organized school. This may be done for one or two people, but it must begin right away. Take new Christians out on visitation and preaching tours so that they may learn to witness for the Lord and at the same time absorb teaching. Bible Conferences, short or long (even up to periods of a month) are advisable, apart from an organized Bible School. The emphasis to be on teaching the Word, so they know how to apply it to themselves and give it out. Bible Schools may be started later, but care must be taken on what principles they are started and operated–it

must be self-supporting and should conform to
principles put forth by the Bible School committee.

When there is more than one missionary on the station:
a. Learn the language first.
b. Other projects and institutional work may be
    started, but these are to be in accordance to the
    needs of the work as these needs arise, with the
    consideration of the future—what if missionaries
    must leave? How will these projects be carried on?
    Institutional work should, if possible, come as
    meeting the demands of the people (the church, not
    a few individuals), not the primary burden and
    responsibility of the foreign missionary. Care must
    be taken in special projects and institutional work so
    that dependence is on the Lord for the supply of the
    needs, not depending on the government. Projects
    should be started with the agreement of other
    missionaries (not just one person or even one
    station, for the benefit of succeeding workers). Note:
    Any new project must have the approval of the Field
    Council before it is started.

The underlying principle, in both new and old works,
large or small staff is to be achieving the above stated aims,
with priority given to providing the Word of God (and
teaching for Christians) in their own language. So that with
increased self-government or independence (politically),
even if missionary activities are curtailed or suspended, the
indigenous church may carry on. Two prerequisites are (1)
the Word of God, and (2) the Holy Spirit in and through the
lives of believers. Organizations and councils, must be
secondary, not primary, not pushed by the missionary.

These aims should be reviewed at least annually and
consideration given to see what definite progress has been
made toward achieving them. If no progress, discuss why
and what should be done about it.

McDougall Strategy Report 1965

In a strategy report given at the District Conference of February, 1965, Field Leader, Stewart McDougall stated that:

Top priority must be the producing of materials the African church can use.

Priority two must be the training of national leadership. Other goals were to place leadership in the hands of competent nationals and the nationalization of our institutions.

Strategy Report by Roland Pickering December 12, 1971

STRATEGY: Thanks to the Lord's faithfulness, the past five years of our work in Dahomey have seen a steadily increasing movement towards a church-centered program with missionaries taking on a fuller role as partners in close co-operation with the churches. For the most part this has meant a continuance of our double offensive — strong vernacular programs on the one hand, and accelerating French programs through urban evangelism, youth retreats, and crash French course for preachers on the other.

Special efforts have been made to relate in a meaningful way all thirty odd projects of the S.I.M. to local or national church councils and these bodies have accepted this new responsibility in a most encouraging way.

Chapter 4: Translation Strategy

"The wide ethnic and linguistic variety of this small republic has presented S.I.M. with one of the greatest challenges to missionary strategy of any of her areas. None the less, the twenty-five years since the work started in Dahomey the Lord had brought fifty churches into being. As a result of the strong linguistic Bible translation programme in Bariba, Boko, Pila and Dompago, churches have sprung up everywhere, some in as little as three years."

The story of the translation work in these four tribes is one of hard work and perseverance over long years. The missionaries found the Bariba language as difficult as anticipated. Marguerite Morrow made a small beginning and Edna continued the work but it was slow going. Dr. Eugene Nida, who was a linguistic specialist with Wycliffe Bible Translators, had said "call for help when you need it" so they wrote inviting him to visit. He was unable to come to Dahomey but did invite the McDougalls to meet him at a conference in KanKan in May of 1948. They desperately needed his help to analyze the language and help finalize the alphabet. There were six missionaries studying, all were eager to make advances and accomplish something accurate and usable. However, attendance at the conference proved impossible for them so they struggled on.

Dr. Nida continued to try to help and in June he wrote about a Dr. Welmers of the University of Pennsylvania, who was then working with the Lutheran Mission and might be available to come. Dr. Welmers did agree to help with the project and sent lists of suggested materials to prepare. The missionaries' expectations were high as they awaited his arrival over a year later. He came with his family and stayed with the McDougalls for five weeks.

They appreciated his approach to the needs of the missionaries for his knowledge, training and expertise while treating their struggling efforts with respect: their dictionary of nouns, verb findings, stories of tribal customs, and ideas of the grammar structure. He was a workaholic and, in the short time he was with them, he was able to lay the foundation for the study of the language which proved invaluable over the life of the project.

His interest in the language and the progress of the project continued through the years. The McDougalls and the Welmers sought each other out when in the U.S. and visited each other, especially after Dr. Welmers began lecturing at UCLA.

Though a foundation had been laid and some translation was being worked on, the progress was slow because of the lack of missionaries prepared and designated for this ministry.

Bariba Translation

S.I.M. had long experience in reaching new tribes following proven principles and practices that God had honored with much fruit. This rich heritage and wise counsel of earlier pioneers guided the translation team as they faced the challenge of finding an entrance into the hearts and homes of a new people.

The missionaries also were keenly aware that underlying all their efforts, love was the key, and total dependence on the Holy Spirit to open doors was the only way.

Each tribe was unique and different. God, who knew the hearts of this people, would guide His servants by His Spirit into ways to express love and open doors for the entrance of His Word.

First, the missionaries needed to find acceptance so, as people watched with open curiosity, they were constantly reaching out. Learning their language, putting it to writing and doing translation was unquestionably a priority need. But there were other competing needs like one the McDougalls discovered when trekking. Early in their time in Nikki, Stewart and Edna went to Tontarou village. It was a new experience for the village to have missionaries but they were graciously received. The couple slept and prepared meals in the village blacksmith shop. Stewart had a continuous audience as he answered questions, talked to groups of men or preached to gatherings. The women were very open to Edna as she sat in their homes or walked with them to get water (it had been a dry year and the distance was long). At the end of their visit, the village elders said the words were sweet and asked the McDougalls to take some of their sons to train. Their ministry was accepted.

Some days later a few elders came and brought three boys. The McDougalls eagerly took them in and soon there were others. That was never a conscious part of their plan but clearly it was the plan and sure guidance of the Spirit.

As other stations opened, missionaries found that fathers were willing to send children to them for teaching, so schools for training them seemed a priority need to accomplishing their stated objective of planting churches. Once the schools were established, the demand for teachers always seemed to exceed the supply. So, though the need of translation was recognized as urgent and essential, it wasn't until 1960 that Jean Soutar and Rosella Entz could be freed from their teaching assignments for full-time Bariba language and translation.

Jean Soutar was working on needed language materials along with her responsibilities at Tchaourou Girls' School. In 1960, she was freed from teaching and joined Rosella in Parakou where Rosella was already working with James Odjo Boro. Together they had completed several New Testament epistles in mimeographed form. The gospels of Mark, Luke and John were in first draft, each done by a different missionary. There were primers and a reader used for literacy. Mary Draper prepared a new set of primers on the Wycliffe model which was nearly ready for publication.

From the start, the work load was heavy and demand-ing and Jean requested prayer for "stick-to-it-iveness". The team would need it in order to meet the needs, all of which seemed urgent, such as: a finished primer, a dictionary, a revision of the rough drafts already in hand and more.

The translation team was greatly helped by the visit of Dr. Wesley Sadler from the Literacy and Writing Center in Central Africa. At his week-long seminar and workshops in December, 1960, they developed their production plan for the next year. They were able to incorporate his program ideas for introducing Christian literature gradually. The Jean Soutar story illustrates the problems faced and how a sovereign God directed the project.

Jean Soutar's Story

Teaching was never a vocation I would have chosen. I didn't know what I was looking for but when the Lord led me to take teacher training I went into it whole-heartedly and enjoyed it. And I have used it almost continuously ever since.

When I applied to SIM, I applied as a teacher in Ethiopia because of an article in *Teachers' Christian Fellowship* magazine asking for teachers for Ethiopia. Then, during my year at Briercrest Bible Institute, Helen Peters came and talked about the need for teachers in Nigeria, an area with a much more difficult climate. We were then studying Old Testament and just at the point where David said he would not offer a sacrifice to God which cost him nothing. I took that as God's leading to apply for West Africa, not Ethiopia.

Before I went to Toronto to candidate classes, a friend said I should take Wycliffe's Summer Institute of Linguistics if I were going to learn a foreign language. I went in spite of Mr. Oliver's assurance that it wasn't necessary. I wanted training in a regular language school. I had enjoyed the phonetics course during Bible School, and found the summer course both enjoyable and challenging. This was what I was looking for and hadn't known it existed. It fit my type of mind: mathematical. The most challenging thing about it was the fact that it was the tool that would give a people the Word of God in their own language. That would be exciting.

But I had already changed my mind once since applying to SIM, so I wondered what would they think if I now said I wanted to do translation work? I went to the SIM candidate school after SIL and was accepted as a teacher for Nigeria. But a few months later I was asked if I would consider going to

France to study French and teach in French West Africa. That
was the first step. The first door opened. Later I was stationed
to Dahomey, the only place where translation was being done
in SIM. While in France I was re-stationed to Maradi Girls'
School to replace a teacher who had married and moved to
Upper Volta. But before I left France there was an urgent need
at Sinendé and I was re-stationed again.

      Once I arrived, I was to teach not translate, but I was
there. The first year I was supervising the African teacher at
Sinendé Boys' School and learning Bariba, getting to know the
culture and the way Baribas thought, through visiting in
villages and dealing with palavers in the school. Then I taught
two years in the Boys' School and three years in the Girls'
School at Tchaourou, but all available holidays I was pursuing
language study and language analysis.

      In 1960 a replacement was found for me and also for
Rosella Entz, and we were assigned to full-time language and
translation work. Rosella and others had translated some New
Testament books but we decided to revise everything and
translate what was left to do. The road ahead seemed clear.
One of the original group of boys who formed the nucleus of
Sinendé Bible School, Bio Doko, became our first informant.
Besides Bio, Pastor James Odjo also helped from time to time.
Then began a series of set-backs in our work. Bio Doko had to
be disciplined by the church and left us. There were times we
had nobody, times when one of the pastors would help for a
while. Then another good prospect and again disappointment.
The first one who stayed was Dogani who had asked for the job
through the church, and the church posted him to us. He stayed with the team over 20 years. We had others along with him
(he knew no French), but they left or were asked to leave as

well. Many problems we encountered were linguistic, others
needed answers and assurance from a linguistic consultant.
But consultants were far away and very rarely accessible. It
was tempting to wish for language helps that translators with
Wycliffe had. And several times when we had a real need we
were privileged to attend Wycliffe workshops and get help. But
the challenge of a newborn church needing to be equipped:
literacy materials, Bible School helps, daily reading notes, a
newspaper, etc. made the struggle worthwhile. In 1974 Rosella
left to marry Ivan Pettigrew, a missionary in South America,
but this coincided with finishing the New Testament except for
the final revision. Two more years were required for this revision with the help of typists and then the opportunity came to
have it typeset in Toronto where the Dompago New Testament
was also being published. The day finally came in June, 1978,
in Miango when I was handed a parcel which had come on the
charter flight. It was a Bariba New Testament! My first
reaction was praise to God for all the way He had guided and
protected His word and brought it to the Baribas. My second
reaction was to wish Rosella was there to share the day.

We had seen glimpses of what the Word could do in the
responses from informants while we worked on the translation:
hearing the sermons they preached, watching people become
believers and grow and churches be born and growing, as parts
of the New Testament were mimeographed and distributed.
But now they had it all in one book and could read any part
they wanted. The church had done a lot of growing and had
become a Union of churches of all the tribes where we worked
(UEEB), but we had not seen among the Baribas the kind of
growth or enthusiasm we longed to see. In the years after the
New Testament came out we began to see more growth and

more confidence on the part of the evangelists as they
preached.

But they still didn't have the whole Bible. They knew
there was much more because they had a series of Old Testament stories we had used for evangelism in the villages but
only some Psalms and a few key passages of other books had
been translated.

There was no missionary replacement for Rosella so it
was Dogani and I who tackled the translation of Genesis at the
beginning of 1978 when we had finished reading all the proofs
of the New Testament and waited for it to be printed.

I had 9 years left till I was due to retire and from time
to time, since contracting hepatitis in 1972, I experienced
health problems, so I wondered whether I would be there to see
the "Bible for the Baribas" completed. But during a time when
the doctor ordered half-time work only, and I thought maybe
only the New Testament was my part and someone else would
have the privilege of doing the Old Testament, the Lord drew
my attention to Jeremiah 29:11: "I know the plans I have for
you . . ." and I was satisfied His will would be done.

The summer of 1978 Pierre Barassounon, a graduate of
Sinendé and Daloa (Ivory Coast) was on holiday from
Yamoussoukro Bible School and Gabriel Doko (President of
UEEB) asked if I could use him. I said "Yes" and he came and
enjoyed the work. He had one more year at Bible School and
could choose at the end if he wanted to do pastoral work per-
manently. In the spring of 1979 he wrote that he would like to
work in translation with us. Gabriel asked what I would do
with him. I said I thought I could train him to take over from
me. So Gabriel agreed to assign him to us. He proved to be
good material. He was a student, a good exegete and later,
when he took an SIL course, he was good at semantics. Dogani

was all (almost) that Pierre was not. Dogani had "the gift of gab." He could express himself well in his own language and, because he knew practically no French, he was valuable in that we knew the translation was understandable to a Bariba who knew no other language. In 1975 Barka Boni (the orphan Yaki had brought up) came to us for work and learned to mimeograph. Later he asked to join the team as a translator. He had lived in Nikki most of his life so his Bariba was good. He'd had two years of secondary school so his French was quite good and his special talent was one neither Pierre nor Dogani had— attention to detail. He was our proof-reader and later the one who learned to key in a lot of the Old Testament on computer. With such a team, hand-picked and called of God, I was confident the Bariba Old Testament would be finished.

I was one year into my last term when I turned sixty-five. I said I planned to stay one year longer, then retire. Pierre asked if I would stay three years and I agreed if my health remained good.

Little by little the team took more and more responsibility for first translation and I went over it with them asking questions and checking and suggesting. The first draft was finished in May, 1988, while I was home on holiday. We had two years to revise it and to do a limited revision of the Old Testament and smooth it out in places. This we were able to do and I left March 23, 1990.

The team re-read the entire manuscript, then I re-read it all at home in Canada. The Bible Society checked it and it is ready for typesetting. Someday I'll receive a parcel and the Baribas will receive a shipment of "The Bible for Baribas." To God be the glory.

Jean Soutar–1995

Chapter 5: Education Strategy

Most of the missionaries' strategic objectives depended on the priority of translation, literacy materials and training. The strategies for education were clearly planned to be secondary and would not be open for consideration for many years. Education strategies were to be developed in such a way as to remain independent of government subsidy or to require the long term involvement of foreign missionaries. Whatever institutional facilities were built were to be only to meet the stated needs of the indigenous church and were to be developed under the national church's direction and care. The emphasis was determined to be on the development of an independent, indigenous church, and institutions that might become dependent on the continuing support of foreign missionaries was deemed unwise. However, the Holy Spirit forced the issue to the fore in early 1950 when Stewart and Edna McDougall rode their bicycles to visit a village near Nikki called Tontarou.

The village sent a total of seven boys to them for training and, strategically convenient or not, they had to build facilities and dedicate precious time and unprepared personnel to the project. The project became the responsibility of the first Yoruba pastors, David Ajibola and Elisha Olufemi. More boys came and the school operated in Nikki until government permission to build a school for boys in Sinendé was granted in 1953 and opened in 1954. The same year, a girls' school was opened in Tchaourou by Sarah Buller because of the strategic importance of training wives for pastors who, after their training for ministry, would need partners who were also prepared to help build a strong, indigenous church.

Miss Pat Irwin was the principal of the school as it developed into a government accredited primary school. Her account of the development of an education strategy follows.

Patricia Irwin's Story

When I arrived on the beautiful grounds of Tchaourou Girls' School in September, 1961, I discovered that the senior missionary, Miss Annie van den Brand (replacing Miss Sarah Buller during her home assignment) would be teaching a class of girls in the Bariba language. In addition, a niece of Pastor Augustin, Mlle. Salome, would be teaching girls in Yoruba. Also, there would be two French classes, covering four grades. I was to teach CE I/II (grades 3/4), while Pastor Augustin's daughter, Mlle. Marie, would be teaching the upper classes of CM I/II (grades 5/6). I was to be the principal of the French section. My instructions from SIM leadership were that I was to phase out the lower French classes, even as the first two grades had been disbanded. The following year the remaining classes would be closed.

As the year progressed, I saw the difficulties encountered by the teachers of the vernacular classes. Each evening they had to create their lessons as there was very little material in either Bariba or Yoruba. I had the advantage of using the government curriculum in French, largely based on the "Mamadou et Bineta" textbooks. It became increasingly clear that there were great advantages to conducting a French school, especially for younger girls who were beginning their education while older girls would profit from a vernacular course complete with household science subjects.

Since Dahomey had become independent a year earlier, it seemed wise to follow the country's official school curriculum which was based on six years of education in French with all the courses, literature, mathematics, science, geography and history, available in textbooks. Because of the conviction that there should be a change in direction from an emphasis on training in the vernacular to an education in French, the Tchaourou School Board was convened and asked to vote on this matter. It was unanimous that the parents wanted a French education for their younger daughters. Therefore, rather than phase out the existing French classes, the previously phased out classes of grades CI/CP were re-opened in 1962.

The girls were recruited from SIM local churches throughout the province of Borgou, in northern Benin (it was a boarding school). Many of these girls came from areas where there were no primary schools or they were already overcrowded. The School Board wanted to provide a Christian education so as to strengthen Christian families.

Morning prayers were conducted in the dormitory courtyard. A new hymn was taught each week during evening devotions in the chapel. Classes began each day with a half-hour Bible lesson in each classroom. During the second semester a Day of Evangelism was held annually with a pastor invited to conduct morning and afternoon services. This was to provide an opportunity for students to make a decision for Christ, if they so desired. As much as possible, those who responded were channeled to a teacher/staff member who spoke their mother tongue so the way of salvation could be made clear to all.

The students attended the local churches on Sunday: Bariba in Guinèrou, or Yoruba in Tchaourou. I often drove a group comprised of older and younger girls, according to a roster, to visit the churches farther away at places like Papanè,

Kilibo, Ikèmon, Agrammarou, Alafiarou and Tchatchou. This group was always prepared to sing hymns to the congregation. In this manner, the girls became acquainted with the Bariba, Fulani and Yoruba churches in the area.

From time to time, a staff member and a group of girls would walk the paths leading to more remote villages in order to witness there, after requesting the chief's permission.

The school had a Bible motto, Colossians 1:27-28. Realizing the task of directing this school was so enormous, I asked the Lord for a passage to guide me. This was our Heavenly Father's reply: "[Jesus] Christ . . . whom we preach, warning every [child], and teaching every [child] in all wisdom; that we may present every [child] perfect in Christ Jesus." I then asked the Lord for guidance so as to fulfill this large order. The answer was contained in I Thessalonians: "to be gentle among them even as a nurse cherisheth her children" (2:7), "to exhort and comfort and charge every one of them, as a father doth his children" (2:9), and for the staff to work together as brothers and sisters in Christ ("brethren", 2:14, 17).

These verses were often repeated during staff prayer meeting conducted prior to classes, Monday through Friday. These were the verses we prayed when we received word that the government school inspector would visit us that next day. He did come, spent the whole day in our midst, sitting in on each class, visiting all the boarding activities. In his very favorable report, he concluded by saying: "The teachers and staff are motivated by a desire to serve rather than for monetary gain." We could only thank the Lord.

So as to have godly, well-trained teachers, the two schools of Sinendé and Tchaourou sent highly-qualified graduates to attend a Christian high school in Daloa, Cote d'Ivoire. Upon their return, they took on teaching assignments in their respective sending school. It was soon apparent at Tchaourou, however, that the women teachers married and left to accompany their husbands. This led to the creation of a separate compound for male teachers to join the staff at Tchaourou. After the closure of Sinendé Boys School, Tchaourou Primary School opened its doors to a few transfer students who either found lodging with the male teachers or accommodation with a family in town.

In the mid-70s when a communist government nationalized all private schools, our teachers were sent to public schools where they carried on a witness for Christ through their lives. One senior girl who was transferred to a public school in her area, had the courage to confront her teacher who repeatedly said there was no God, saying that she knew there was a God and that she talked to Him in prayer each day. Knowing the pressure on her, her parents removed her from the school. She later became the wife of a pastor.

After the take-over of the Tchaourou property, there was a decline in maintenance of the buildings and grounds. Years later, I met a former student who said she wept every time she saw the former school. I told her not to weep over buildings and property but to rejoice for the "living stones" (1 Peter 2:5) scattered throughout Benin.

Many of the graduates went on to serve the Lord in various ministries, as pastors' wives or staff at Bembèrèkè Hospital. Others have been faithful wives and mothers throughout the country.

Years later, the UEEB Church, recognizing the important role that Sinendé and Tchaourou graduates had played in the growth of the church, opened a Christian primary school in Parakou, and more recently in Bembèrèkè.

To God be all glory for what He performed during the ministries of the various Christian schools in Dahomey/Benin.

Patricia Irwin–2004

Part II:

The McDougall Story

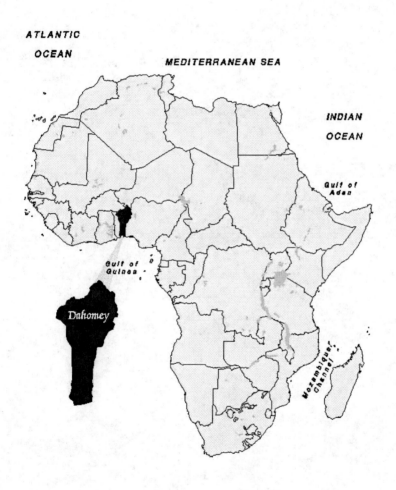

Chapter 6: Jesus Saves

Stewart Minto McDougall arrived without fanfare on June 15, 1910, in Brandon, Manitoba, Canada, to Colin and Lillian McDougall. His older brother and sister had three months to fuss over him, and then their attention was diverted by packing all their earthly belongings. Hoisting them onto the train one crisp September morning, the five McDougalls sat swaying as their car clacked over the tracks from Manitoba to Vancouver. When they finally stood, dusty and rumpled, in the Vancouver station, Colin had no job and no housing for his family. Undaunted, he set out that very day to hunt for work, and by evening had found employment at Pioneer Laundry. Though his training was in pharmacy, he knew better than to scorn the job. Times were hard and, since his marriage to Lillian in 1906 he had even sold ice cream for a living.

Despite the humble family circumstances, the McDougall heritage was a noble one. Stewart received the pluck and highly motivated diligence characteristic of his long ancestral line of teachers, pastors, missionaries, doctors, and professionals. His mother brought him flexibility and equanimity; his father, initiative and discipline.

He was a happy child. Being third in a line of seven children made him a tease, and teetered his life precariously on occasion. A knitting needle choked him once in early childhood, and boiling soup scalded him twice. He hammed up mealtimes and sang Scottish ballads with uninhibited zest, delighting his musical father, who had emigrated from Scotland during high school.

Had he lived in more affluent times, Stewart's life might have spun itself out in careless entertainment. Indeed, one frustrated teacher exclaimed, "McDougall, you'll never amount to anything!" But God never allowed him the luxury of forgetful self-indulgence. At the age of eight he nursed his whole family back to health during the flu epidemic, succumbing only after their recovery. When Lillian reluctantly granted approval, he dropped out of high school at age fifteen to work at the mill for a year, supplementing the family's income. Tedious hours and heavy responsibility sobered his thoughts, wrapping his wages in growing heart-bonds to his family.

They were a loving household, staunch Presbyterians, woven in tight loyalty around the hub of the home Lillian created. Stewart's father graduated from the laundry. When World War I beat its drums, Colin enlisted in the Canadian Army Medical Corps and sailed for active duty in Europe, finishing high school through the army's educational program. When the War ended, he stepped back onto Canadian shores with a dream: a career in education. Back to the laundry he marched, this time merely to feed his family while he attended teachers' college. In 1920, he triumphantly accepted his first teaching position at Robert's Creek. In 1924, a new teaching job opened in the interior of British Columbia at Campbell River, and young Stewart accompanied his father into those backwoods for the year. While his father taught, Stewart studied, never dreaming one day he would return to that same area of Canada as a changed man with a new focus.

Bachelor life ill-suited those two. In September of 1926, renouncing all further separation, Colin moved his family to Maple Ridge, British Columbia, and lived there till his death in 1961, happily settled in a rambling house he built for Lillian on ten acres of land. Here the McDougall family put down their roots, claiming Maple Ridge as home for the next two generations.

Stewart's days soon hummed with activity as he plunged into his last year of high school classes, sports, and year-book staff. One afternoon in the spring of 1927, Stewart stumped through town selling yearbook subscriptions. His cheerful smile and easy good manners were those of the natural salesman, and prospective customers smiled in spite of themselves as he presented his offer. One man's smile was especially wide. Bill Fuller, owner of the Fuller-Watson Company, not only bought a subscription but also offered Stewart a job at Haney's Department Store! Stewart accepted the offer on the spot. After graduation, the job expanded to fill his time.

The Fuller connection brought more than a job, however. Bill Fuller, his father, Owen, his wife, and all their family drew Stewart into their circle, adopting him as their own. He fished with them, played tennis with them, vacationed with them, and, since they shared their work and play with him, it seemed natural for them to share their worship too. In the Fuller's case, this meant attending the Maple Ridge Baptist Church.

For the first time, Stewart sensed reluctance in his parents' response. As loyal Presbyterians, they regarded the Baptists with uneasiness. Stewart honored his parents, but when they allowed him to attend, he and his elder sister, Beulah, sat listening to the Baptist preacher, Rev. A. J. L. Haynes. Gradually Maple Ridge Baptist became their church. Happily, in December 1928, while attending a Christian camp in Washington, Stewart trusted Christ as his personal Savior. Beulah followed his example, and both were baptized before the bells rang in the new year.

The Fullers rejoiced. Now Stewart belonged to them in more ways than one, and as the years passed they demonstrated their commitment to him with loyal generosity. It was the Fullers who sent the funds to build Stewart's first mission station in Dahomey, in memory of Bill's father. Time after time their contributions came, addressing special needs in burdened situations. When Stewart died, the Fullers paid for his eldest son, Colin, to fly out to meet his mother and bring her back to America.

Not long after his salvation, Stewart felt God wanted him to be a missionary with China as his destination; perhaps that was the farthest end of the earth he could picture. Certainly this was the natural outworking of his character. From the time he trusted Christ, Stewart burned with bright passion for serving His interests. At Maple Ridge Baptist Church, he threw himself into developing a young people's fellowship. The group mushroomed. But the path for Stewart to get from his home to the mission field was unclear.

In the wisdom of God, an evangelistic team from the Bible Institute of Los Angeles (BIOLA) held gospel outreach programs in Vancouver that summer, and Stewart began musing over the possible benefits of a Bible Institute education. Through the slow summer afternoons, he and his friend, Jitsuo Morikawa, discussed the logistics of attending BIOLA till spurred by each other's enthusiasm, they applied together and waved acceptance notices like banners a few weeks later, grinning widely.

Stewart's parents, who had expected him to attend a full-fledged university in Canada, were surprised by his new interest in a Bible Institute in California, but as his intentions solidified, so did their support and encouragement. Beulah, of course, was thrilled. Putting aside her thoughts of the wrenching separation, she indulged Stewart as he planned and packed and speculated aloud about every detail of life in the big city.

It was a small-town boy who, in the fall of 1930, steered his Model A Ford, affectionately dubbed "sphizzerinctum", down the winding roads through the forests and towns of northwest USA, past the broad valleys of central California, through the bustling downtown traffic of Los Angeles to arrive at the tall building with the red neon "Jesus Saves" signs on the roof lighting up the sky. The chimes in the belfry hung hymn-notes in the evening air and Jitsuo sat up in the seat beside him, yawning. The city glittered with an enchanted aura, though as Stewart learned, under the glitter there lay gutters.

Chapter 7: A Mind of Her Own

Edna Mae Luft was born on January 1, 1914 in Mariposa, California. Henry Luft, at that time, was the manager of an orange grove and Bertha Brown Luft was a housewife. Edna had three younger sisters but the family was together a very short time because their mother died in the 1920 flu epidemic leaving six year old Edna to be nurse, housekeeper and babysitter. Henry Luft then moved his family to Armona, California, where he found employment as a mechanic in a cannery, where he remarried and where he lived the rest of his active life.

Edna's family was unchurched but she trusted Christ for salvation when she was thirteen and was baptized a year later in a local Church of the Brethren. Her parents discouraged her "religious trend" and often tried various tactics to prevent her from attending Sunday School and church but she seemed always to find a way to work it out. She particularly enjoyed teaching a Sunday School class of primary boys and girls through high school and it became her ambition to become a Kindergarten teacher. Teaching, however, required a college education which she could certainly not afford so she worked and saved through the summer of her high school graduation and the following semester and, in February, started Junior College in Tulare. She lived with the Bergmans who became her greatest source of encouragement.

After completing one semester there, she was offered the opportunity to go to Los Angeles to work at keeping house for a family. She jumped at the opportunity because the family promised to see that she was able to continue her education while doing her work. Her parents, however, did not approve so

Edna turned to prayer and gradually their attitudes changed
and they gave their consent.

Not long after Edna arrived in Los Angeles, she went to
visit a friend who was attending the Bible Institute of Los
Angeles (BIOLA). The students who were there "by faith"
challenged Edna, but she was determined to be a teacher and
Bible College was just not the way to get there. But getting the
Lord to change His mind wasn't as easy as convincing her
parents. Finally, she spoke to the lady of the home where she
worked and lived and her employer agreed that Edna should go
to BIOLA and do her housework around her class schedule.
She enjoyed the classes and the atmosphere but it was during
the annual Missionary Rally that she was challenged to yield
her all to Christ. She gave up her plans to become a teacher
and the Lord directed her attention to Africa. The chairman of
the Africa Prayer Band was Stewart McDougall. His passion
for lost souls in Africa fired her imagination and commitment.

In November, 1933, she met Stewart personally for the
first time. She was a waitress in the BIOLA cafeteria and he
was the manager. However, he was a senior, graduating in the
spring of 1934 and planning to head directly to Africa with the
S.I.M. They planned and prayed together and Edna wrote,
"Then it was even more difficult for me because I didn't want to
go to Africa because of some one but because of a definite call
from God. One Sunday afternoon in May after I had taught my
class of High School girls the 28th chapter of Matthew, the Lord
spoke very definitely to my heart. There was no longer any
room for doubt as to His will for me. I promised to go and teach
depending on His 'Lo, I am with you always.'"

Chapter 8: Two Loves

For young scholars BIOLA proved a teeming world of Bible knowledge. Systematic study of the books of the Bible, doctrine, theology and languages left Stewart in a whirl of discovery. His professors proved to be men who considered teaching more a ministry than a job and did not count their hours of duty by the clock. Stewart's respect for them grew as he observed the personal righteousness which adorned their instruction.

And dormitory life was fun. In spite of Depression times, in spite of long hours managing the school's dining room, in spite of scrimping to pay expenses, Stewart found time to play. In the evenings the boys stood on the fire escape and serenaded the girls across the echoing courtyard. Together with his friends Stewart walked the city shops, libraries, museums and parks, strolling with fresh youth's grand disregard for previous hours of long labor.

Nor was his leisure time spent in purely selfish pursuits. The city's homeless, children, destitute and drunkards were all the focus of BIOLA's outreach efforts. Stewart reached out to the alcoholics. Patiently he learned to know them, their habits and backgrounds. He talked earnestly with them about the Lord Jesus, Who came to save them from the power of sin, and visited them week after week in the slums. Back in his dorm room, he prayed earnestly for those men, wrestling for their deliverance from the tyrant which burned their throats and dominated their lives. Here he learned patience and long-suffering love, for even the most fervent converts were likely to cover up alcoholic breath when he returned the next week. When he sailed for Africa, his thoughts still lingered with them. He wrote begging a friend to pay two of the men a visit and send word on their progress.

But not all objects of his interest proved so unresponsive. In his second year at BIOLA, Stewart found himself face to face with a young receptionist selling stamps in the dorm lobby. "It was love at first sight," he declared later, and promptly set out to court Miss Edna Mae Luft with gentlemanly forthrightness. In this he was aided by two things: Edna's instant, if slightly shy response, and the cooperation of Miss Culter, the Dean of Women. "Miss Culter favored us, I'm afraid," Edna later twinkled ruefully, as she recalled that worthy woman's instructions to Stewart to escort Edna home from her waitressing job at a downtown restaurant declaring it was too dangerous for her to return alone in the evenings. Those walks afforded conversational starts to their heart throbs, and Stewart soon learned that Edna's devotion to Christ matched his own. They interspersed lofty topics with such sentimental trivia as claiming one star for joint ownership.

Edna grieved over her unsaved family, and Stewart found himself newly appreciative of his own. His parents were honorable, righteous people, his home peaceful and safe. Yet even as gratefulness warmed him, Stewart found himself wondering if they truly knew Christ as their personal Savior. This burden he revealed to Edna, and she, with a sharer's sympathy, added her prayers to his for assurance of his parents' salvation.

They prayed about other things too. In fact, prayer became the meeting-ground for all other facets of their relationship. Even after Stewart finished his BIOLA training and journeyed to Toronto, England, and Nigeria, their letters centered around prayer as the sphere of their greatest expressions of love for each other. Through prayer they met at God's throne simultaneously, meticulously calculating differences in time zones so as to be one at an appointed hour. Through prayer they cared for each other's needs, lavishly pouring out heaped-up blessings. Through prayer they soothed each other's discouragements and came alongside in spiritual battle.

Their courtship proceeded steadily. After Stewart finished BIOLA's two-year Bible course, he enrolled in their one-year course on Missionary Medicine. Edna often had opportunities to serve at special events in the school's dining room, settling into the team under Stewart's adroit management. A bittersweet aura haloed the year as they pushed aside thoughts of parting.

Parting had been hard enough for just one summer. Stewart had driven Edna home to northern California, then returned to the backwoods of British Columbia, no longer the schoolteacher's son but a home missionary with the Canadian Sunday School Mission. He and his friend, Neal, tramped unflaggingly from house to house, sometimes miles apart, to invite children to the meetings in the country schoolhouse. They organized Scripture memory contests, sang lively choruses and narrated Bible stories with enthusiasm, never omitting a gospel presentation. Edna followed his travels by letter, aching to be with him and praying for each of the children he mentioned. Yes, that separation had been difficult and before them loomed another that dwarfed the first, though they did not guess by how much.

During BIOLA's annual missionary conference in his first year, Stewart had met a man representing the Sudan Interior Mission named Mr. Tommy Titcombe. They were mutually impressed by that meeting. Stewart was struck with the need for missionaries in West Africa. He began considering that field, and the more information he received, the more convinced he became that he should go to Africa rather than China. Mr. Titcombe encouraged him to apply to S.I.M. Over time, he rose to be Stewart's close friend and mentor. But Stewart could not anticipate the years of combined effort they would share across the ocean one day; he simply liked the man he met at the conference and yearned to take the gospel to people who needed it.

Africa seemed almost as far away as China. Edna would not have dreamed of asking Stewart to wait for her graduation although he knew of her desire to go to Africa as well. Their common conviction was that getting out to the mission field was such a rigorous, demanding, consuming business that nothing–not even blooming romance–should distract one's focusing all energies toward that goal. So at Stewart's graduation in June, 1934, Edna held her head high and clapped bravely as Stewart strode across the platform. After all, he might come visit her once more before he sailed overseas.

He returned home to raise support. Maple Ridge Baptist Church ordained him as a minister of the gospel in a solemn ceremony of dedication, and through the summer he dug wells and chopped wood to earn bus fare to S.I.M.'s headquarters in Toronto. It was during those days that he marked a change in his parents, especially in his father. He wrote,

> Edna, I wish you could have seen my mother and dad last year and then again this year. Mother and my aunt were both out to the service (where Stewart was speaking). Mother has said nothing, but I know that she is thinking. Dad has taken a very definite stand for the Lord and his life has been the greatest blessing to me in the past few days. Dad used to be opposed to missions and said that missionaries should mind their own business. Now he is fully in favor with my going! Tonight when I came in, Dad was alone in the kitchen reading the Bible. When I came in he hurriedly put it

away, but it is something I have never seen before. On the way home the other night he was telling me about some books he read about the inspiration of the Scriptures and their structure and he said, "Only God could have written such a book." Edna, God has heard and answered our prayers. . . .

When October, 1934, arrived, he had collected enough money to travel to Toronto and pay half his fare to Africa. S.I.M. invited him to come out to their headquarters, hoping the rest of his needs would be covered by the time the next group of new missionaries sailed from there at the month's end. He watched USA and Canada's expanse slide past the Greyhound bus with growing excitement. In Toronto, he met the other members of the outgoing group, packed his belongings, and spoke enthusiastically to church groups in the area. But the funds he needed did not come in. Some of the other team members also lacked money, so the group delayed its departure till mid-November. When it became evident that several people would have to delay indefinitely while the others sailed, Stewart asked S.I.M. if his passage money could be put to their account so that all could sail except himself.

He waved goodbye cheerfully, but it was hard, and Christmas that year was his loneliest ever. He had hoped to visit Edna once more before leaving but now it became clearly impossible. Full of loneliness, he proposed to her by letter, but her first tender response discouraged him: she would consider it; she loved him; but she needed God's peace that their lives and work would most honor Him together.

Chapter 9: Canuck in Yorubaland

"I am afraid all my preconceived ideas of African life and Africa were all shattered the first few hours. Instead of a barren desert, the first thing that meets your eyes at Lagos is lovely green lawns and a lovely hedge of trees and beautiful big buildings," wrote Stewart to his parents upon his arrival in Nigeria.

Edna had finally accepted his proposal joyfully, confidently. And the remaining amount he needed to sail arrived in a fat lump sum from a teacher who had held him dear in childhood. On February 8, 1935, at 1:05 PM, the Montclair pulled out from Canadian shores, bound across the Atlantic Ocean.

He had stood on deck and watched the teeming shore with the feeling of a prisoner about to step out of a cell. The journey was long and tedious, on occasion rough, and at two ports passengers were forbidden to debark because of a yellow fever quarantine. When their ship finally lumbered into Lagos on a breezy Thursday afternoon, April 3, 1935, he and the rest of the small group of S.I.M. missionaries waited over an hour before a launch shuttled them from ship to wharf, where customs officials inspected their passports and luggage. The sun set as the ordeal proceeded, and by the time they were told they could return to the ship for the night, it was eight o'clock and the last ferry had gone. They took a taxi, having bargained the driver down from ten shillings to four to drive them nine miles. "This is the craziest place," Stewart thought, in silent echo of the others' sentiments. They moved wearily to their cabins for a last night's sleep in the narrow bunks.

Morning sun cheered them, as did the sight of a well-stocked lunch box, courtesy of the ship's kitchen crew. Since customs was behind them, their goal this morning was simply to get from the ship to the train, which proved to be another test of fortitude. The hand luggage had to be carried to the taxi, and upon arrival at the station Stewart stood guard over the jumbled pile like a watchdog, fending off swarms of eager boys while the others went to locate their seats on the train.

That was a fairy tale ride. A kind guard moved them all into a first-class compartment though they had paid for second-class, and Stewart wrote later, "I enjoyed the train ride I believe more than all the time on the boat." Periodically they lurched to a stop and vendors swarmed to hawk their wares–pineapples, papayas, bananas, oranges, mats, baskets, wood carvings. Outside, the scenery grew greener, more lush. He couldn't help comparing it to the interior of British Columbia. Oddly, he felt a sense of exotic familiarity.

The familiarity wore off as he stepped out into the blistering heat at Minna, but the enchantment lingered. He met the veteran missionaries through a haze of unreality and plunged into activity.

Sunday morning he sat with a group in the market-place, singing loudly in their tongue and listening intently to the garble of testimonies, though he understood not a word. That afternoon he and a veteran missionary wound their way through the maze of straw huts that was the mining camp, settled under a shady tree, called the people to hurry and come, preached for an hour, and retraced their steps–with a little difficulty, since the huts all looked alike.

He could have settled happily at Minna but was assigned instead to Egbe for his year of language study. Before going he was warned by the Field Director that Egbe would not be an easy place to work, although it was one of S.I.M.'s oldest stations. Many of the Christians had fallen back into the sins of their fathers. The missionaries were few and burdened with heavy demands. Looking Mr. Playfair in the eye, Stewart asked, "With your knowledge of the field, if you had a life at your disposal, where would you invest it?" Without hesitation, Mr. Playfair replied, "In the South." So Stewart went to the Yorubas rather than the Hausa tribe, and for the next four years, Egbe became his home.

It was a large station compound. In addition to the main house and two smaller houses, the property held a dispensary and a school. The church building sat nearby, between the town and the mission station. Two single women, Miss Kuntzelman and Miss Lang, teacher and nurse, occupied one small house, the Playfairs lived in the main house, and Stewart moved into the other small one, a cottage of mud brick walls tar-coated on the outside, thinly cemented mud floors, and a grass roof. Stewart borrowed furniture from furloughing missionaries and settled in. Soon after he arrived, Adeyemi came to him. He was small for his fifteen years, but eager to earn money to buy clothes and books for school. For one shilling a week he swept floors, made beds, hauled bath water and shined shoes, cheering Stewart by his ready grin and eagerness to please.

Stewart soon found that solitude was a luxury. From early morning to late evening the visitors came, many of them schoolboys wanting to laugh at the pictures in his Montgomery Ward catalogue, or practice arithmetic or English, or gaze at his snapshots of Edna. The constant stream of people was both a help and a hindrance to his language study. Each day his goal was to study Yoruba for six hours. He found it a difficult

language, full of subtle tonal differences which his Canadian
ear could hardly distinguish and his tongue struggled to
reproduce. Moody, his language teacher, repeated phrases and
words with the patience of a man long accustomed to the white
people's ineptness. Though Stewart felt his progress to be slow
and his mistakes myriad, when the language exam was given
to him five months early, he sailed through it, outscoring his
fellow-examinees who had been studying more months than he.
It was a pattern for him: in high school he had won the French
award for his fluency in that language, and later would learn
others with equal ease. He never thought of himself as
particularly gifted; in fact, his reaction to his exam scores was
astonished relief.

It was difficult to devote himself to studies when he
longed to be with the Yoruba people. Surrounding the station
nestled villages with a few believers, many of whom begged for
a preacher. One Sunday morning as the missionaries sat
together at breakfast, a man came in from a village about five
miles away. He pleaded for someone to come speak the Word of
God to them, but each missionary was busy with other responsibilities that day. In the end one of the men promised to come
later that week. Stewart sat silent through the exchange but
that evening by kerosene lamplight he wrote burningly to
Edna, "As I see these things and the great need of the people
here, it spurs me on to more diligence in the study of the
language. You spoke . . . about us going on long walks to tell
'our people' about Christ. Dear, if the Lord should tarry and it
is His will I feel that much of our time will be spent in that
way. It is not so nice, and possibly that is why so few do it, yet
if someone doesn't, how can they hear?"

Like all other missionaries he suffered bouts of
homesickness. The mail arrived every week, carried fifty-seven

miles by a boy in the village who took their outgoing mail and
returned with letters from home. Those letters eased the
parched places in his soul like ice water on a sweltering day.
All the while he was nursing a sick child, repairing a car,
supervising construction work, or repeating phrases after
Moody, images of home intruded ghostlike into his conscious-
ness, stirring up bittersweet pangs. The days for mail delivery
he sat distracted, glancing out the window, and, when the
carrier appeared, Moody knew enough to go home rather than
spend his afternoon competing with letters. Stewart wrote
prolifically during his first two years on the field, hungry to tell
his family about his life as though to narrow the enormous gap
of miles between them with pen and paper.

They answered warmly, though without his urgency.
After all, their circumstances had not changed and they still
had each other. But if their letters seemed infrequent to
Stewart, Edna responded with all the fervent emotions of a
hearing heart. She had finally graduated from BIOLA and,
rejoicing in her father's permission to pursue missionary work,
she applied to S.I.M. and trusted God to help raise her support.
They waited patiently through several delays and, in April,
1936, she arrived at Lagos. When the ship docked, a message
came that Stewart would be unable to come meet her.
Disappointed, she sat in her cabin, struggling to compose
herself and feeling lonely in the bustle of a foreign port. A
slight tap came on her door and a steward put in his head to
say a visitor waited for her in the upstairs lobby. Bracing her
head high she went up. There stood her beloved in all his
mischievous delight, twinkling from ear to ear! He had cajoled
permission to drive a load of gold down for a couple of miner
friends, conveniently timing his arrival with hers. Happily, she
climbed into the pickup truck with a suitable single-lady

chaperone to drive home with Stewart. She wrote later to her sister, "Finally Martha went to sleep!"

Chapter 10: Soldier of Two Armies

Their joy in reunion bordered on euphoria, but S.I.M. had stringent rules for engaged couples. Edna must spend a year in language study and pass her exam before the wedding. They must live on separate stations and Stewart was allowed one weekend visit per month. A chaperone must accompany them at all times. Some evenings they gratefully watched the boy carrying the lamp lengthening the distance between them, his small figure diminishing, the lamplight flickering faintly through the tall grass. Though the waiting was hard, it was infinitely less difficult than being separated by an ocean, and on May 22, 1937, they were finally married. The best man in the wedding was Orville Thamer who would later join them in Dahomey.

During the last year of their engagement Stewart had been promoted to station manager. The Playfairs moved to Jos, leaving him in charge of the Egbe dispensary, school and church, as well as a parish of some twenty villages in the surrounding area. Miss Lang and Miss Kuntzelman gave long hours to teaching and nursing, and Stewart focused on pastoring the churches.

It was a demanding job physically, emotionally and spiritually. The long, brush-crowded trails could not always be traversed by motorcycle or bicycle, so he trekked across those footsore miles with his luggage carriers. When he arrived at a village, he would often be called upon to settle a dispute or publicly rebuke a church leader or member who had fallen into sin. Everywhere he saw untrained leaders and congregations like sheep without a shepherd. Many Christians reverted to idol worship and pagan practices. He preached passionately and spent long hours after the meetings counseling with people who begged to be heard.

The role of disciplinarian ached painfully. When his beloved language teacher, Moody, married his daughter to a pagan man, Stewart knew that such a public sin called for public rebuke, and that he must give it. On a hot Sunday morning in the Egbe church Stewart knelt before Moody in front of a startled congregation. "I must rebuke you for this sin," he said, "but I come to you as a son to a father."

These were days of gradual maturation for the new missionary couple. While he was on his own, it was fine for Stewart to make objective appraisal of those missionaries who had gone before him. Now that he was gaining a supervisory role, however, he had to learn patience and an attitude of understanding if he ever hoped to lead anyone.

The last twenty years of the colonial era in West Africa were excruciating for missionary leaders. Nigerians were pressuring missionaries for the incompatible concessions of greater direct support and greater autonomy. The more senior mission leaders often resisted attempts at Nigerian control of the church, and the more progressive leaders like young Stewart were vulnerable to detractors from both sides. If Edna were to be a help to him in his new position, she must learn to defend her man without being defensive, and to maintain an open heart to her Nigerian neighbors without being overwhelmed by the demands of some.

Actually, relationships between missionaries and nationals in the area were particularly strained during those years. Denominational mission boards had started schools for their followers; now the S.I.M. converts begged for schools of their own. "You want to plunge our nation into darkness," they complained. But S.I.M.'s missionaries were few even for evangelism, and money was scarce. When Stewart and Edna were married, they listened to the pleas as they continued to travel the circuit of the churches. "All right," Stewart replied to each one, "You make a building available and raise the money for your teacher's salary for a year. Bring it to me, and I'll make sure you have an African teacher." This system of incentive and reward blossomed into an overnight success. The teachers trained at Egbe or Igbaja and settled happily in the villages, usually teaching in the church buildings, with salaries in hand. The villagers worked hard to collect the money for the next year's wages, thus avoiding debt while educating their children.

Stewart understood the parents' concern for their children better since the birth of his own son, Colin, in June of 1938. When he and Edna trekked to visit the villages, often for weeks at a time, "wee Colin" went along, bringing delight to children and adults alike. As they shared meals and slept in homes, whole families responded to Stewart's preaching, and many were baptized.

In 1940 they went on furlough. Though that meant thousands of miles of weary traveling across both Canada and the United States, at the same time they basked in the refreshment of renewed friendships. Churches welcomed them with

open arms, family eagerly became reacquainted and Edna bore
a second son in Vancouver whom they named Donald.

Then came the War. It shook the nation and left
Stewart wondering if he should enlist as a chaplain. The
decision was not by any means clear-cut in the social
environment of 1940 Vancouver. For the son of a WWI veteran
whose brothers were either in action or on the way, there was
the family tradition to uphold. National service was also the
honorable thing; if a "man of God" ran out on his country in
war time, would he really be above reproach? A great number
of rural Canadians that year were prepared not to think so.
Christmas, 1940, dawned and set upon a soldier of two armies
and a man of two minds.

Chapter 11: The Greater Good

Stewart would have been honored to serve with the Allies but his Prince had already given him his commission in Africa and on May 15, 1941, the McDougalls boarded the <u>S.S. El Nil</u> and looked across the Atlantic. The ship's regular route had been Egypt to France, and most of the crew did not understand English, so a system of sign language emerged, accompanied by grins and chuckles.

Upon arrival in Europe, they received news that the previous month their sister-ship, the <u>Zam Zam</u>, had been sunk. This caused considerable dismay to some of their fellow passengers who immediately decided to disembark and return to New York. Stewart wrote, "I really don't see any advantage in doing that for no matter when you cross the water you do so at a certain amount of risk. . . . We are not the least bit worried so don't worry about us." They landed in Lagos without incident.

But even in Africa the War affected them. Stewart befriended the Canadian soldiers he met, and they soon learned the way to Edna's kitchen, hungry for her fresh bread, a cup of tea, and the warmth of a devout, happy home. They began "dropping in" regularly, often with gifts in hand to show their appreciation for the unflagging hospitality. So earnest was their loyalty that when Stewart's car broke down on the way home from the hospital after the birth of Murray in September of 1943, the soldiers who discovered them escorted them home with exuberant pomp. Stewart found God had made him a chaplain though he had not enlisted in the army!

They did more in their second term than simply minister to the soldiers, however. In 1941 they returned to

Egbe. They had been working there only a few months when
the mission asked them to move to Mopa, which closed for lack
of a missionary. This was the first of a series of compromises
for the greater good, as Stewart gained an appreciation for the
overall strategy in Nigeria. In order to contribute to the
national effort, he had to be willing to sacrifice his special
interest in Egbe, to become a temporary stop-gap in a less
conspicuous post.

They settled in happily, however, content in the
responsibility for oversight of the area churches. Stewart often
trekked out to the villages, though Edna's responsibilities for
the children kept her at home. She prayed for protection on
those nights when Stewart had to be gone.

One night she awoke with a sense that something was
wrong. She padded through the house, investigating, and found
to her horror than an army of driver ants had reached the
screen door of her back porch. In a panic, she roused the
household workers, who rapidly spread hot ashes from the
wood stove in a ring around the house, blocking the ants' path.
In the morning she found that the ants had marched through
both rabbit hutch and chicken coop, stripping the animals to
the bone as they ate them alive.

Most of the time, life was not this dramatic. But just as
she and Stewart began to feel quite "settled", they received a
new request from the mission. The station of Igbaja needed a
missionary to run the Bible school. It was the only S.I.M.
institution for training Yoruba/Yagba leaders, and the
churches needed pastors desperately. So, six months after
moving to Mopa, the McDougalls packed their belongings and
moved yet again for the greater good.

The suddenness of the move gave them no time to
prepare for the demands which met them. Edna taught English

to the fifteen students, and Stewart plunged into an all-day
Bible teaching schedule, studying for the next day's classes
after he came home at night. He wrote his lessons out in
longhand and Edna spent evenings typing them at the kitchen
table. The urgency left them a bit breathless. In addition to
being the only teachers at the Bible school, Stewart also was
responsible for the station's upkeep and the administration of
the dispensary. Many of the Bible school students were
married, and all the students and their families lived on the
station and thus fell under Stewart's care as well. On
weekends he supervised the students' training in evangelism
as they bicycled out to preach in various nearby churches.

Edna was busy too. Besides caring for her home and
children and helping Stewart in the Bible school, she housed
and entertained any visitors who might be passing through,
taught the women, and supervised the local elementary school.
Her housework was made more difficult by the scarcity of
supplies due to the War. As much as possible, they imported,
and after that they had to live off the land. Honey could be
strained; milk could be boiled; flour could be ground.
Complicated preparations lengthened her working hours.

While at Igbaja, Stewart was recommended by the Field
Council and voted in by his fellow missionaries to be District
Superintendent of their area. This meant yet another move
back to Egbe, since that was the administrative center for all
the Yoruba/Yagba stations. Fortunately, Missionary Bill
Crouch had returned from furlough and was able to take over
the responsibilities at the Bible school so the McDougalls could
leave.

This new job was mainly one of administration. Stewart
had oversight of both missionaries and churches among the
Yoruba/Yagba stations, which kept him busy with conferences,

consultations and travel. For two years he listened, talked,
reasoned, shepherded and nurtured the people in his care. He
learned to hear both sides of a story, to give a word of hope to
discouraged hearts, to acknowledge and praise hard work, to
make difficult decisions, to put aside his own weariness in
order to give attention to an important issue, and to organize
his co-laborers strategically for the greater good. At two years'
end he put aside his own weariness one more time as he
listened to other members of the Field Council discuss Lagos.

Lagos was Nigeria's major port and capital. Many of the
Yoruba young people from the rural areas were going to Lagos
to work, and the Field Council began to see that they needed a
place to worship while they were living in the city. Without
nurture, their interest in spiritual things often waned
noticeably. Moreover, the missionaries who arrived by ship
needed someone to meet them when they landed in Nigeria. It
was recommended that S.I.M. open a station in Lagos and

Stewart volunteered to do it, disregarding the fact that he was due for a furlough. He and Edna moved there for nine months and built the station buildings on Montgomery Road before finally sailing to Canada for furlough late in 1945 with Colin, Donald, Murray and new baby, Janet Rose.

After visiting Church of the Open Door and other supporting churches, they stayed several months in Armona, California, with Edna's family and moved to British Columbia to live with Stewart's family for the first six months of 1947. The McDougall family had found a house which they moved to the family property, and so they were able to enjoy having their own space.

Chapter 12: Starting Over

To meet the challenge of the half million inhabitants of this area . . . seven well-staffed stations are needed and needed at once for more reasons than one. . . . . The longer the delay the harder will be the task. The door is wide open. Never have we known the French officials to show a more sympathetic and friendly attitude towards us and our work. God has wonderfully answered the many prayers sent up over a period of at least ten years for the creating of this very attitude and the opening of these very doors.

--Osborne and Strong,1944 reporting to Field Council regarding Dahomey

Yes, from the standpoint of S.I.M., the Dahomey effort was by now ten years old; but the battle for those half million souls had begun twenty years before that in the heart of Miss Frances Boyce. Sometime missionary to China, sometime schoolmarm, valiant warrior in prayer, Frances Boyce heard a lecture in 1914 on the degenerate state of the tribes of Dahomey and, in that hour, received a prayer burden from God which never left her.

For years this woman prayed for Dahomey. At the head of her bed she kept a list of prayer requests, and Dahomey's tribes sat in full view as she repeatedly asked her Heavenly Father to send the gospel there. When she moved to British Columbia to teach school, she little suspected the import one Sunday School pupil named Stewart would have for her prayers.

It was this Miss Boyce who, upon hearing of Stewart's need, forwarded his passage money from London for that first missionary journey after his friends had gone ahead. It was this Miss Boyce who met Stewart in London and took him to Westminster Abbey where he read the last prayer of David

Livingstone: "I pray that heaven's richest blessing may rest
upon the soul who attempts to heal this open sore." As he stood
in the great cathedral, the force of the words poured over him.
He wrote home, "That had come from the heart of Africa, and I
could not but praise God that He had privileged me to share in
the prayer of that great hero of the cross of the Lord Jesus
Christ."

Years later when Stewart was District Superintendent
in Nigeria, he happened upon the British Colonial District
Officer in the streets of Ilorin. "I've just been visiting in
Dahomey," the D.O. commented, "and those people are the
most degraded I've ever seen." The missionary to Nigeria
began to ponder the contrast: here among the Yoruba,
second-generation believers studied the Bible in their own
seminary and led their own churches, while just over the
border the Baribas sat in darkness without even a written
word in their own language to show forth the light of Christ.
The Yorubas had heard the gospel for over forty years! Grieved
and burdened for Dahomey once again, Stewart began to
discuss the Baribas with his Yoruba seminary students, hoping
the Lord would move in their hearts and that one of them
might go but, in the end, the burden remained his own. He
asked the S.I.M. leadership if he could be released from his
position in Nigeria and go to Dahomey to begin a new work.

The mission's reaction was one of surprise. Why leave
the Yoruba work at its peak? Why leave the group whose
language he knew so well to begin all over? Mr. Titcombe,
Stewart's mentor and colleague in the Yoruba work, was
especially puzzled. Even the leaders at Church of the Open
Door back in Los Angeles shook their heads at the news.
Stewart patiently discussed with each group his deep desire to
go. "I don't want to leave the Yorubas," he explained, "I want to

lead them to a wider outreach." It also meant leaving their two older sons, Colin (8) and Don (6) in the S.I.M. missionary children's home in Ontario, Canada. His objective was to begin a work which his Yoruba students could continue and sustain as they learned to be missionaries themselves. The strategic nature of the decision and Stewart's certainty of God's leading made their action unavoidable.

So it was that by faith in 1947, Stewart and Edna returned to Nigeria after a short furlough to gather the few essential belongings they would need for setting up house in Nikki. A truck driver named Jimoh, who had driven them many miles in the past, agreed to carry them as far as his "lorry" would go. Never having been to Dahomey before, they were not sure what condition the bush roads would be in, or even necessarily which road led to Nikki. They agreed with Jimoh that if the road became impassable he would set them down with children and belongings, and head back home. There is no way to imagine just what the outcome of the venture would have been had this happened. The roads proved to be just two parallel walking paths with high grass on either side and down the middle but Jimoh proved extraordinarily persistent, roaring down steep banks into river-beds and up again until finally they arrived at Nikki.

The French Commandant received them with courtesy knowing they were coming and what their purpose was. But the rest of the community would surely be mystified. They had seen many troops in the past few years due to the War; were these new foreigners with the Military? Or maybe traders, like the Muslim missionaries they knew? Stewart and Edna were conscious of the intense curiosity which met them on their arrival. Little could they know how God had been preparing people's hearts for their arrival.

Chapter 13: Bonding

On a hot, dusty afternoon a large rickety truck roared into the village called Nikki. The passengers sensed excitement rising through their weariness as they sat up, stretched, and looked into the passing faces of the people who would be their neighbors for the next four years. When at last they pulled up to the front of the Commandant's house, both Stewart and Edna were wide awake.

The French official and his wife greeted them with gracious hospitality, and for the next few months the McDougalls lived in a small guest house on their property while Stewart began clearing the piece of land they had been given on which to build their own house. He was hampered by lack of money and no means of transport except a bicycle. The first building that went up was only a simple two-room mud house with mud floors and a grass roof. Nearby, he built a kitchen of similar construction. They did not live long in these quarters because the Fuller family from British Columbia sent money to build proper brick-and-stone buildings. He made forms and mud bricks but had to return the seventy miles on his bicycle through wilderness where lions and elephants were plentiful just to order another truck delivery of supplies from Nigeria. On one such trip, his bicycle hit a root and threw him to the ground smashing his pith helmet. The wheel was bent so he repaired it the best he could and rode the rest of the way to Nikki suffering a serious sun stroke and exposing their real vulnerability. Over the next year, they were preoccupied with construction, planting a garden, landscaping, and settling in.

Their main object was to reach the Baribas with the gospel of Christ, and they began efforts toward that end almost as soon as they arrived. First they focused on the Bariba language, recognizing that this was a prerequisite for communicating the gospel. They recognized further that they would have to eventually provide a Bible for them. In this they felt very inadequate, since neither of them had linguistic training. Then one day they received news of a linguist named Dr. William Welmers who would be willing to come for six weeks to help them if they would simply pay the price of his passage. Gratefully they accepted the offer, and on August 22, 1948, they received him into their home. In six weeks of intense study they sketched a Bariba grammar together, meanwhile learning principles from the scholar which would help them in their language-learning long after his ship returned him home.

And language-learning was slow, much slower in Bariba than Yoruba had been. Part of the reason for this came as a great surprise: many of the Baribas also spoke Yoruba! This was true not only in Nikki but also throughout the rest of Dahomey. Furthermore, the Yoruba people, hardworking and enterprising as they were, had spread into many places throughout the country, doing business and prospering. As soon as these people discovered Stewart's proficiency in Yoruba, they became very interested in the white man who had mastered such a difficult language; and of course, thereafter they addressed him in Yoruba. This impeded progress in Bariba, and his feelings about his knowledge of Yoruba became ambivalent: gratitude for the instant rapport it produced, frustration with the impediment to learning Bariba. But then, he reasoned, he was certainly making friends. In fact, both he and Edna were bonding to the Bariba of Nikki, almost instantly won over to them by their warmth.

These people had watched them move into a mud-and-thatch house just like their own, their belongings few, their furnishings sparse. The Nikki villagers began to feel that their new white neighbors were somehow akin to them. If they dropped by the McDougall home on their way from working in the fields, they often brought a gift of some fruits or vegetables they had grown. Edna soon grew a garden of her own so she could return a gift of her tomatoes when receiving their pineapples and yams.

During his brief stay, Dr. Welmers was also impressed by the generosity of the Bariba people. One afternoon as he sat at the kitchen table reviewing notes with Edna, they heard chanting and clapping in the front yard. Several women from a nearby village had each brought a load of firewood on her head to give to Edna. They marched in single-file to the house and then, one by one, they each circled the house while the others chanted and clapped. As each woman completed her round, she threw down her head-load with a flourish while her comrades sent up a cheer. Dr. Welmers was quite moved by this expression of goodwill toward cultural outsiders; but Edna was even more so as she realized that the town from which these women came was one where regular evangelistic outreach had begun.

When the McDougalls' household belongings finally arrived, there was multiplied rejoicing. People had come to see them as "our white people", and with a great sense of propriety they watched Edna unpack. Each item was subjected to scrutiny, comment, and final approval. Edna found herself giving praise in her heart to God for delaying the arrival of her belongings (despite the inconvenience those delays had caused) so they could be a means of bonding rather than a barrier.

Chapter 14: No Strategy of Man

David Ajibola and Elisha Olufemi were two of Stewart's students at Igbaja Seminary. Whereas they had not caught Stewart's vision for the Dahomey outreach in the classroom, the Lord gave them their call at the appropriate time, and now they came to Nikki fully supported as missionaries of the Yoruba/Yagba church.

The foreigners were now two black and one white making a circuit of all the villages surrounding Nikki, building friendships and explaining the gospel through interpreters to the Bariba people. As the people in a village began to believe in Jesus, the missionaries would agree to hold regular prayer meetings there on the condition that the believers build a prayer hut in which to meet. Occasionally the missionaries would be presented with the request: "Take my son home with you and teach him about God and His Word." Thus after some time, there came to be seven young boys living on the Nikki station.

A supporting church in Oregon shipped a truck to them for the work in 1948 so, in January, 1949, Stewart was able to drive to Lagos, Nigeria, to pick up Colin and Donald who came from Canada to join their family. In June, William was born to complete the picture. Now there were four McDougall boys with seven eager playmates and seemingly endless options. Imagine the possibilities for mischief among the boys of Nikki station in those days!

As Edna began to know the women of her neighbor-hood—washing clothes with them in the river, shelling beans with them in their homes, trading vegetables with them from her garden–she noticed that many of them suffered from sores on their bodies which they wrapped in leaves. One day she said impulsively to a neighbor, "If you come to my house tomorrow morning, I will give you something that will make you better." The woman came and did not come alone. Soon Stewart and

Edna had more requests for treatment than they had expertise. In response to their cries for help, the Lord sent an S.I.M. missionary nurse, Miss Alice Wilkinson, formerly serving in Ivory Coast.

Miss Wilkinson was an asset to the ministry team in many ways. Her ministry of healing greatly expanded the audience for the gospel message, and she particularly reached out to the children using Vacation Bible School curricula and teaching the hour of religious instruction at the school. But Alice never allowed her schedule to become too cramped for a few moments of conversation with her fellow missionaries, the most recent addition being Gus Fredlund, formerly serving in Niger. Gus Fredlund had the same passion to present Jesus to the Fulani tribe as Stewart had for the Baribas. As Miss Wilkinson grew to share Mr. Fredlund's point of view, their colleagues began the happy preparations for a wedding.

The first three years of the evangelism of Nikki were very much like church planting strategies elsewhere, except that there was no way any one could have planned it. The McDougalls went alone to Nikki as the Morrows went alone to Kandi. After three years of God's superintendence the missionary staff had tripled, the horizons of ministry had broadened, the Baribas were not only receptive to the gospel but were also giving their children. No strategy of man could orchestrate this kind of expansion.

As Alice Fredlund settled into her new role as missionary wife, Edna shared her joy and excitement. No human strategy brought these women together in ministry, and who knew then the awfulness and grace of His billows?

They were beginning to see the vision develop. Their family was settled; they had a handle on the language and a strategy for translation; they had committed and well trained colleagues; they had the confidence of mission leaders; and now they had a truck to facilitate the building expansion would require, but the roads and access would continue to demand all their imaginative resources. On one medical emergency trip during rainy season, they were able to log only twenty-five miles in twenty-four hours.

Looks like we have a problem.

Can I get some help here?

I think it'll work.

Maybe not.

Chapter 15: Expansion

The McDougalls' furlough in 1951-52 entailed a decisive strategic shift away from their earlier Yoruba work. When they returned to the field in 1952, it was to plant the church of Jesus in all of Dahomey beginning at Nikki. Stewart left his family in Canada to take six months of French language study in Paris. Once this retooling was complete, Colin was left in the home for missionary children in Canada for high school, but the other children returned to Africa to study at Kent Academy nearer their parents.

They were in for a shock—a shock that led to the greatest era of expansion for the church in Dahomey. J. B. Williams decided not to return to Parakou after his furlough but to take a position in the home office which required a significant change in field operations. This came at a time when the S.I.M. was preparing to send increased personnel to geographically expand the evangelism effort in Dahomey and, since Stewart was superintendent at the time, he had to leave Nikki and take the reins in Parakou.

One detects a hint of bitterness over this change of direction when Stewart writes of Williams' decision, "I don't understand how a man who has been involved in the work over here can ever be satisfied to go back." He was, in fact, chagrined to leave Nikki—the strategic center for outreach to the Bariba tribe—to be installed in the administrative head-quarters. But this was where he was needed, and it was from Parakou that the great expansion was directed.

Roland Pickering, the delightful and fun-loving bachelor, was already evangelizing the Dompago tribe in their own language, and was audacious enough to think that he and

his Dompago colleagues could translate the Bible. Stan
Dudgeon joined the Fredlunds in Kandi, strengthening the
team and freeing Gus Fredlund to finish translating Mark's
Gospel in Fulani. The Thamer family, who were already fluent
in Yoruba, were recruited from Nigeria to open up the southern
station of Tchaourou.

Stewart found there was plenty to do in Parakou
besides administrative correspondence. He felt the most important ministry in Parakou town was the Bible school, and he
recruited some of his former students from Igbaja days to help
teach. Stewart was dismayed that the courses were being
taught in French (in which few of the Yoruba students were
proficient) and that they were being taught by a European
woman. In short order, he had Yoruba teachers instructing the
Yoruba students in the vernacular. There were both Yoruba
and Bariba congregations, and, on one Sunday in 1953,
Stewart took part in six church services. In that year Sunday
school attendance jumped from twelve to one hundred twenty-
one.

While the opportunities were abundant all across
Dahomey, the outlook was especially promising in the South
where land grants were wide open to the S.I.M. But finances
were lagging for the development of Tchaourou and Cotonou,
and these towns were a day's journey by wood-burning train
from Parakou. Moreover, at the same time the southern
expansion was held up by lack of finances, the local government in Parakou was pressuring the S.I.M. to build a
respectable urban church building near the town center.
S.I.M.'s policy was for local churches to build indigenous
edifices with local funds; but the land they were given in
Parakou town was ideal, and the mission agreed to let Stewart
build the building if he could raise the money. Finally it was

Neil Barnes, Stewart's friend from Coos Bay, Oregon, who donated the $2,000 which enabled them to build the Yoruba church in Parakou.

Stewart's original strategy for Dahomey seemed to be coming about just as he had envisioned: the Yoruba teachers from Nigeria were evangelizing and making disciples among the Yorubas in Parakou and these young disciples were reaching the local Baribas. Stewart left the evangelism more and more in the hands of his disciples as he administered the growing construction machine—six pairs of pit-sawyers could just barely keep pace with the mission construction boom of 1953-54.

It was just when the missionary personnel were stretched to the limit that the Fulani people movement began to gain momentum. Gus Fredlund and Stan Dudgeon were simply unable to keep up with the conversions. The semi-nomadic Fulanis were hard to keep up with anyway and seemed closed to Fredlund's ministry in Nigeria where Islam had preceded him. But as the missionaries developed personal relationships with individual men and as their ministry operated more and more in the vernacular, the Lord began calling out whole households for His Name. Near the close of 1953, Stewart urgently requested help of his friend Dogon Yaro, a Hausa/Fulani evangelist with a great love for Jesus. It was the wisest choice he could have made.

Dogon Yaro and Fredlund became the most successful crusade team among the Fulani up to that time. Dogon Yaro's dynamism and Gus Fredlund's amicability and love for his listeners attracted Fulani men and their households. In Sinendé, the elusive Fulanis assembled in great numbers for the government-sponsored inoculations of their cattle, and by God's synchronization, the crusade arrived when the Fulani

population was at its peak. In Parakou, the crusade gave rise
to a church of two hundred fifty Fulani at a distance of twenty
miles from town, seemingly born overnight.

The growth of the church among this formerly closed
tribe gave an encouraging lift to the Field Council when they
met in Jos, Nigeria, that June of 1954. How strange that as
Stewart gave his reports with the other churchmen and looked
to future growth, the seeds of disease were already
germinating that would take him out of the expansion.

Friends: Billy and Boni

Chapter 16: Needles

Janet had celebrated her ninth birthday in May. After the District meetings in June, she was not feeling well. Their trusted doctor at the nearest Baptist hospital in Shaki, Nigeria, was puzzled by her continued fever. He suspected tuberculosis but was not satisfied with that diagnosis either, so unfortunately, she would have to be admitted to the hospital. During the fall of 1954, the family relocated temporarily from Parakou to Jos, Nigeria.

By the time Stewart was able to arrive in Jos with five year-old William and eleven year-old Murray, it was apparent to all that Janet needed the care of pediatric specialists in the United States. But with the outreach boom underway in Dahomey, the Field Council could not afford to have the district's superintendent take an early furlough. The compromise was for Edna to take the four children back to North America while Stewart returned to Parakou to be assisted there by the Cail family. Edna agreed this was the best way and, in early November, she arrived with some trepidation in New York: her only daughter sick of an undiagnosed disease with the vague hope that if the tropics had caused the illness, leaving the tropics might cure it.

Edna admitted Janet to St. Luke's Hospital in New York and took the younger boys up to Canada to be with their oldest brother, Colin, while Janet was under observation. Her symptoms included lesions in her throat and mouth and later on the nasal septum, and of course, the fever. The sores were painful and she was almost constantly being punctured for blood samples or medications, so that it was distressing to her mother to watch her daily progress, if progress it was. The

sickness seemed to come in tides, waxing and waning, and still
it had no name. Janet's case was taken over by Dr. Spiers, a
personable woman who was able to put Edna at ease.

Meanwhile in Parakou, Stewart moved out of the family
house so that the Cails could move in, and he continued to
administer the Bible school. By now the school had both Bariba
and Yoruba students as well as six of the students' wives. The
women studied Bible co-educationally with the men and in the
afternoons they took instruction in reading and cloth-weaving.
On weekends all sixteen students were going out to minister
the gospel in the community, and every Monday they brought
back news of God's blessing. Roland Pickering was also far
ahead of projections for the church in Dompago, and, in fact, he
was planning to start a Bible school within the year. He had
already translated the Gospel of Mark into Dompago, and, in
Pila, the Gospel of Mark was also ready for printing.

But now the spiritual battle took on the aspect of a war
of attrition. As Christmas approached, Stewart felt his
motivation slipping. The energy required to keep the expansion
going was more than the man could sustain alone without his
family, with his heart and concentration divided. On the one
hand he couldn't see how he could pass the Christmas season
alone with his family in crisis but then to whom would he leave
the work? and who could solidify the gains of the last three
years? and who would sustain the momentum? The doctors still
seemed confident of a cure and Stewart and Edna felt that if
Janet were to get well soon they could all be reunited on the
field and then could take their scheduled furlough in 1956.

The war began to take its casualties when the
protagonists were already tiring. David Ajibola, Stewart's
Yoruba disciple from Igbaja days and his first colleague in the
Dahomey frontier, drowned off the coast of Nigeria near Lagos.

Seeds of discord and dissension were being sown among the
saints in the Yoruba church in Parakou, much as discord had
been fomented among the Nigerian Yorubas when Stewart was
superintendent there. And Janet's symptoms were worse. The
lesions were still painful, but now her joints were sore and stiff
as well and she could no longer fully extend her arms. Dr.
Spiers' prognosis was revised from two months to six, and Edna
finally requested S.I.M. to free Stewart to come home.

      The details were finally worked out at the end of May
for Stewart to leave the field in August, but in the meantime
Edna had become overwhelmed by her crisis in New York. As
soon as seventeen-year-old Colin got out of school she wrote for
him to come take care of her while she continued to care for
Janet. Meanwhile Janet's condition deteriorated during the
summer of 1955 until she had to be readmitted to the hospital,
and then the McDougalls fell victim to the S.I.M. rule book: a
furloughing missionary could only use the airlines if there was
no cheaper means of travel. Edna began to realize that if
Stewart had to come by ship, she still had a long wait ahead.

      God provided for the family that summer through the
generosity of an upstate New York farmer named Albert Gibbs.
He was a concerned layman. His daughter, Alberta, was with
S.I.M. in Dahomey and his son, Alan, would one day join them
in the work. The Gibbs made room for the McDougall boys on
their farm in July, and the country life seemed to suit them
quite well.

      When Stewart finally arrived in America at summer's
end, there were only a couple of weeks left before schools
opened on the West Coast, so the family immediately left for
the Church of the Open Door in Los Angeles where they were
housed at the church's missionary cottages. Janet came under
the care of Dr. Jacques and the Los Angeles Orthopedic

Hospital for tuberculosis of the bones, or whatever it was that by now had begun to cripple her.

Chapter 17: Civilian Life

By Christmas 1955, Stewart McDougall, man of action, was at a dead end. S.I.M. had no work for him on the West Coast. Because he was still a Canadian citizen, he could not take ordinary employment to provide for his family. Worst of all, he was out of his Dahomey commission for a period of indefinite duration and there was nothing he could do about it.

Dr. Darroch, North America Director of S.I.M., offered Stewart several regional representative positions in the U.S. and Canada, which Stewart was at first inclined to reject. Eventually he was able to accept the prospects and the challenge of the S.I.M.'s mid-western states including Chicago and mission representation at the Moody Bible Institute. The challenge of this assignment arose from the fact that S.I.M. had lost credibility in the region during the early 1950's and many associations would have to be restored or created anew. Unfortunately, the job would require a great deal of travel (three weeks per month, in fact); so when the family relocated to Wheaton, Illinois, in the summer of 1956, they still had to get along without Dad much of the time.

Each child dealt with his father's absences differently. Colin grew into independence quite early, since he rarely lived with his parents after age six. In fact, when the family re-settled in Wheaton he decided to stay in California to attend BIOLA although he later joined the family and attended Moody Bible Institute. Donald was also independent, preferring the public school system to the private Wheaton Academy, but he found it difficult to accept the absence of his dad and expressed resentment at times. Murray was the most gregarious and easy-going of the children but seemed to have

the most difficulty adjusting to boarding schools until he
entered Wheaton Academy where he thrived. Bill never did
find a context away from home where he could be productive
and content and so was always a concern to his parents.

Of course, the relocation to Wheaton meant that Janet
would have to leave the care of Dr. Jacques in Los Angeles who
was now convinced that her affliction was not tuberculosis
anyway. When Janet came under the supervision of Dr. Adolph
in Chicago, she was still without a diagnosis after two years of
treatment. It was not until April, 1957, almost three years
after her first symptoms, that filaria was diagnosed and treatment begun. It was then discovered that all seven McDougalls
carried the filariasis parasite and each had to take a course of
Hetrazan until it was eliminated.

After completing one year at Moody, Colin announced to
his surprised parents that he was leaving school to become
assistant manager of an auto parts store. The other addition to
the household was Stewart's unmarried sister, Islay, who came
as his secretary and, of course, there were numerous overnight
visitors according to the custom of missionaries everywhere to
give and receive hospitality. It was actually a welcome relief for
the McDougalls to return to American civilian life, to be near
their children, to hear other men expound the Scripture, but
four years was enough. Janet's health had improved signifi-
cantly so Stewart applied for, and, in 1959 received, a new
commission to Dahomey as administrator of the boys' boarding
school at Sinendé; they were to leave for Africa September 1. A
final deputation trip was scheduled for the summer, tickets
were booked, and the mid-western region was turned over to
another S.I.M. representative. Then came Colin's second
surprise: he and fiancee, Virginia, were going to be married
August 28 in Illinois. The summer of 1959 was even busier

than they had imagined, but by September, the McDougalls
were headed overseas.

McDougall Family 1958
Colin, Murray, Donald
Stewart, Janet, Bill, Edna

Chapter 18: Statecraft

The Sinendé assignment lasted less than a year, though it was full of its own excitement. Stewart organized and built his most commodious and civilized mission home ever with even a flush toilet. The school was an administrative challenge in that Sinendé was experiencing drought and he was responsible for a school of hungry boys. Edna, of course, was mother to the whole crowd, and the fierce heat together with her rowdy charges often left her exhausted. During their brief tenure, nineteen boys trusted Christ and, as the drought broke and the climate cooled a bit, the McDougalls found themselves gaining enthusiasm for their new work.

Sinendé was, in fact, the kind of work a man could put his heart into with potential for growth and multifaceted ministry, much like the days at Egbe or at Nikki. But God had other men chosen to build it. Dahomey was embroiled in a controversy that would change forever the missionary effort there. The nation needed statesmen, and if Stewart had never before been called in that capacity, he must fill it now. His peers chose him to return to Parakou as their superintendent and to chart a new course for the church.

When the McDougalls returned to Parakou, they found several problems simmering. The outgoing superintendent had been handicapped in dealing with the local church because he was not conversant with Yoruba language and culture. The Yoruba penchant for politics was now manifest in the church as the people separated into the party of polygamy and the party opposed to polygamy with the pastor silently aiding the politically powerful polygamists. The polygamists had effectively handcuffed the superintendent by recalling their

Methodist heritage to gain credibility and by painting those opposed as the party of the white missionary. Any statement the missionary made against polygamy would merely prove the polygamists' point.

On the national scene, Dahomey gained independence from France and the new republic turned almost immediately to the communist Chinese for patronage. The Methodist secessionists began to plant the seeds for the expulsion of S.I.M. expatriate missionaries from the country, gaining confidence from the new political climate.

The change of government also forced Stewart back to the beginning with the plans for Bembèrèkè Hospital. Plans had already progressed to the point of extensive fund raising, but now fresh approvals were needed. The Bariba Literature Center was established by the memorial fund of Mrs. Bergman (Edna's early mentor), and Stewart felt an urgency to launch that project immediately. He envisioned a center for both the production and distribution of Bariba literature and scripture portions.

Roland Pickering's Dompago outreach was still a bright spot: the Bible school was well-established and the translation was going ahead. The Fulani outreach was now beginning to mature with whole villages practicing the Christian faith. The Bariba Bible School moved from Parakou to Sinendé under the supervision of the Zobrists, and Jean Soutar, a fully-trained linguist, took over the Bariba New Testament project in Nikki. By the end of 1960, Stewart had delegated almost all of the Bariba work to other missionaries at other stations and was able to concentrate his energy on the Parakou Yorubas.

Stewart entered this stage of ministry with some admixture of regret. He was certainly in the place God wanted him, and he was certainly the leader for the hour. God had carefully trained him to deal with Yoruba churchmen, but his great desire had been for the Baribas. The people he had most wanted to reach were eventually reached by others; in fact, to his chagrin, he still did not feel himself fluent in the Bariba language. But then, just before Christmas, the Lord provided a three-day conference that greatly consoled the pioneer in him, as twenty-seven of his Bariba Bible School students came to Parakou for a reunion. He wrote, "On the closing day we knelt in prayer, and I lifted my eyes and looked at those twenty-seven young men kneeling and pleading with God for their own people. And my eyes clouded with tears as I thought of just a little over fifteen years ago when Edna and I stood alone at Nikki and prayed, 'Lord, give us souls among these people.'"

Both Stewart and Edna fought loneliness during this period more than ever. After five years of being together as a family, they and the children were all separated. Bill, now twelve years old studied at Kent Academy in Nigeria. Janet was sixteen, living in a home for MKs and studying at Perry High School in Michigan. She spent Christmas 1961 in Chicago with Colin who now had two children still unseen by the grandparents. Murray, eighteen, was writing home with enthusiasm about his romance with Jan (whom he would eventually marry), and Donald was driving a bus between the downtown campus of Bible Institute of Los Angeles and the new BIOLA College campus in La Mirada.

The loneliness was heightened at times by recurring leadership crises both from above and from below. On the field, the man whom Stewart had replaced as superintendent began to challenge the church's new direction, and the mission personnel began to divide into parties just as the national church was doing. Some were for appeasement, some for confrontation. The ministry team seemed to be weakening just

as it faced its greatest test. At the same time, the Field Council
for West Africa was facing a crisis of confidence in their home
directors. Stewart was elected to represent the council's
unanimous feeling that the current director-designate ought
not be confirmed.

Stewart did, in fact, attend S.I.M.'s 1962 general council
to vote against the appointment of Mr. Ray Davis as S.I.M.'s
General Director. He was not confirmed on the first ballot, but
was confirmed unopposed on the second. Stewart was asked at
that time to consider taking the post of West Africa Field
Director in Jos, Nigeria. It may have been tempting to accept
such an assignment rather than return to the storm at
Parakou, but both Stewart and Edna felt they could not
abandon the church to chaos. Fortunately, Bill Crouch was
available and was chosen for the post which enabled Stewart to
travel to Chicago for a month with the family. Murray was at
the climax of his high school track and field career and was
glad to have Dad along to share his celebrity. Then off they
went to Los Angeles: Murray to enter BIOLA College and
Stewart to congratulate Don and Perlene on their recently
announced engagement.

Back in Parakou, Edna had her own responsibilities.
For years a liaison between women of the Yoruba and the
Bariba tribes, she had established an adoption program for
unwanted Bariba babies. Bariba women had the pagan custom
of abandoning babies whose top teeth came in before the
bottom teeth, usually with fatal results. Edna accepted these
babies and found Yoruba Christians who would adopt them.
During her husband's absence, Edna hosted the Skullman and
Wiebe film crew who were producing the S.I.M.-sponsored <u>This
Child Shall Be a Slave</u>, which documented the plight of
abandoned children. Within a few years Edna would have the

joy of seeing Bariba Christians take over the program to adopt the outcasts of their own tribe.

By August, 1962, when Stewart returned to the field after his three-month absence, he could sense the looming crisis. Despite months of prayer and attempts at persuasion, there was no easy way to heal the rift. If the polygamists were allowed to lead, polygamy would become the accepted practice of the church. Therefore, to protect the integrity of the Yoruba church it seemed that a confrontation would be necessary.

Chapter 19: Schism

In September, 1962, the McDougalls took the unusual precaution of moving into rather cramped quarters on the church compound. It had become apparent that the polygamists were prepared to forcibly take over the church. Those of Stewart's colleagues who felt the issue of polygamy was minor were openly critical of the move, calling him reactionary and blaming him in advance for splitting the church apart.

The annual conference was held in Tchaourou that December with delegates sent from all over Dahomey. Stewart described it in a letter as "the best conference we have ever had." After he left, however, his long-time friend and colleague, James Odjo Boro, met separately with the Bariba delegates. As pastor of the Yoruba church in Parakou, he presented the Baribas with his plan to secede from the evangelicals and join the Methodist denomination. Had the Baribas agreed, this would have marked the end of the ministry of S.I.M. in Dahomey. As it was, the Baribas were scandalized by Pastor James' plan saying, "In the fifteen years before the S.I.M. came to Dahomey you never tried to tell us the gospel; the white men of the mission evangelized us. You did not care about us in the past, so why should we join you now?"

The fallout from this confrontation can hardly be exaggerated. The choir director had already been dismissed because of his multiple wives, and now the elders from the north were insisting that polygamists no longer be allowed to stand for election as church elders. The Yorubas from the coastal regions made the eldership their rallying ground, insisting that polygamists also be allowed to hold the office of

elder. Pastor James refused to take a public stand on the issue
of polygamy, believing it to be an issue of primarily political
significance. Mission-trained evangelists and elders felt that
the Bible's stated condition that elders be husband of only one
wife made the issue fundamental. In a meeting that lasted
three-and-a-half hours, they forced Pastor James to either
state his position or resign his pastorate—and resign he did.

The ensuing schism was near-fatal for so young a
church. The Yoruba Methodists established a church
immediately next door. Polygamists were welcomed as elders
there as was Pastor James. The Yorubas from the south,
accustomed as they were to political intrigue, also managed to
take all of the church finances and fully seventy-five percent of
the church membership and would have taken the church
property itself if the missionaries had not been physically
occupying it. The entire population of Parakou was scandalized
by the feuding Protestants. In this environment it was easy for
Stewart's fellow missionaries to find fault with him.

However, once the shock passed, the church made rapid
recovery. The elders who had been true to the last called a
morning prayer service for 6 AM every morning. The prayer
meeting began with fifteen regular attenders and grew. Soon
they felt compelled to set Fridays aside as a day of fasting and
prayer. One woman said it was the first time in years she had
felt free to pray in that church, but now the Spirit of God
seemed to be at liberty among them. The elders exhorted the
people not to be bitter, but to receive back the defectors
whenever God chose to bring them back.

Adamu Dogon Yaro who had been so effective with Gus
Fredlund in Fulani evangelism had moved to Dahomey with
his wife to teach at the Fulani Bible School. Roland Pickering's
disciples were running the Dompago work well enough for him

to leave it in their hands for eighteen months while he pursued
further linguistic training. He was pleased to find them
maturing to independence. Seeing the strength of the Beninois
believers, Stewart and Edna decided to carry on with their
1963 furlough as planned.

Chapter 20: The Cities Southward

Stewart and Edna returned to the field in November, 1964, the church schism behind them and a new era about to begin. Their furlough had been so packed with activity that it seemed almost restful to go back to work.

The previous June, Bill had left Kent Academy to accompany Stewart, making overseas stops in Switzerland, Italy and Scotland. From Chicago they drove, helping Colin and Jinny move their household to California (a 72-hour marathon) less than a week before Stewart was to officiate at Don's wedding in North Hollywood, California. After the wedding, Stewart handled Don's preaching responsibilities while Don and Perlene went on their honeymoon.

The three-bedroom furlough house across the street from BIOLA College was packed with Stewart and Edna and their three unmarried children plus Colin and Jinny with their two and infant Kevin added in December. Stewart was away for three months in the spring with speaking engagements in Canada and the American Midwest. The expanding family had plenty of motivation when an opportunity came for Colin and Jinny to buy the home of Stewart's friend, Al Brandt, in La Mirada. Colin was coaching track at BIOLA and was offered a full-time position which he accepted and the family moved in. Stewart added on an apartment to house Janet during her freshman year at BIOLA. In the summer, it was Murray and Jan's turn to get married. Stewart and Edna then drove back to Michigan to enroll Bill in his new high school before returning overseas.

The outreach about to be launched in Dahomey would require a different kind of transportation. Stewart bought a

small Opel suitable for urban work and started putting miles
on it. The McDougalls moved back to the mission compound
(since the church was no longer threatened), leaving the church
manse available for Edna's Bible classes, and construction
began on the Parakou Christian Bookstore. After eighteen
years of mission to the rural tribes, the new focus was upon the
emerging educated class in Dahomey's urban centers,
especially Parakou and Cotonou. On June 1, 1965, the bookstore opened.

The big news at the Bariba women's conference that
year was that the Baribas wanted a change in the adoption
program for abandoned Bariba infants. To this point the
evangelical Yoruba women had run the program and adopted
the Bariba outcasts, but now the Baribas were ready to adopt
their own, in effect ending the pagan custom of abandonment.

Janet continued to have symptoms of filaria: lethargy
and pains in her joints and her doctors wanted to operate. Bill
was also having difficulties with academics in his new school,
so Edna went back to the U.S. for the summer. As it turned
out, Janet had improved by the time her mother got there, but
it was a bonus to be on hand for the birth of Don and Perlene's
baby girl, Susan. Trusting the Lord to provide the higher
tuition, Edna withdrew Bill from his school in Michigan and
enrolled him in the school of his choice, Wheaton Academy near
Chicago.

Edna was back in Dahomey in time to be met by her
husband before he left for a special trip to Nigeria to address
the leaders of the evangelical Yoruba church there. He had a
once-in-a-lifetime opportunity to present the needs of the
Yoruba church in Dahomey and to enlist Yorubas in Nigeria to
reach their own. As he had attempted to inspire his Nigerian
students at Igbaja years ago, now he spoke to his colleagues in

ministry. Would they undertake this new missionary thrust into Cotonou? Cotonou was a largely Yoruba city, the largest in Dahomey. Would the Yorubas accept the challenge?

After his sermon and his words of challenge, the pastor who had invited Stewart rose publicly to commit himself to reaching his tribesmen in southern Dahomey, but he did not stop there. "Who else will stand with me?" he asked, and his colleagues stood to a man, committing their energies to advance the gospel in the South. Within a month they had appointed two men to serve the church in southern Dahomey.

Stewart lost no time once he had these commitments. Progress had to be made while the men were still on fire. In less than a month he was in Cotonou with his colleagues Gordon Beacham and Jim Cail looking for property, hoping to build a youth center and to open an office and a guest house. These plans appeared tenuous for a few days before Christmas when the military overthrew the civilian government in Cotonou, but even then Stewart was sanguine, feeling that once the communists were gone from the civil government there would be greater opportunities for the gospel. In Parakou, at least, the coup came peacefully without bloodshed. During the second half of 1965 much time was spent organizing the evangelistic crusade of Yves Perrier through French West Africa including Upper Volta, Niger and Dahomey. The Methodist mission cooperated with S.I.M. and ECWA to plan the largest crusade in the history of Dahomey with a two week campaign in January, 1966, at Parakou and then two weeks in February at Cotonou. The publicity was thorough. The music provided by ELWA radio from Monrovia, Liberia, was quite professional, attracting great crowds. Edna was hostess for the Perriers during their Parakou campaign, but she was freed

from those responsibilities in February and was able to
accompany Stewart to Cotonou for the meetings.

The first week of that campaign was exhausting but
thrilling to those involved. Stewart was especially excited by
the response and dreamed of the follow-up they could have
there, particularly among the young and educated listeners.
The Lord was truly giving them the cities! The team took an
afternoon break on February 11 and went by car to the beach.

The morning of February 11, 1966 carried no sense of
premonition as Stewart and Edna quietly left their sleeping
fellow-missionaries in the little bungalow and went to watch
the sunrise on the beach. They were still marveling over the
results of the previous night's evangelistic meeting: sixty new
believers in Jesus Christ. As the grey dawn had warmed to
gold, Stewart read aloud, "But I would you should understand,
brethren, that the things which happened to me have fallen out
rather unto the furtherance of the gospel . . . . According to my
earnest expectation and my hope, that in nothing I shall be
ashamed, but that with all boldness, as always, so now also
Christ shall be magnified in my body, whether it be by life or
by death. For to me, to live is Christ, and to die is gain"
(Phil. 1:12, 20, 21). He had observed thoughtfully, "Nothing
ever happens to God's child by accident." After prayer, they had
stood side by side, talked of the greatness of God as displayed
in the sea, and sang. It was a fitting way to begin a new
morning, especially this one—heads thrown back, throats full of
praise. None of the sea's menace had shown itself then.

Nor had it later when, after a picnic lunch on the shore
with several of their fellow-missionaries, Edna watched
Stewart and Gus Fredlund and Al Cross dive into the waves for
a brief swim. The water was warm and the sky was blue. Edna
walked along the beach, kicking the edges of the waves into

spray. As she walked, she quoted the words to a poem by Annie
Johnson Flint:

> They are God's billows, whether we are toiling
> Through tempest-driven waves that never cease,
> While deep to deep with clamor loud is calling,
> Or at His word they hush themselves in peace.
>
> They are God's billows, whether He divides them,
> Making us walk dry shod where seas had flowed,
> Or lets tumultuous breakers surge about us
> Rushing unchecked across our only road.

She said aloud, "They are His Billows," little guessing what an
added dimension of meaning those verses would shortly hold
for her. She glanced at her watch as she turned back and
thought that the men had been swimming a long time. Then,
with that suddenness which nightmares share, Al Cross lay
exhausted on the beach, gasping urgently that Stewart and
Gus could not return to shore.

There were a number of people in the party, but very
few swimmers among them, and it was not until Al Cross
returned gasping on the shore that any alarm went up. The
ELWA team ran up the otherwise deserted coastline to get
assistance from fishermen who happened to be there mending
their nets. These jumped into their boats and searched the
area until they were able to recover the bodies of Stewart and
Gus Fredlund. Stewart was found in knee deep water close to
shore and the ELWA team administered resuscitation efforts
while the car was brought near to the shore. Stewart's heart
continued to beat for more than two hours giving signs of hope.
Gus' body was found later farther out to sea.

Edna found herself on her knees saying over and over,
"Lord, glorify Thyself" as she watched the men trying to revive
her husband. Finally she calmed down enough to be quiet, and
into her stillness came the reply, "They are My billows." God
comforted her at the hour of her beloved's death.

The physician staff of the hospital was on extended
lunch break, and frustrating minutes passed with him
unattended on a gurney as a doctor was paged. Edna was
separated from Stewart in a waiting room. When the doctor did
finally arrive, it was to inform her that her husband of thirty
years was dead.

The crusade organizing committee came to the decision
that the campaign should continue to its scheduled conclusion,

but Yves Perrier was unable to continue preaching; the cumulative exhaustion followed by the drowning accident overwhelmed him. The missionary staff were also stunned at the loss of two colleagues and their leader, and only by great force of will were they able to complete the series of meetings. The U.S. ambassador handled arrangements and provided cars to the entourage returning that night to Parakou. A car was also sent to Kandi for Mrs. Fredlund to bring her the shocking news and transport her to the funeral held the next day at the Parakou church.

Chapter 21: Grief and Farewells

Edna's entourage returned home, reaching the Parakou compound in the darkness of early morning, February 12. Even at five o'clock, the compound was a sea of people who stood at Edna's approach and then in unison bowed low to the ground, the African expression of profound respect. Once the Western rituals of grief were over, they made way for the Yoruba rituals to begin.

That day, masses of cars, motorbikes, bicycles and pedestrians moved from church to cemetery to pay their last respects to a missionary and his colleague whose arrival in Dahomey, West Africa, nineteen years before had gone almost unnoticed. The variety of mourners reflected the wide influence of their outreach. Present were the Catholic bishop accompanied by priests and nuns, Protestant missionaries from bush stations near and far, French government officials, every shopkeeper in Parakou, and, of course, crowds of the Africans to whom Stewart McDougall and his friend, Gus Fredlund, had dedicated their lives.

The group's mourning held an aura of stunned disbelief. Grief beyond speech muted their expressions of sorrow to Stewart's widow, Edna. Occasionally one or two blurted out words of their loss to her. One said sadly, "Our father has gone," and another managed, "The great tree in the middle of the compound has fallen."

Their shock was understandable. Vigorous, healthy, busy as District Superintendent of the Sudan Interior Mission's Dahomey missionaries and most recently conducting a week of evangelistic meetings in an effort to begin outreach in the port

town of Cotonou, Stewart's life had ended with an abruptness
that seemed as unrealistic as a bad dream.

According to the custom, Edna stationed herself in the
parlor and received her mourners by ones and twos, resting
only at intervals. The mourners kept coming for a solid
week--even those estranged by the church schism came to
speak with her. According to the wishes of both widows, the
men were interred at the public cemetery with simple
headstones rather than the elaborate monuments the church
people had proposed.

But the loss of Stewart McDougall was not just a
bereavement to his wife. As the letters and telegrams of
condolence poured in, one colleague mourned, "Some people are
missed only by their own families, but Stewart will be missed
by our whole missionary family. He was so much thought of.
What ever is Dahomey going to do?" Another wrote, "The dear
African people are heart-broken along with us to lose a prince
among men." Yet another wept,"Oh my dear, dear Edna,
perhaps I have never said so . . . because we do often foolishly
coat over our real feelings with banalities, but you and Stewart
have long been among my most *favorite* people on the face of
the earth. I have loved you completely, without reservation . . .
So of course there is a terrible gaping void in the niche where
Stewart belongs in my heart and in my mind."

One African summed up the general feeling: "The center
pole has fallen; now what do we do?" That was indeed the
recurring question. For Stewart McDougall, unobtrusive and
unknown upon his arrival to Dahomey, had come to a central
position in God's work there.

Colin was able to secure compassionate leave from his
teaching assignment at BIOLA College and come to Dahomey.
By the time he arrived, Edna had already come to the decision

that she should return to the U.S. rather than finish out Stewart's term. Colin was able to dispose of his dad's tools and belongings as well as cover severance expenses for all of Stewart's workmen. It was astounding how many relationships of trust he had established: there were schoolboys, students in technical school, the workmen, his colleagues; all of these relationships entailing "loose ends" to be dealt with and only a few days to do it.

Being unsure of her future and whether she would ever be able to return to Africa, Edna asked Colin to take her back to Nigeria to the stations where they had served and where they had so many friends. They visited Igbaja where Stewart had been principal of the Bible School (now a seminary), Egbe where they had enjoyed many years of fruitful service and Isanlu where Edna and Stewart were married and finally, Lagos station on Montgomery Road which Stewart had built.

Two incidents stand out beyond the warm and crowded receptions they were accorded. At Igbaja, the elders of the church asked to meet with Colin alone and they had only one question: "Why does the church in America send us no more missionaries like Titcombe, Playfair and McDougall? All you send us any more are book-keepers and school teachers." Colin's response was that the mission had told American churches that the Nigerian church was now mature and was to be considered a sister rather than a daughter. Did the elders want him to return to America and tell the churches that the mission had misinformed them? Do they really need more missionaries or have they become mature enough to need only book-keepers and school teachers? After considerable discussion, the elders told him that they would be satisfied with book-keepers and school teachers and thanked him for meeting with them.

In Egbe, the woman who had been Colin's nurse when he was a small child walked a full day and slept across the entrance to his apartment all night on the cement porch and could not be convinced to find a warmer and softer place to sleep. She remained sitting on the porch for two full days and lying across the entry for three nights until Colin and Edna left for Lagos. Many very kind words and impressive receptions were held for them but these two encounters were the most remarkable.

By April, Edna was in Wheaton with Bill, thirty years of missionary work behind her.

Chapter 22: Edna's Final Effort

Edna enjoyed the prospect of living near her children and grandchildren in Southern California. She had furlough time accumulated and was eligible to stay for a time in the Church of the Open Door missionary cottages in Glendale. However, Glendale was a long way from La Mirada; she had no vehicle or driver's license and housing was expensive in California. She unexpectedly received a life insurance check from a policy taken out on Stewart by a supporting church in Coos Bay, Oregon and began to look for ways to afford a home near her children. She found a home where she and Janet could live and soon after was offered a job at BIOLA College as Correspondence Coordinator, answering mail from donors and questions from radio listeners to the BIOLA Hour broadcasts. Dahomey, however, was never far from her thoughts and always in her prayers.

By 1969, her family was starting to move back to Africa. After graduating from Talbot Seminary, Don and Perlene were accepted by S.I.M. to teach at Igbaja Seminary where Stewart had taught twenty-five years earlier. Murray and Jan were headed to Swaziland under The Evangelical Alliance Mission and Janet was planning to apply to S.I.M. to teach in Ethiopia after graduation in 1970.

Although she loved her job and her home, in early 1971, Edna applied to S.I.M. for another assignment to Dahomey, this time to Cotonou to attempt to carry on Stewart's unfinished vision to evangelize the capital city. She was accepted but her French language skills needed sharpening so she left for Switzerland in the summer of 1971 to study French. While there, she slipped on the ice and was hospitalized for

several weeks before completing her studies and flying back to
Africa. She visited Murray and Jan in Swaziland before flying
on to Nigeria to spend Christmas with Don and Perlene in
Nigeria and finally to Cotonou in January, 1972. That summer,
Colin was asked to coach a U.S.A. Track and Field team of
fifty-six collegiate athletes under the State Department to
compete in pre-Olympic competitions in fourteen countries. He
was able to visit Edna in Cotonou between meets in Nigeria
and Uganda at which time all of her family were in Africa
except for Bill. Colin's visit was propitious because, by that
time, Edna was completely frustrated with her assignment and
was ready to give up.

　　Both the District Superintendent and the Cotonou head
of station were experienced bush missionaries and had little
concept of the kind of measures required for reaching an
educated, urban population of young people. Edna had just
spent four years on a college campus and six months in
Switzerland watching and listening to young people and
planning how best to reach them. The methods and costs of
ministry in the city required imagination and a level of
commitment far different than pioneering in rural Africa.
Neither the budget allocated nor the leadership assigned were
ready for the task. Edna along with her co-laborers, Jean and
Soula Isch, felt side-lined and frustrated. Edna groused that
she was treated with condescension as though she was the
grieving widow returning to the scene of her loss in order to put
her life back together instead of as a serious missionary. Colin
advised her to write her observations in a letter to the Field
Council and let them decide what to do. She did.

　　In August, 1972, she was asked to move to Niger at the
request of Dr. Howard Dowdell to help set up the new S.I.M.
Francophone Field Director's office in Niamey. She served with

distinction until December, 1973, when she retired from active
service and returned to La Mirada, California.

Edna accepted the position of Missions Secretary for her
sending Church of the Open Door in downtown Los Angeles
and later worked closer to home as a proof-reader for the
Lockman Foundation working on the New American Standard
Bible and Concordance.

Part III:

Building the Church

Outline of Stations

1946	Kandi
1947	Nikki
1949	Parakou
1950	Djougou
1951	Sinendé
1952	Dompago
1952	Tchaourou
1952 [1975]	Tchatchou
1954	Ségbana
1959	Simpérou
1960	Bembèrèkè
1967	Cotonou

Chapter 23: Kandi (1946)

1946	Station opened in October by Ed and Marguerite Morrow.
1947	Morrows forced to leave due to Marguerite's illness. Gus Fredlund and Earl Playfair: Fredlund reached out to Fulanis.
1948	Church organized. First Aid medical work started.
1951	New church building dedicated.
1957	Weekly medical outreach to three villages by Stan and Jane Dudgeon.
1961	French Bible College started by Ted and Addie Emmett.
1965	Church at Tissarou. Strong Church at Kassakou. Pastor Baguiri: 8 Baptized.
1966	Death of Gus Fredlund. Station closed.
1973	Station reopened with Dr. and Mrs. Gordon Beacham. Language work: Monkollé with Grace Birnie and Barbara Wright.

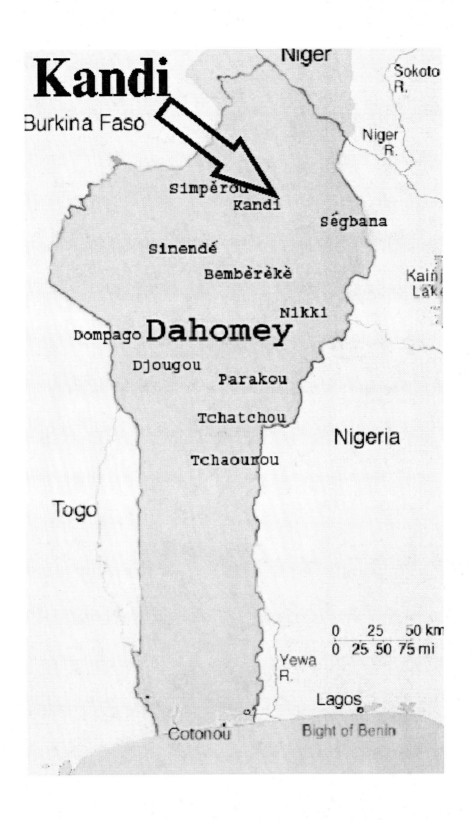

Kandi

Kandi, in the northern district of Dahomey, was the first station to be occupied by S.I.M. missionaries. Ed Morrow arrived there in October of 1946. His wife, Marguerite, with sons Charles and Richard, joined him in December. The Morrows had labored for seventeen years in a difficult Muslim area in Zinder in the Colony of Niger and responded to God's calling to open a work in northern Dahomey. They came from the north to Kandi which was the political center for the district where French government offices and trading firms were located.

Ed found a group of professing believers already meeting together and they welcomed his ministry. The group included some Yoruba tradesmen and others from Southern Dahomey and a dozen or so soldiers from the Ivory Coast. He taught them in French and had it interpreted into Yoruba.

Building a place to live was a primary and urgent need since they were living in a garage, using a store room as the kitchen. Ed had many difficulties finding materials and men. Here is Ed's description of the process:

> . . . And so our house is going up, from God's good earth to our dwelling.

The walls have been put up with sun-dried mud bricks made right here on the compound. The plastering is done with the same kind of mud with some additional "ant hill" clay to make it extra sticky. The ceiling is made by laying many bamboo sticks on rafters made of split palm logs. The bamboo is tied onto the logs with bark. On these sticks are placed mats on which goes a thin layer of mud for extra coolness. The frame-work of the roof is made of the same kind of split palm logs and bamboo sticks and a heavy thatch of grass. All this is tied together with ropes made from a strong reed. The floors will be laid with pounded laterine rocks dug from the ground. The doors and window shutters will be made from trees cut from the bush some five miles away. . . . We have been interrupted several times to purchase headloads of reeds to supply the 25 rope-makers who are working out there in the shade of the mango tree. [The Sudan Witness, September 1947]

Marguerite started her study of Bariba, the major language of the area. This was an unwritten language and there were no helpful materials. The tasks seemed formidable and their days were filled with activity. The services, the

building and language study along with adjustments to a new place challenged them.

It was not for long, however, because in May of 1947 Marguerite became ill with a fever. The fever continued and on June 12 the Morrows left for medical help in Jos, Nigeria, nearly 1,000 miles by jeep and small plane. On August 8th, the family went home to the U.S. for further help. The report at that time reads, "The ill health of Mrs. Morrow deprived this station of the founder so soon. Many mourn their loss and pray God will heal and restore their beloved missionaries." But this was not to be. Marguerite Morrow died in New York on October 8, 1947.

Gus Fredlund came to Kandi station in June, 1947. The McDougalls had arrived in Nikki in March and Gus had been assisting them as they settled in. He came to Kandi to keep this developing work open. He continued the meetings with the existing group of believers even though he felt inadequate in French and lacked confidence in his faithful but inexperienced translator. Earl Playfair arrived soon after and joined Gus in preaching which was a happy assignment for both of them since they had been friends from student days. For Earl it was the realization of a desire on which he had long set his heart. Together they made many contacts with the nationals and the increasing French population. They sold Bibles and other Christian literature and were well received.

Both young men went to Nikki to spend Christmas with the McDougalls and, upon their return, found that their houseboys had stolen goods from them. They fined the boys and suspended them for a month instead of turning them over to the police. At the watch night service one of the boys, Abdoulaye, a Fulani, responded to Gus' invitation to accept

Christ. His sense of sin was real and his desire to accept pardon and cleansing through the blood of Christ was clear.

Gus had a special interest in the Fulani people and had studied their language. In fact, his decision to come to Dahomey was because of the many Fulanis. Earl had just come from the Gourma tribal area in Upper Volta and quickly sought out Gourma soldiers stationed there. They listened attentively to his witness but did not join them for services. He tried to find a Bariba-speaking Gourma to be his informant but was unable to do so. Gus was quick to use Abdoulaye with his radiant testimony as they trekked together to Fulani villages. He diligently sought out the Fulanis and found the interest very high in villages like Podo. When the Adjoint took the census in Sonsoro, Gus accompanied him and witnessed to hundreds of Fulanis. Another time he trekked for a week to Guéné near the Niger River where eleven Fulani villagers made profession of faith. These new believers agreed to meet in the chief's house each Sunday.

Along with these outreach efforts they continued the services and literature distribution. Joseph, a carpenter with the military, was an encourager, helping them with the teaching on Sundays. Another encouragement was the four prayer group meetings held in homes each week. These fostered increased attendance at the mid-week service.

The building continued and, with the laying of the cement floors and making of wooden shutters, it neared completion. Gus' plans for marriage spurred on these efforts. He had been making frequent visits to Nikki ever since Christmas to visit Alice Wilkinson. They were married on June 2, 1948, at a lovely wedding in Ilorin, Nigeria.

Earl also was ready for marriage. His bride-to-be was in the U.S. and he was eager to return home on furlough. He had spent several years in Gourma country before coming to Kandi so it was time for his furlough.

Gus and Alice settled in at Kandi after their honeymoon in Miango, Nigeria. As a couple they had friendly contacts and social interaction with the French community. There were many families with children and some were open to their witness. Classes at the chief's compound flourished with stories, singing and memory work and several children trusted Christ for salvation. Further encouragement came from the first two Bariba believers. Aboudou, a former Muslim, made a clear confession and witnessed unafraid. Yara Mayi was an old man to whom others listened with real interest when he gave testimony. They formed a class for Baribas and the chief showed special interest.

In October, 1948, Stewart McDougall and Ed Morrow with James Odjo Boro came for special meetings. McDougall researched the history of the Monkollé people, a group of around 3,000 pagans, and found they were closely related to the Yorubas. The men agreed they should be evangelized by the Yoruba evangelists. Market meetings were held and they preached in several languages: McDougall in Yoruba, Morrow in French and James Odjo Boro of Parakou in Bariba.

During the visit, plans were made for organizing the local group of believers into a church. McDougall and Morrow interviewed candidates for baptism and three were recommended. Fredlund followed through with baptism and immediately formed a class for preparing other believers for baptism. They formed the church with three members and a large group of adherents. A site was chosen, which the Bariba chief approved so application to the government was made.

At the end of 1948, the Fredlunds left for furlough in England. It burdened them to leave the work so newly planted and fragile but there was no missionary to replace them. Emmanuel Gnonlofoun, who had training as a lay-preacher with the Methodists, kept the services going. A Yoruba couple, Solo and Dorcasi, from Nigeria came in March of 1949 and had an effective ministry to the Yoruba people there.

Ed Morrow returned to Kandi in October, 1948 and remained until the Fredlunds returned in 1950. Some special efforts during his stay included a catechism class twice a week for Protestant children attending the government school. He taught in French; six children were enrolled and some accepted the Savior. Morrow took a team on a five day trek into the Banikoara district where they were warmly welcomed in eight villages. It seemed a promising center for expansion, but the Catholics were established there with a national catechist who was teaching children from the government school.

The Monkollé were revisited when McDougall came with Yoruba evangelists, Samuel Afolabi and Elisha Olufemi. They went to three villages located north and east of Kandi: Angaradébou, Kutakourkou, and Saa. The desire to speedily send someone to these people was greatly strengthened and Morrow strongly urged this in his reports.

Early in 1950 the Fredlunds returned from furlough freeing Morrow to proceed to his new assignment: to open the station at Djougou. Newly arrived missionary, Stan Dudgeon from Ireland, joined Ed in Kandi and together they left for Djougou in March.

Fredlunds

Fresh from furlough, Fredlunds were happy to find some continued interest and they began again with enthusiasm. Then difficulties showed up when their friend, Abdoulaye, proved unfaithful and showed no interest in the scriptures or the church. The Fulani chief died. He had been friendly and encouraging about a beginners' class in Fulani with reading, writing and scripture memory work. His son, Pullo, who succeeded him, appeared friendly but forbade his immediate family permission to attend. The children's class in the chief's house had to be transferred to the mission site when a Catholic priest made objection on the grounds that the mission permit to teach applied only to the mission compound. The formal application for the church site was refused. The chief tried to alleviate the situation but was unable to do so. The church building would now have to be on the mission site. The reasons given for this decision were: 1) to prevent overcrowding the town, and 2) to avoid provoking Muslim opposition and unrest.

These difficulties were problems meant to be overcome, meant for change and not defeat. The compound became a very busy place with the children's class there, the foundation for the church completed, and a "first-aid" medical work started. These activities seemed to spark an interest in the church services. Local Bariba, Dendi and Fulani peoples started to attend.

There were other encouraging activities at this time. M. Reuter, the French commandant who helped so much in the beginning, returned to his post. The Yoruba evangelist, David McIntosh, arrived to assist. He was responsible for the new and recently opened outstation of Kassakou. The people there were very eager and wanted to build a church. Permission was granted for catechists' schools at Kassakou, Angaradébou and Ségbana. The prospects for these places looked bright for Nigerian evangelist, Amos Ayorinde. He came in November of 1951 and was stationed in Angaradébou to begin a ministry to the Monkollé. He had a willing people and started almost immediately to hold Christian Religious Instruction classes every evening. The texts and songs he translated kept the classes interesting. In six weeks he had reached out to thirteen villages within a ten mile radius; ten of them with a first time witness. Later he went out to Fouè, Fafa and Tia. There was such a good response in Tia with twelve professions of faith that he began a regular service there. Amos was called home to Nigeria because of the illness of his son. When he returned he brought his family with him. They continued the outreach to the Monkollé people until the end of 1953. Angaradébou and Tia were then closed.

Gus was excited over the interest in Ségbana where the chief had appealed to him for an evangelist or a missionary. This man was chief over 7,000 people who were almost totally pagan. He said he was ready to put up a church building if someone would come. There was no one available to send so Gus continued to visit and always found the people receptive. His prayer was that God would protect them and keep them free from Muslim infiltration until a resident missionary could come.

The Fulani work progressed during these years and a great step forward was taken when evangelist Dogon Yaro came for a visit early in 1953. Gus' special burden for the Fulani shows in this quote from his report:

> I had the privilege of accompanying Adamou Dogon Yaro of Kano on his month-long evangelistic campaign among the Fulani and Gando of Northern Dahomey. We estimate a total of over 400 professions of faith. It is already evident that they will not come through for the Lord but we know that there will be much lasting fruit nevertheless. We look forward to the time when he can return again to work in this fruitful field. I have for a long time prayed concerning the establishment of a Fulani Bible School for the training of evangelists that shall be able to go and live among these people and teach them. My comfort through the years has been these words 'If the vision tarry, wait for it!' So, I have waited and prayed these last nine years. It now seems that the time is approaching for the fulfillment of this vision. There are already three students ready to begin with several others in prospect. Is Dogon Yaro God's man to take the burden of teaching in this school?

So Gus' hopes were high as he took his family home to England at the close of the year.

A number of missionaries and evangelists made significant contributions to the growth of this work in the next few years. Stan Dudgeon thoroughly trekked the area. Apart from time out to build his house and to help Pickering in Dompago to build his house, he pursued a heavy trekking schedule. He went to Banikoara and Sonsoro preaching in fifty villages around there. For thirty-five of these villages it was the first time anyone had preached the gospel to them. He trekked south to Ouéré and together with James Odjo Boro and Augustin Adjaoké he visited the key villages of Gogounou and Gamia before he left on furlough and a study time in France.

Augustin Adjaoké came to Kandi in 1954 to cover the
station while Gus and family were on furlough and Stan was in
France. A house was built for him and he carried on the work
faithfully for four years. He did literature distribution from the
Bookstore, pastored the Yoruba church and visited the nearby
villages, especially Kassakou and Sonkparé. During this time
the grass church building at Sonkparé was rebuilt with mud.
In 1958 they had a baptismal service for three believers from
Sonkparé and two from Kandi. In 1960 five more were baptized
from Kassakou and Sonkparé. It was noted in each report that
Pastor Augustin had instructed the candidates very well.
Augustin also trekked some with Stan and Oswald Zobrist.

In 1955 Oswald came to Kandi to remodel the house in
preparation for Irene to join him there. They moved in
December and Oswald took over the responsibility of the
Yoruba church. This church was a matter of deep concern and
much prayer for, even though the attendance remained high,
the moral standards were questionable and the spiritual tone
was low. This had been a pattern almost from the beginning.

There were some special features of this ministry.
Oswald made good contacts through hospital visitation. Also
notable was the short term Bible School held in the out-
villages. It was thrilling when their Bible School sent three
single men and two couples to Parakou Bible School for further
training. Evening studies with young men from the military
was an effective outreach. Oswald and Augustin made a trek to
Toura, which put them in contact with an area of 35,000
people.

When Stan Dudgeon returned from furlough in 1956 he
continued his trekking to the villages and found continued
interest and encouragement. He and Janey Younkers were

good friends and, after spending their holiday time together at Miango, they became engaged. It was a special occasion of joy and celebration when they were married on December 13 at the close of the annual conference. Shortly after their marriage, they were visited by a young adventurer named Nicholas Mosley who recorded his experience in a book entitled, <u>African Switch-back</u>.

In Kandi the missionaries were Mr. and Mrs. Dudgeon, he an Irishman . . . and she a tall Canadian with fair hair who looked, as she was, someone who could be good at nursing. They lived in a three-room house of which the roof had recently been blown off by a whirlwind. He had been in Kandi seven years and she for three months.

We went out with them one afternoon when they took medicine to a village. . . . In the small straw church in the  village about 40 people gathered and stood quietly in a queue by the pole-benches. The scene had an eye-catching quality. . . Children hardly of an age to speak were trying to be accurate about what was wrong with them. They described pain by noises, a headache went, peep-peep; a stomach, boop; and eye, aaah. Mr. and Mrs. Dudgeon talked to them about facts. They understood.

Watching this, I felt myself to be an observer of acts of unequivocal goodness. This is rare. Almost any human act is suspect, or can be imagined to be suspect, in terms of being an imposition of the personality by him who acts. But here there was none. There was hardly any talk. No one was "putting anything over." For the first time I understood why the missionaries didn't preach and didn't even at first instruct but simply were, in deeds, what they believed they should be. They were serving. People who think missionaries are bigots who seek to impose their complex ideals upon people who are happy in simplicity should visit an animist village where through their obscure beliefs the inhabitants are frightened and starving. . . .

Talk rationalizes after belief; it is necessary because it keeps belief true. But belief comes, and spreads through what men are. In the straw church with two large white figures bending to catch the whisper of a child of three this seemed, for a moment, to be evident.[London, 1958]

Gus Fredlund was detained in England because of the fragile health of some of the children. His desire was to return but the mission was reluctant to give permission for a separated family situation. In late 1956, however, permission was granted and in this quote from his farewell letter to his friends at home you will feel his heart beat:

The Fulani tribe numbers over five million, and there are to my knowledge, less than a thousand who profess to be Christian. Over five hundred of these are in Dahomey, and I am the only missionary of SIM who speaks their language. Thus it is essential that I go at this time to help and guide these babes in Christ as they storm the citadels of Satan to set his captives free. May I count on your prayer support? be assured that you will stand with me? that this great evangelistic campaign may be an eternal success.

Of course you realize that my heart would prefer to stay by the comfort of my own fireside, with my wife and children about me, the security of a good job, and all that means, but as we prayed together, we were convinced that our personal comfort and pleasure have no right to stand in the way of the eternal salvation of these millions. Alice will especially need your prayers, as hers is the more difficult part, taking the burden of being both 'mother' and 'father' to five active children while I am away on the King's Business.

So in November of 1956 Gus returned to Kandi, not to head up the station work, but solely for Fulani evangelism. He found good response as he traveled among the villages. Stan and Janey returned to Kandi in 1957 and settled in the main house. In February they started medical work in three villages. It was a simple procedure as they set up a table in the back of the church and nurse Janey treated all the needy who came.

The Zobrists opened a new station in Simpérou. In May, 1958, Oswald started building there and stayed in the

Gomparou Rest House. Irene and the family remained in Kandi until the housing was ready for them.

The interest Morrow, Fredlund and McDougall had in the Monkollé from the very first occupation of the Kandi area never flagged, but it was difficult to establish a stable work among them. Sarah Buller came from her place of service in Nigeria in July of 1959 for a six month stay to research the Monkollé and, with Sabi Koukou, they translated ten chapters of John, then hymns and a first reader. They found the people still friendly and open, however, they were almost totally illiterate. Sarah left with a burden for these people and a prayer for a young African man to learn their language and evangelize them. Sabi Koukou settled in Pèdè and reached out to three other villages each week. He held Sunday services at Pèdè, Tissarou and Borodarou and he supported himself through his carpentry work.

Charles Carpenter spent some time in Kandi in 1958 studying Fulani and ministering as he could. In 1960, he and Elaine moved in to Kandi from Ségbana and Charles pursued his work among the Fulani. He found most of them had already heard the gospel from Gus but the need for further teaching was there and the interest was good. He worked on a primer for them with guidance from Gordon Beacham.

1960 closed with the lighthouse at Kandi sending out streams of light to Yorubas, Baribas, Monkollé and Fulani.

On August 1, 1960, the territory of Dahomey became the Republic of Dahomey when it gained independence from France. All concerned trusted strongly in God, who is sovereign over all, to bless His fledgling church and continue to give freedom to preach and teach His Word.

In 1965 the Fredlund family was in Kandi. Neither
Simpérou nor Ségbana stations had resident missionaries, so

Fredlund Family

Gus was overseeing the work in those stations as well as
Kandi.

In the Kandi area the most responsive villages were the
Monkollé villages of Tui, Loro and Podo and in Tissarou, a
Gando village where the group now numbered twenty-five and
several had burned their fetishes publicly. The chief,
Sinaourarou, witnessed enthusiastically as he played records
for his friends. This group continued to grow spiritually as well
as in numbers and applied for permission to build a church.
The Monkollé believers were calling for someone to come and
teach them but Gus was not able to respond to all their needs,
limited both by time and language.

In February of 1966, Fredlund joined the team going to
Cotonou for the Evangelistic Campaign where he lost his life

and Alice was left alone. Shortly after this tragic loss Alice took her wounded family home to England and the station was closed.

The Kandi station remained closed until 1973 when Dr. and Mrs. Gordon Beacham came to reopen the station and study the Monkollé language. This assignment enabled Grace Birnie and Barb Wright to move forward in their study of the language preparatory to working among these people. So the lighthouse was shining again. Ouorou Mark, who was running the Bookshop was also in charge of the Yoruba Church. Grace Birnie and Barb Wright had a Sunday School class in French for students and the Beachams held a Pila prayer meeting in their home. Kandi station had been restored to its strategic objectives.

Pickering, McDougalls and Morrows with French official

Chapter 24: Nikki (1947)

1947   Opened in March by Stewart and Edna McDougall.

1949   Yoruba Church in Nigeria (EMS) sent two pastors: Pastor Elisha Olufemi and David Ajibola.

1950   Seven boys moved to Nikki compound to be instructed. Medical work started by nurse Irene Zobrist.

1952   N'dali opened by Elisha and Elizabeth Olufemi.

1953   Medical work reopened by Annie Van den Brand. Zobrists left and Cails arrived. Pastor Timothée came to work.

1962   Bariba Bible School moved to Nikki.

1963   Nikki became the Bariba Language Center headed by Jean Soutar and Rosella Entz. Jonathan and Rosalyn Maxwell started the French Bible School at N'dali.

1964   Language Center very active. Vernacular School for Bariba and Fulani Girls opened with Margaret Bevington.

1966   Séko Damagui came to pastor the Bariba Church. Church built at Djega.

1968   Wurumo built their first Church. Simoni pastored the church at Bouca.

1971   Many believers. Church built in Sin. Paul Yonduro became Pastor. Pierre Aliou replaced Simoni as pastor at Bouka.

1974   Rosella Entz left for Latin America. Village work progressed at Monno, Alaga and Gbausi.

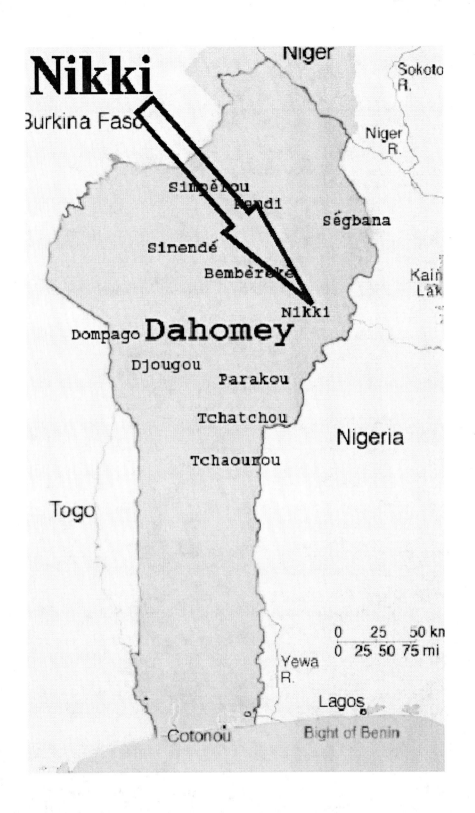

Nikki

Stewart McDougall's decision in 1945 to move his work and family to pioneer Dahomey went against all the professional advice he was offered, against all his aspirations and work objectives and against his own best judgment. His decision meant leaving a field where he had proven his leadership and where he was highly respected by veteran missionaries and church leaders alike. It would eventually mean giving up furlough time with his aging parents to go to the Alliance Française in France for language study. His language skills were adequate but he would have to learn a new language from scratch and reduce it to writing—he would have to become a translator—a task far beyond his skill and training. It meant leaving his two older boys in Canada for schooling for at least two years while he settled the rest of his family in Dahomey. It meant leaving a British colony, where official business was done in English and Protestant missionaries were tolerated if not understood, and moving to a French colony which was predominantly Catholic and where all his efforts would be resisted. It meant risking the health of his young family because the road out to medical care was completely impassable during rainy season. After all, he didn't even have his own vehicle to move his goods or provide for emergency exit. Surely, if God had really called, He would have provided for these essentials. All the arguments were sound, but God had called him, as a disciple, to leave all and follow Him.

Stewart and Edna, accompanied by their two youngest children, Murray and Janet, entered Nikki in March, 1947,

thanks to the courageous driving of the hired lorry driver and Stewart's insistence. The driver suffered broken springs, several flat tires and was having to coast down the hills for fear of not being able to purchase gas in Dahomey and unsure of having sufficient on board to make it back to Nigeria. The family had to take turns riding on wood benches in the back of the truck since there was not enough room in the cab. Their safe arrival in Nikki was a great relief to all concerned.

Alice Wilkinson had a large part in these beginning events in Nikki. She joined the McDougalls in October, 1947, coming from WEC ministries in Ivory Coast. Alice's fluency in French and knowledge of French culture and customs gave her ready acceptance with the school children, and her classes in town were well attended. She ministered in Nikki until her marriage to Gus Fredlund in June, 1948 when she moved to Kandi.

The beginning seemed slow but each new missionary who joined the effort brought encouragement. Ed Morrow came in 1948, returning from home leave after the loss of his wife, Marguerite. He had many years of experience ministering in French. He gave instruction to the other missionaries in the French language and reached out to French-speaking nationals as well.

On January 8, 1948, Mr. and Mrs. J. B. Williams and
their daughter, Judy, arrived in Nikki. The government guest
house was again made available so they stayed there until
Stewart built another house on the mission property. They
studied Bariba and French and prepared to start up another
outpost station.

James Odjo Boro came from Parakou to stay briefly. He
was the only Bariba believer they were aware of and had been
trained as an evangelist under the Methodist mission. James
encouraged the missionaries as he taught them Bariba, his
fluency in Yoruba making communication and translation
easier for the McDougalls. James explained the gospel message
clearly to interested Baribas and, during his stay, they were
able to translate some scripture and work out other messages
for use later.

In March, 1949, their sons, Colin (age 10) and Donald
(age 8), were able to join them having traveled by air from
Canada accompanied by a family friend. The Baribas
immediately claimed them, giving them Bariba names. Colin
was named Ouorou Nikki and Donald, Sabi Nikki. Edna was
then pregnant with their fifth child, William, who arrived
safely in June to complete the family picture.

In 1949 Stewart was invited to return to Nigeria to
speak at the Yoruba Church Conference at Egbe, their former
home. Stewart's prayer for many years had been that the
Yoruba Church would catch the missionary vision. At the
conference, three Yoruba pastors responded to Stewart's
challenge to join them in Dahomey to minister among the
Baribas. These were the first missionaries sent out by the
Yoruba Church and signaled a coming of age as they took this
important step of collective faith. It was here that Stewart
made an important discovery concerning God's sovereign

wisdom. The Yorubas of Nigeria, among whom he had
ministered so effectively, had no way of knowing what it meant
for the disciple of Jesus to leave all and follow Him because
they hadn't seen from where the missionaries had come or
what they had left. Stewart had been their teacher and, as far
as they could measure, had it all. By giving them an example
of what it meant to be a disciple, leaving all to go to a tribe
they considered cannibalistic and beyond the pale—it now
became clear. Stewart had been their trusted leader before and
would continue to help them make their way if they would only
obey the call of God on their lives.

Solomon and Dorcas went on to Kandi while Pastors
Elisha Olufemi and David Ekundayo Dada stayed in Nikki to
minister, studying Bariba and leading children's classes.

As missionary activity increased so did the opposition.
There was a noticeable change in the attitude of the Muslims.
From the start they did not show much interest in the mission
work and were rather friendly on occasion but this changed
into definite opposition, causing some who came to meetings to
fear persecution. This was especially felt during the fast of
Ramadan. Children who had been attending for two years were
suddenly forbidden to attend by their parents.

As the message continued to be preached, however,
some good things were happening. A church building was
completed in Nikki providing a gathering place in town. Those
who attended were mostly Yorubas but some Baribas joined
them and the message was interpreted.

Stewart and Edna rode together to neighboring
Tontarou on their bicycles over a path well worn by the women
bringing their produce to market. They stayed three days and,
as they were preparing to leave, some fathers requested that
they take their sons and teach them so they could return to

instruct the village. The McDougalls eagerly accepted and soon had seven boys resident on the Nikki compound. David and Elisha taught them and the missionaries rejoiced to find another means of reaching out, realizing that the walls of resistance were coming down.

The struggling missionary effort was making tiny steps forward but received a tremendous push when Dr. Welmers came for a month in 1949. He was a student of modern languages and on a scholarship from Cornell University. In his short time in Nikki he completed a sixty page study of Bariba. He discovered there were four distinct tones and suggested changes to the alphabet they were using to make it conform to the international phonetic alphabet. New missionaries would then have a better understanding of the language from the start.

However, Welmers challenged Stewart on another, unexpected front. The Bariba tribe was essentially matriarchal. Since a tribal man may have many wives and divorce one for almost any reason, her children had no security in her husband. Therefore, since the mother's eldest brother could not divorce her, he was the titular head of her family. It was the child's uncle that decided whom the child could marry or whether he or she would get an education and where. Welmers argued that to translate the "Lord's Prayer" as "Our Father" would transmit the wrong idea of the believer's relationship to God, therefore, to be accurate, they must translate it "Our Uncle who art in heaven." Stewart paced the floor for two nights before deciding they could not do that. He decided that a missions strategy based primarily on the translation of the scriptures was inadequate. One must at the same time equip "faithful men who will be able to teach others also." This was a watershed event.

In 1950 Irene Archer arrived to take over and expand the medical outreach. Needy folk came in large numbers. Soon after, her fiancé Oswald Zobrist arrived from Switzerland and they were married in early 1951. They stayed on in Nikki and had a fruitful ministry even while occupied with language studies. Oswald visited extensively in the villages.

The Pèrèrè region with eighteen villages to visit was a challenge and Oswald made friends as he took his medical kit and treated ulcers wherever they needed him. Seeing the great need of those people left him with a greater burden than ever.

In a report he wrote about the opening of N'dali, Nikki's first outstation: "Pastor Elisha with wife Elisabeth had moved there and were received with great interest and expressions of joy that a teacher would live in their town. Even the

Pastor Elisha Olu preaching at N'Dali

chief rejoiced and he with some elders encouraged everyone to attend the meeting." After they had been there some months, Zobrist reports that this chief and some of his men gave their testimonies of faith in the Lord Jesus Christ. The Muslims didn't like it so they came to the chief and told him he would die, but if he would give them a sheep or a goat or some money they would pray that he would not die. He replied, "My life is in God's hand and I fear not to die because I know where I am going. Just go away and do not come back to my house again." About eighteen months later the N'dali believers were celebrating the opening of the church they had built and the chief joined in their celebration.

Other encouraging signs included Annie Van den Brand from Holland joining the missionary effort in June, 1951. Among her many activities she taught Borori, a Fulani believer, and his family while they were in Nikki. He then witnessed in the Fulani settlements regularly.

Even so, McDougall reported in 1954, "The response to the gospel has been very slow."

Cail wrote, "Only with regular visitation over a period of years will we see fruit among this people."

Annie said it this way, "Sometimes one is made to believe that there is an advance towards accepting the gospel, other times we are disappointed to see those who once made profession and gave signs of growing in grace turning their backs on the Lord."

The testimony was still there but the response was slow, and interest seemed to flare and then die. But the faith of the missionaries remained strong, knowing that seed sown would sprout and grow when watered.

All of them understood that Islam was the chief hindrance to growth in Nikki itself. For even though its presence in the villages was felt, it was not oppressive. In Nikki it was strong. Followers of Islam were staunch and it was politically the only choice for a man who wished to succeed. This is illustrated in the actions of some who wanted to believe.

In Ouénou a man was going to be baptized and, though he was present at the service and ready, he stopped and, addressing the people gathered, said, "I cannot be baptized," explaining that if he were baptized it would not please the people of the village where he was the chief.

Chief Baba N'dari was another. He was a dear and trusted friend but when he was being considered for King of the Baribas, his attitude toward the missionaries changed greatly and the friendliness did not return until after he was named King. Only then were the children of his household allowed to attend the meetings.

Tradition was strongest in the villages. In one village the plan of salvation was preached with the explanation that God had given His Son to be the sacrifice for sin and that God did not accept sacrifices of chickens and animals. One old man responded, "No one ever told us before that there was any other way to worship God. We offer these sacrifices because our fathers did."

Another hindrance for the missionaries was their collective lack of fluency and understanding of the language and the culture of the people.

They reached out to the children from their time of arrival and the children responded eagerly. Every evening a group gathered to sing and hear what little the missionaries could teach them. Many came regularly. Try to imagine Edna's excitement one evening to overhear one little fellow trying to teach another boy one of the choruses. To explain it, he put his feet together to show how they nailed the Savior's feet and then held out his arms to show how they drove the nails in His hands. The message was getting through if ever so falteringly.

Their "faltering" was understandable in the early days but inadequate for planting a mature church. One day their language informant remarked upon answering question after question, "I didn't know our language had paths to run on." This was an exciting moment because he was beginning to see some reason in all the repetitions and probings. His language had a grammar.

After many months, when the alphabet seemed settled, Edna wrote some simple sentences and made a small book by hand. Some of the children learned over time to read these. One day the McDougalls invited the chief and a group of older men to come to their home and had the children read to them. One man exclaimed, "I never thought I'd see the day a book would talk my language."

During this time, there was a great deal of activity. The McDougalls left for furlough in May, 1951 and upon their return were stationed in Parakou. The Thamers, who had worked with the McDougalls in Nigeria for many years, came on temporary stay, prepared to move on to Tchaourou when it was opened.

Annie Van den Brand remained busy with her teaching and doing medical work out her back door. Pastor Timothée Ogouchina had come to minister to the church. Zobrists went on home leave in 1954, and Mr. and Mrs. James Cail moved to Nikki but then were needed to help out in Parakou for a year and Nikki was closed. When the Cails returned in 1955 they found the villages still receptive and whenever Jim visited, the people would beg him to return soon and teach them more. The village of Ouénou was encouraging both in children's classes and a strong testimony of six or eight men. They reported that the power of the fetish had greatly decreased and that their desire was to follow Jesus. They had started to build a place to worship.

In Sumaru where they seemed eager to learn to read and to follow the Lord, eight young men were ready for baptism, and Sakarou near N'dali was very promising. Annie had spent seven weeks there living in the mud church during the week and staying in Pastor Elisha's house in N'dali on week-ends, spending her time with the people—visiting and holding meetings.

This interest continued through the end of 1957-58 while Cails were in the U.S. and Annie kept up the visitation accompanied by her companion, Esther Foundohou, a graduate from the Tchaourou girls' school. The village of Ouénou had finished their building of a little mud church and Elie Olodo, from Parakou Bible School, went there to teach them for three months and to lead them in witnessing to surrounding villages.

Annie became ill and left Nikki for a long period of time but returned in time to welcome the Cail family in June of 1959. Ouorou Sidi Jean from the Parakou Bible School came soon after to assist them in the ministry and carried on the work at Ouénou. Jim Cail trekked the area together with him and said, "His eagerness to learn more about the Word is continually a challenge to me."

It was encouraging when the church in Nikki took the responsibility of a portion of Ouorou Sidi's support while he worked at Ouénou. Jim and Ouorou Sidi did the preaching. The Nikki church people wanted this to be a Bariba church so the preaching was now in Bariba and translated into Yoruba.

August 1, 1960 was Independence Day. Dahomey had graduated from being a French colony to a sovereign state among the nations of the world. It was a day of great solemnity and celebration.

Abel Dogani preaching near Nikki, 1962

1962 was full of activity as the Bariba Bible School moved to Nikki from Sinendé. Jim Cail had ten students and the teaching was a challenge. They completed a six month term with two graduating and closed for a time when Jim left again for furlough and medical attention.

Margaret Bevington moved to Nikki with her Bariba Girls' School. Jean Soutar with Bio Mati as informant was concentrating on linguistics and translation work and also teaching language to missionaries Shirley Hyman, Mary Carney and Irène Sossauer.

When Cails returned they were re-stationed to Bembèrèkè to be near a doctor because of Jim's diabetes problem. Rosella Entz and Jean Soutar had worked together in Parakou on the translation work and now Rosella, back from furlough, was stationed in Nikki to continue this partnership. They both attended Bible Translators workshops in Accra,

Ghana and received much help. Upon returning they spent months on Bariba syntax and a dictionary.

In 1966 Ouorou Sidi followed the Cails to Bembèrèkè to assist as they reopened the Bariba Bible School there. Séko Damagui came as the new pastor for the Nikki church. He had a real burden for the church and a vision for the potential of a strong church with good witness in the villages. The attendance increased at both Sunday services and prayer meetings but the anticipated revival did not come. However, the village outreach had an impact: Kawo led the way to evangelize his home village of Djega; the believers in Bouca built their church and welcomed Pastor Simoni and his wife, Esther, to lead them.

Nikki was always a hub of activity with missionaries coming and going—some families en route to Nigeria with their children going back to school, others going to Gurai to catch a SIMAir plane. Gurai was the closest air strip in Nigeria which made air travel to school and holiday easier since mission planes would not have to cross over the border into Dahomey. The Biafran secessionist war in Nigeria had made flights into Parakou impossible.

Rosella Entz and Jean Soutar were a very good team and worked well together as well as with the national evangelists and pastors working in and around Nikki. However, while Jean was away for two years, 1967-69, Rosella was alone and managed her heavy load well. In an article in the British edition of "The Sudan Witness" of July, 1969, Rosella is quoted as follows:

At the district church Conference, 111 delegates

Jean Soutar with Bariba
translation team

attended, representing seven languages, so a good deal of interpretation was involved. After one of the business sessions, the Bariba pastors met to discuss some matters which were pertinent to their particular area, and at that time I presented a need for a language informant for the translation work. Realising the importance of the task, the pastors offered to come and help, one at a time, for periods of some three months each. Although there were 'pros and cons', this was a solution to an immediate problem, and I could foresee that it would be of benefit, not only to me, but also to the pastors themselves.

When the first pastor came with his wife and little boy, we began translation the following morning. I am thankful to say that with the Lord's enabling–and in spite of the heat–we were in due time able to complete translation of the Book of Acts. It still has to be checked

Pastor Paul Yonduro

and then stencilled and mimeographed. The pastor's reactions to the work have been most interesting. He is undoubtedly enjoying the task, but is sure that he has never worked so hard in his life, and feels as if he is taking higher seminary training. One day he told me that he had always wondered why it was taking us so long to get the entire New Testament translated.

When Jean returned, the translation team finished I and II Thessalonians. Dr. George

Peters of Dallas Theological Seminary came in March, 1970, to give a seminar on Evangelism using the Old Testament as a foundation. This had an important effect on the village work in the Nikki area. The team started writing up Old Testament stories and the pastors used them extensively in their preaching in the villages. Interest and numbers grew, as did understanding. There was a real spurt of growth in the nearby Sin area and, by the end of 1971, they had a group of fifty who came regularly, built a meeting place and started women's meetings with good attendance. By 1972 they were strong and ready to receive Paul Yonduro as their pastor. They reached out to surrounding areas, resulting in a growing work in Alaga. Dogani, gifted as an evangelist, found the Old Testament stories especially effective as he worked and taught in Gbausi, Monno and Wurumo. Pierre Aliou replaced Simoni as pastor in Bouca and continued to visit Djega.

When preparing a strategy for Dahomey, the McDougalls had studied missionary pioneer efforts in other places. They were persuaded that the proven strategies S.I.M. had used in her many other pioneer contexts were most valid: translations and literacy, evangelism, medical work and education. Missionaries had ministered in these ways in the Nikki area for twenty-five years and were now seeing fruit from their labors.

Nikki had become a quiet station where gifted and highly motivated missionary ladies focused on translation and were working in a support role to the national church leadership many years before the birth of the UEEB in 1975 and subsequent turnover of all the work to the national church five years later. Jean Soutar is quoted below from an article on translation in the sixth "SIM NOW" magazine, describing her view of the place of translation work in the development of the national church.

> . . . What has given real meaning to translation work is the fact that we are not simply translating the Bible as a project in itself, but making a major contribution to the establishment and growth of the church.
>
> And now that the church is a reality here, we work in partnership with it. Our job includes feeding the church. In fact, the Beninnois leader of the Bariba Bible School calls our translation base here at Nikki the kitchen—the place where our food is prepared! We don't undertake projects apart from meeting the church's need and helping her in outreach. So we have prepared Bible teaching materials, materials for Bible School students and pastors, preventive medicine booklets and many other things. In the beginning we decided among ourselves what to do; now the church decides along with us.

Chapter 25: Parakou (1949)

1949   Opened by Mr. and Mrs. J.B. Williams.

1950   First baptisms and church organized.
            Bible School opened. Simple medical work.

1952   McDougalls assigned to Parakou after furlough.

1953   Dispensary and in-patient housing opened with
            Millie Davis in charge.

1954   Yoruba Church building completed with David Dada
            Pastor. Bookstore opened.

1960   Bible School moved to Sinendé.

1961-62   Yoruba Church crisis.

1963   "Foyer de la Bible" opened by Moira Alexander.

1965   Bookstore moved to the center of town.
            Yoruba women's conference.

1966   Perrier meetings and death of Stewart McDougall.
            Work at Amanwignon started by Annie Van den
            Brand.

1972   French congregation became a separate church
            organization.

1975   UEEB established with Gabriel Doko as president.

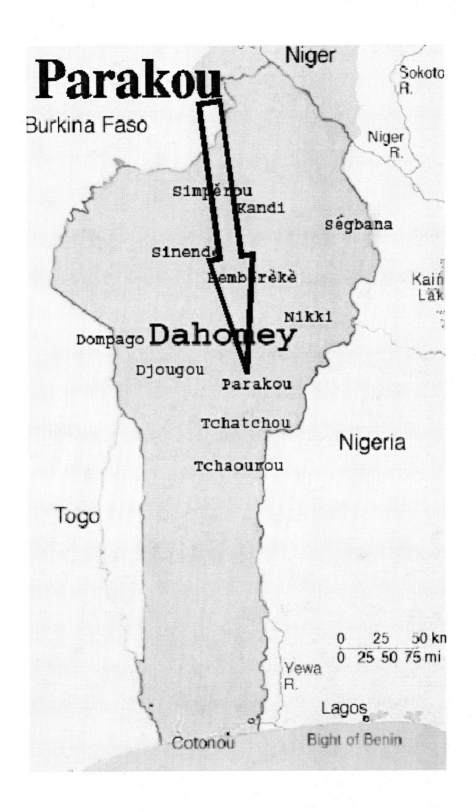

Parakou

The opening of Parakou station was a necessary strategic move and part of the original plan to reach the Baribas. While Nikki was the tribal center for the Baribas, Parakou was the government and commerce center of the North. It is located midway between the North and South districts on the main road from Cotonou on the coast to the Niger border. The railway running up from the coast ended in Parakou enhancing its importance.

Stewart was filled with praise and excitement when the government permits for the site in Parakou finally came through in the fall of 1948. God had already supplied the funds for building the station. Mr. and Mrs. Ivan Lageschulte in Wheaton, Illinois, upon hearing of the need, donated funds they had saved to build a new home for themselves.

The Methodists had interests in Parakou so (since S.I.M. was a fellow member of the Federation of Protestant Missions of French West Africa) S.I.M. was required by agreement to request their permission before entering there. In a letter written in 1946, the Methodist representative stated that their mission had struggled single-handedly in the evangelization of Dahomey for over a hundred years. The strong pagan opposition of the kingdom of Abomey to their work in the South made progress difficult. In the early 1900's they had reached North to the Yorubas in Abomey, Dassa, Savè and Kilibo where they had a growing work. More recently they developed a ministry among the Pila peoples in the Djougou area. The Methodist Director, M. Parringer, had visited villages around Parakou, and they had a presence in that town in James Odjo Boro, a Bariba who was Methodist-trained. A group of Yorubas met in his home. After returning

home, M. Parringer wrote, "If you really can place seven
missionaries in the Bariba Country we shall be only too glad,
and ready to give any help we can. . . . It is indeed urgent to
reach them before they are gripped by Islam." He repeated his
invitation later in another letter, "May we say again how ready
we are to co-operate with you, and that we wish God's blessing
on your undertakings."

James Odjo Boro rejoiced greatly over the prospective
coming of S.I.M. also. J.B. Williams recorded and later
translated and transcribed James' life story which tells of his
conversion, his call to preach to his people and his Bible school
training. Following is James' own description of these events.

> At last the graduation day came and what a thrill it
> was for us all. We were all given our appointments and
> I was to go back to Dassa-Zoumé where I had actually
> begun the work.
> The years passed and the Lord blessed, but all the
> time I was thinking of my own people. I had not been
> back to my own tribe since I first left thirteen years
> before. I knew that no one had ever taken the Gospel to
> them and as far as I knew, I was the only one who had
> accepted Christ. I couldn't bear it any longer and finally
> told the missionary that I wanted to leave and go back
> to my own people. He finally gave me permission to go
> back and my wife and I started back to my own tribe.
> We reached the Southern border of our tribe but I
> was ashamed to go home. I had been away for years and
> my people would expect that I had become wealthy. I
> decided to stay in the large town where I could get a job
> and make plenty of money. I closed my eyes to the need
> of my people and my ears to God's call and for five years
> I tried to make money.

After describing his unsuccessful, fruitless struggles to
make the money he wanted, he continued his story.

> I got back home tired and discouraged. My wife met
> me at the door and gave me a drink of water and went
> to prepare food for me. A few minutes later, however,
> she came back and gave me a small parcel that my
> younger brother had sent me. I opened it and there was

an old pair of pants and a shirt. He had heard about my
condition and sent them to me. I put them on, and I
could have cried. Anyone could see that they weren't
made for me, but they were better than what I had.
Never since I accepted Christ had I had to wear clothes
like these.

A few days later a Christian from Dassa Zoumé
came to see me. He too had come to Parakou to work.
He said that there were five of them and they would like
to have services on Sundays. For months my Bible had
been packed in my box and I was completely out of
fellowship with my Lord. That night I took out my Bible
and for the first time in months I knelt in prayer!

The following Sunday five of us gathered together in
my room which was the first Protestant service ever
held in Parakou. In the weeks that followed we met
regularly each Sunday and the Lord blessed and added
to our number. Soon our room was too small and we
decided to build a small building where we could meet
together.

All those who met with us were strangers but there
were none of my own tribe. One day I decided to visit a
village where I knew the Chief. What a thrill it was as I
preached to my own people in my own language and
told them of Christ. I had thought that they would not
accept my message but what a joy it was to see the
eagerness with which they listened. Far into the night I
sat around the open fire and answered questions. When
finally I lay down on my mat that night, I was tired, but
I had never before known such joy and peace in my
heart.

About three in the morning, I suddenly awoke as I
heard somebody call my name. Again I heard a voice
say 'James, take my name to the heathen.' It was the
voice that I heard twenty years before. God was
reminding me of the first call to preach and there on my
mat that morning, I rededicated my life to Christ.

I asked the Methodist missionaries to send someone
to my people, but they didn't have anyone to send. I
began to ask God to send someone to work among my
people. One day I heard that some missionaries had
arrived from Nigeria and they were going to live in my
town [Nikki]. Who were they? Would they love my
people? Would they preach the same gospel that I
preached? As soon as I could, I went to see them. I only
planned on staying two or three days, but instead I
stayed two weeks. These missionaries [McDougalls] had

the same Bible I had, they could speak the language I had spoken in Nigeria, and in which I had studied in Bible School. They loved my people and asked me to teach them my native language so that they might preach to them. What a thrill it was to me when the first verse of scripture, the first hymn, the first chapter of the Bible and then the first gospel was translated into my own language.

Mr. and Mrs. J.B. Williams were ready for the opening of Parakou station. They had been in Nikki for nearly a year, and had made good progress in language study. They were well suited for this pioneer effort. Since there was no house yet in Parakou, Mrs. Williams and Judy stayed at Nikki during the construction. The men built a grass shelter for protection from the heat of the day and a sleeping place for themselves while building.

The parcel of land, three hundred feet square, was covered with thick brush and tall grass, and water was a problem. But soon there was activity everywhere: crews clearing the land, crews breaking stone, men making mud bricks down by the stream. Stewart joined them, bringing Joeli Gbogundjoko and his building crew from Nikki and stayed to haul lumber from the cutting site sixty-five miles away.

The chief and elders of Sinagourou (now part of Parakou) came the first day to observe. When the missionaries explained why they had come, the men nodded as if to say, "We will wait and see." Almost daily they returned to check on the crews' progress.

In January 1949, the Williams family moved into the partially finished rooms of the main house while the work continued. The corrugated metal roofing was delayed in coming and the rains came early, so they put grass roofing on instead. By the end of the month they had the first Bariba service with about fifty present.

At that time Parakou had a population of about 6,000. It was a Bariba town but, since it was a government center, many tribes were there with at least six languages spoken. The nomadic Fulani settlements were all around the town with an estimated 10,000 people but the Fulani were bilingual and understood Bariba well.

Williams started trekking the area on foot as soon as they were a bit settled. The response in the villages was immediate. When he would miss some villages the elders would send a message requesting a visit. Some promised to build a

hut for meeting if he would bring them the "sweet words of Jesus." J.B. recorded: "It is not uncommon to have someone stop us in the middle of a message and say, 'We are sinners and we believe Jesus is God's Son that you are telling us about. Just tell us how to accept Him and we will do it right now.'"

The response in Parakou itself was slower with personal contacts bringing better results than mass meetings. The Bariba chief made a profession of faith and invited the believers to meet in a house inside his compound. Children's classes were held daily on the compound and some younger boys were learning to read.

Borori, son of a Fulani chief, came to visit and listened raptly to the message. It was the first time for him, and he asked for it to be repeated until he understood. The next morning he returned with all the leaders of his village. After

they listened and listened, they stated that they were well
pleased and wanted to follow this Savior.

The Yoruba church group was continuing to meet but
when Baribas and Fulanis joined them they were crowded for
space. The churches went to two services with Baribas meeting
at early service and Yorubas later. Soon the Yorubas built their
own meeting place in Quartier Gah. Surely this was God's
timing and His messengers had come to a prepared people.

Rosella Entz joined the Williams in January of 1950
and that fall the Bible School was started. From the beginning,
they had six boarding students and sixteen day students, some

, of them enrolled in the literacy
classes and others in the Bible
School. Classes were held
three weeks out of the month
and the fourth week they went
out evangelizing in the
villages. The students often
chose a central village for their
gatherings and people would come in from surrounding areas
to hear them.

By the end of 1950, the Bible School buildings had been
constructed. The Yoruba Church had been organized and had
their first baptismal service with twenty-six baptisms. The
village work, nurtured by the students, was very encouraging.
Women came to Mrs. Williams' classes and brought their children. Much time had been spent in translation, working on the
Gospel of John and preparing materials for the Bible School.
James Odjo Boro was involved in many of these activities,
preaching, teaching, translating and mediating palavers. God
had indeed answered his prayers for missionaries to love his

people. He was finally and joyfully obedient to God's call to service.

In August,1951, the Williams family was ready for furlough. They had planted well and had seen much fruit in a short period of time. They left, anticipating their return to the work started at Parakou but God led otherwise since S.I.M. reassigned them to the U.S. home staff. They had turned their responsibilities over to Orville and Ethel Thamer who had been in Parakou waiting to open the new station in Tchaourou.

Annie Van den Brand from Holland joined the Thamers and Rosella Entz and together they kept the witness going on all fronts. The Bariba believers completed their church building and continued to grow in number. The attendance was up to one hundred in afternoon Sunday school as well as morning service. There was a large class of men, a group of fifteen women, and two classes of teen-age boys with other children coming as well. This response in all ages was very encouraging.

The Bible School was an integral part of the Parakou work. Rosella carried heavy responsibilities as she managed to keep it going with the assistance of James Odjo Boro and Pastor David Dada from Nigeria. Upon their return from furlough and study in France, Stewart and Edna were assigned to Parakou in July of 1952. Stewart took part of the teaching load and reorganized the school curriculum. Most of the students were not well read in French so he divided the students into Yoruba speakers and Bariba speakers providing instruction in their tribal language while teaching them French as a subject. David Dada and Orville Thamer taught in Yoruba and Rosella in Bariba. He also found the buildings had not been adequately maintained so much of his attention was devoted to the building program. When the school term ended

in the fall of 1953, they celebrated their first graduation, graduating four Yoruba young men. Three of these left immediately to fulfill their assignments to local churches and the fourth found his place of ministry in the Kandi Bookstore.

In 1953, Stewart supervised the building of a duplex for single missionaries and a dispensary for outpatient medical treatment. Mrs. Williams and Rosella had begun an unofficial but effective medical ministry in 1951 serving up to one hundred thirty-eight patients in one day. Nurse Millie Davis joined them in the work but was unable to open the dispensary until inspected by the government doctor. The medical work showed a steady increase, reporting treatment of over one hundred patients a day in 1954 and nearly two hundred a day in 1955. The government had agreed to grant funds for medicines to operate the dispensary but was slow to follow through and the financial burden on the mission, which had agreed not to charge for medicines, was heavy. Medicines were imported from Nigeria, the U.S. and France with great difficulty. Finally, in June of 1956, funds were forwarded and in the fall of the year additional funding was given to the Parakou work as well as to the dispensary at Sinendé. Evangelistic outreach at the dispensaries brought new families into the churches every week.

The most important development of 1953, however, was the visit of Fulani Evangelist, Adamu Dogon Yaro from Kano, Nigeria. He came for a month at the invitation of Stewart and

Gus Fredlund, and the response of the Fulanis was immediate and powerful. From the beginning the Fulanis had been the most responsive tribal group. Heads of households would bring their entire family to hear the message. There had been set-backs in the early stage, however, when the ritual initiation beatings took place Sunday after Sunday, the tug of the old ways, practiced for generations, drew them strongly [see pages 269-270 for description]. The mocking and persecution for non-participation was severe. There had been a withdrawing. In time, however, they returned bringing friends with them.

Dogon Yaro had been invited because of the numbers of believers and their sincere interest to learn. For two months he traveled with Gus Fredlund, visiting Fulanis wherever they gathered. Dogon Yaro was used to indifference and antagonism in Kano so the friendly, welcoming, accepting reception in Dahomey filled him with joy. When his visit ended he expressed reluctance to abandon these new friends but did return to Kano, leaving behind him several hundred converts and scores more who were interested. One young man, Borori, who had already trusted Christ, dedicated his life to ministry during this time and became a fearless witness and evangelist among his people.

A freshness came to the Fulani believers from these wonderful times together with someone of their own tribe who was overflowing with love for God and for them. New people started coming from villages throughout the area.

Another important development in the work was the beginning in 1952 of an annual church conference including all the churches from the main stations. In 1954, McDougall reported having to translate the meetings into five different languages but, "despite this handicap the Lord spoke to the

hearts of men and women through His word." In 1953
McDougall had been notified that the church building site in
the center of Parakou that he had reserved with the
government, had to be used within the year or their rights to it
would be forfeited. The Yoruba church had grown and was
sorely needing a new building to accommodate that ministry.
The property had been available for some time but, since it was
located on a main street in this important government center,
the specifications and requirements were considerable. This
made the cost of building in that location beyond their
capabilities. In November of that year, the gift from Neil
Barnes allowed them to build the church and a bookstore on
the site and dedicate them in early 1954. The bookstore
became a center for reaching the educated French government
workers and entrepreneurs in Parakou who seemed eager to
read the Protestant Bible to see for themselves how it differed
from the Catholic version.

In 1954, the buildings were completed with great
rejoicing and celebration. David Dada of EMS from Nigeria
was the pastor to the Yorubas and services were also held in
French to meet the need of many, including normal school
students and teachers. Jo Stevens managed the newly built
bookstore and had an active outreach to the French community. Jim and Teddy Cail arrived in September, 1953 for
language study before being assigned to Nikki in August, 1954.
In December of 1953, five thousand copies of the Gospel of
John in the Bariba language were delivered.

The villages were begging for teachers, so each new
class that came in helped to meet their needs. In early 1954,
the "Short Term Bible School", a special six-week course,
introduced many to the opportunity. This was especially

planned for farmers who were mostly free from their farm work
in February and March. The churches were faithful to send
their young men. Twenty-two attended the first year and
twenty-six the next. Some who came stayed on to take the
three year course. In 1954, Stewart reported in a letter, "We
had . . . 25 students in the Bible School, three of whom were
married and had wives and children with them. It meant that
the single men had to sleep four or five in a room side by side.
Apart from being unhealthy, it made it impossible for the men
to study or have devotions in their rooms. We are trusting the
Lord for even more this coming year and it seems almost
impossible to accommodate them." By 1955 the school was
bulging at the seams with students from all three tribes:
Bariba, Fulani and Yoruba. Some of the men had been leaders
in pagan worship; some had been Muslim; but they all studied
together in a wonderful spirit of cooperation. When word came
of a gift from England to build dormitories, they anticipated
getting started as soon as the rains were over.

In 1955 and 1956 the majority of the students were
Baribas, but there were many Fulanis who could also be
taught in Bariba. In 1957 there were eighteen men students
and nine of them brought their wives making twenty-seven
total in very crowded housing. Among these couples was Borori
who had come with his wife, Yoobi. The women had some
classes specially designed for them but shared some classes
with the men. A weaving shed was built for them and several
women learned this skill.

The witnessing and teaching the students did each
week-end in the villages made for great growth and expansion
for the church. All systems were at full capacity in the
language study, women's ministries, Bible School, translation

and medical work, village evangelistic outreach and church
ministries in the Yoruba, Bariba, French and Fulani
communities.

The medical work served all the people in these
ministries. From the small beginning it kept growing and
meeting needs with people coming every day from distant
villages. Every dispensary had an evangelist assigned who
preached the gospel to all the prospective patients before
treatment sessions began each day.

In 1954, the McDougalls' daughter, Janet, became very
ill and Edna returned with their children to the U.S. while
Stewart remained in Parakou until August of 1955 when
Rosella took over station leadership. In 1955, two other needs
became obvious: the need for a Fulani Bible School and the
need for a guest house at Parakou since so many missionaries
came there for official business. The Fosters took over the
guest house, business department and book-keeping, and
Louise assisted in the dispensary three days a week.

The primers for literacy training that Edna had worked
on for many years, then under the direction of Mary Draper,
were finally printed and arrived from the U.S. The bookstore
reported 5000 tracts per month being distributed and the
Bariba women had their first conference beginning
November 12 with an average attendance at meetings of
twenty-eight. One significant event of 1956 was the dedication
of the outstation at Tchatchou attended by three hundred
twenty-five people and pastored by Amos Ayorinde of the EMS.
Another was the first major donation of medicines by the
government to the dispensaries at Parakou and Sinendé. At
the end of 1956, the Fosters moved to Sinendé and were
replaced by the Zobrists.

In 1957, Jean Playfair returned to Parakou to begin reading and writing classes. The dispensary was closed for four months due to the furlough of Millie Davis and was opened again in April by Irene Zobrist until Millie's return the end of June. That year the government declared the drugs for the dispensaries were to come in duty free which lifted a great portion of the financial burden off the mission. The government also granted funds for the construction of a new three-room building and the remodeling of the original one. The first Regional Council of Dahomey Churches met in Parakou in August with four churches represented and the Annual Church Council met in November.

In 1958, Millie Davis opened a medical work in Tchatchou two days a week while ministering in Parakou the other days. The Emmetts moved from Djougou to relieve the Zobrists who left Parakou to survey the Banikoara area for a possible new station. Language study, taught by Teddy Cail, was moved back to Nikki to get the new missionaries away from all the noise and activity. Margaret Bevington arrived and went to Nikki for language study. S.I.M. General Director, Dr. Albert Helser and Edward Rice, accompanied by their wives, visited Parakou station prior to the District conference at Djougou and were a great encouragement. Prime Minister Maga visited the north in 1959, encouraging the citizens to engage in hard work and pay their taxes if the nation was to succeed in its approaching independence. Stewart and Edna McDougall returned and were assigned to the Boys' School in Sinendé.

In May of 1960, when Field Leader and Mrs. Emmett left for furlough, Stewart McDougall was asked to move back to Parakou to take over the direction of the field again. He found

severe tensions in the Yoruba church. It appears that his
strategy to bring Yoruba speaking pastors and evangelists to
assist in the planting of the church in Benin required a Yoruba-
speaking field leader. Lacking one over several years caused
stress between the missionaries and Nigerian staff as well as
renewing old tribal animosities between Yoruba and Bariba
believers. As a result, the Nigerian pastors had been recalled to
Nigeria. In a letter to his family dated April 25, 1960, Stewart
wrote:

> We surely need your prayers for the work there for
> things are in a bit of a state. The church has defied Mr.
> Emmett [previous field leader] on certain major issues
> and he didn't know what to do. It is the Yoruba church
> and . . . we will be able to understand them. . . . There is
> a strong Methodist element that has come in from the
> south and they have been running things. . . . There is
> also a real need in the Bariba work and the villages
> have not been visited for some time. There has only
> been one person who knew any Bariba at Parakou for a
> year so things have been neglected.

Apparently, Ted Emmett spoke excellent French and
was well able to make all the official contacts, which was very
important to the work, but was not equipped to supervise the
work of the churches. Restoring order and a sense of
partnership was going to be more taxing than Stewart could
have anticipated. In fact, the idea of getting missionaries from
the U.S., Canada, Britain, Ireland, Australia, France,
Switzerland, New Zealand, Nigeria and Holland from different
theological traditions to work together as a team was more
than a man should be expected to accomplish, even a very
gifted man.

On August 1, 1960, Dahomey celebrated her independence from France. The missionaries in Parakou sat on the
verandah watching the French forces driving by—first the
military jeep with officers and the Tricolor and then all the

vehicles loaded with soldiers. This was a strategic time in the
history of Dahomey as the forces of Islam, Romanism and
Communism were all bidding for this new nation. All of them
were aware that the future of their mission depended largely
on how wisely they responded to the changes independence
would bring.

Stewart wrote at the time:

> Dahomey became an independent Republic the 1st of
> August. We praise the Lord that the change took place
> without any violence. We know many of the government
> leaders personally and their attitude toward the work of
> our mission has been friendly. We do covet your prayers
> for these leaders that they may be given great wisdom,
> and above all that the preaching of the gospel of the
> Lord Jesus Christ may not be hindered.

The missionaries were well received in government
offices because, as nationals took responsibility, they preferred
to use their native languages in offices and the missionaries'
abilities to communicate in the tribal languages, instead of
French, was appreciated. So the witness continued in all areas.

Later that same month, the Bariba Bible School moved
from Parakou to Sinendé so McDougalls planned a "Home
Coming" for all former Bible School students, and their
testimonies of what God was doing in the villages through the
preaching of the gospel was thrilling. This event provided one
of the most encouraging moments in Stewart McDougall's
career as he heard the students praying for their own people.

In a letter dated August 25, 1960 from Parakou,
Stewart wrote, "A few days ago I talked to a French official
who was leaving, not to return. He looked at me and said with
real feeling, 'McDougall, if ever in the history of Dahomey they
have needed you, it is now.'" In October, the new head of state,
Monsieur Maga, sent a representative to the mission's annual
field conference in Tchaourou. When the missionaries asked

how they could best help the new nation of Dahomey, he replied that they should just keep doing what they had been doing in the past. Although the response was not definitive, it was reassuring that the national leadership was willing to accept their help.

In October, 1960, Stewart and Dr. Dreisbach located the springs in Bembèrèkè that would make possible the building of the mission hospital there. It took months of negotiating with new and inexperienced officials to get the permissions required, locate building supplies and get the funding. However, this was to be the priority project on the field for the next year.

The Bible School classrooms were remodeled and became the linguistic and literature center. Jean Soutar, Rosella Entz and Edna were assigned the task of translation, language and literacy for the Bariba work. Their first informant was Bio Doko. The first production was two hundred copies of a sixty-five page basic baptismal booklet and five hundred copies of a Bariba hymn book. The Gospels and Acts were produced in mimeograph form later, in 1962, and were used with much blessing and gratitude. Earl and Carolyn Bruce were moved from Djougou to Parakou to supervise the bookstore in its new location, to expand its inventory, accessibility and colportage work, and to start a lending library. Their report in 1961 showed a large increase in sales and opportunities and plans to expand locations and reopen bookstores that had been closed at other stations.

The dispensary in Parakou was closed in anticipation of the opening of the hospital in Bembèrèkè and the moving of the nurse, Millie Davis, sixty-five miles north to the new facility. This meant a major shift in strategy since the dispensary had been such an important evangelistic entry point for many

years. The hospital was dedicated July 3, 1961, with joy and
celebration. It was attended by the President of Dahomey,
Monsieur Maga, General Director of S.I.M., Ray Davis, and
many tribal delegations. By the end of 1961, it became obvious
that due to illness and other personal issues, the Dreisbachs
would be unable to continue and a replacement would have to
be found. Three stations were closed due to lack of personnel
and the mood among the missionaries became somber.

Stewart had his hands full with the Yoruba Church
situation. He described the problems in a letter to his children
dated September 17, 1961:

> We would certainly covet your prayers for the work here
> in Parakou. We feel that the Lord is on the verge of
> granting blessing but the devil is surely giving us a bad
> time. . . . A great many of our people in the church are
> really former Methodists or are still Methodists. The
> Methodists sent one of their men to the world ecumen-
> ical movement and now he is back in Dahomey trying to
> unite all the churches in Dahomey under their banner.
> Last Sunday when we got to church there were three
> Methodist pastors (African) in church. We had no word
> that they were coming so went right ahead with the
> service as usual. I spoke and then after the service they
> said that they wanted to talk to me. . . . A group south
> of here left the Methodist church about 9 years ago and
> have been calling themselves SIM although we had
> nothing to do with them except that we trained two
> pastors for them in our Bible School. They have done a
> tremendous work and one of them has a church of about
> 300 attendants. The other is smaller, but about a month
> ago they asked us to come down and baptize those who
> were ready for baptism. An African pastor went down
> and spent a week examining them and then I went
> down with two other pastors for the baptisms. There
> were 64 baptized that day and I never baptized any
> group that had more clear-cut testimonies for the Lord
> Jesus Christ. The Methodists are upset about our hav-
> ing anything to do with the group but they didn't want
> anything to do with the Methodists. There is a
> Methodist church in town but the man drinks and the
> leader of the area has just taken a second wife and they

say they can have no fellowship with them at all. It was
about this matter that the men said that they came, but
they criticized our insisting that Methodist members
who want to become members of our church be exam-
ined regarding their faith in Christ and must also be
baptized. They had a meeting with our elders which . . .
lasted two hours. I think they are planning to open a
Methodist church here and it would surely be a boon to
us if they did. The Methodist people who love the Lord
would not leave us and the ones who want to live in sin
with their two wives are a continual headache to us.

Stewart left for Jos and the West Africa Field Council
on April 16, 1962 and from there to New York for the U.S.
Council meetings and did not return to Dahomey until the end
of June. Edna's letters recount the profound stress of the
situation. In one dated May 14, 1962, she wrote:

Unless the church at home prays through this situation
with us at this time, the work may be lost. If not lost, it
will surely be set back many years. . . . The situation
here is black, no amount of reasoning will make it
lighter. The clouds are heavy, it is a mountain we can't
tunnel through, and a river we can't (at the moment)
see our way across. Faith is down to bedrock. I believe
God for this situation or I don't. . . . In this crisis all we
have given our lives for either stands or falls. You must
beg people to pray, stating the situation as simply as
possible without criticism or complaint.

The issue that predominated was whether polygamists
could be assigned positions of leadership in the church. The
mission had taken the position that polygamists should not be
baptized because once the man was baptized, it would be difficult to keep him from being active in church leadership. Since
tribal status often was accorded on the basis of wealth and
wealth was judged by ownership of cattle and wives, a man of
status in the tribe would also be accorded status in the church.
Therefore the only sure means of preventing trouble in the
church was to declare polygamists ineligible for baptism.
James Odjo Boro had effectively by-passed the elders of the

church and was consulting with a group of men who were
polygamists. With Stewart out of the country, they became
very aggressive. One chorus became the missionaries' daily
theme song:

> Got any rivers you think are uncrossable?
> Got any mountains you can't tunnel through?
> God specializes in things thought impossible.
> And He can do what no other friend can do.

During the French administration of Dahomey, all
European dwellings were required to be at least a mile from
the native town so the mission site in Parakou was a hindrance
to McDougalls' managing of the church crisis. Now under
national governance, those restrictions had been waived, so
when Stewart returned in September, he remodeled the old 12'
by 24' bookstore beside the church into an apartment for him
and Edna, using funds donated by special friends in the U.S.
This dramatically changed the dynamic since the property had
been deeded to the mission and the church had no legal
standing, thus forcing the issue toward resolution.

On February 3, 1963, the opposition pulled out and
started a Methodist Church in the home of one of the men,
Paul Oloubi. Stewart called in all catechists and elders from
the churches, the Conseil d'Administration together with
Orville Thamer and leaders from Tchaourou. Twenty-five men
came for a time of review, consultation and prayer. The whole
question, one which would affect all the work, was: Would
polygamists be permitted to have any part in the governing of
the church? The elders of the Parakou church were against it
and the leaders of all the churches stood with them. James
Odjo Boro did not leave with the first exodus but by the next
Sunday he had gone with the opposition, his family having
preceded him there. He made a determined effort to get all

former Methodist people to leave and in the end seventy-five percent of the people did leave. The nucleus that stayed wanted to cooperate with their missionary leaders.

Those whose attempts to disrupt the work had failed, now turned their efforts into a campaign to influence all the national churches to assert their independence and drive out all the white people. The missionary leaders had a great meeting in Tchaourou with the pastors and evangelists and the Lord was very present as they listened to accusations (some true) and complaints. Public confessions were made and forgiveness sought. The meeting ended in a spirit of oneness and determination to stand together as they faced a new and uncertain future. In a letter to Mr. Emmett dated March 13, 1963, Stewart reported that, before leaving, the opposition group had drawn 90,000 francs out of the Parakou Church bank account which they were using to build another church building. He also remarked, "It is wonderful to have an elders meeting and not have to fight over every point. . . . Instead of retrenching they are planning on going ahead and have raised the amount they are paying to the evangelists. . . . It is in faith for they have such a small group, but their offerings are just about the same as they were before." The opposition sent a delegation to the church at Djougou to persuade the Fulanis to join the movement against the missionaries but Dogon Yaro was present and publicly confronted them and stopped the movement.

Edna had successfully started women's ministries among the Yorubas both in Nigeria and in Nikki and now in Parakou. In April, 1963 she and Rosella organized the first Bariba women's conference. Rosella's report recounts that they prepared for thirty-five but sixty-five women came with an equal number of children. It was a new experience for them and the excitement was high. Some meetings were led by the Bariba women and the testimony time was memorable as they shared stories how God had worked in their lives in very

Annie, Shirley, Rosella and McDougalls

difficult circumstances. The Bariba tribal custom was that babies born face down or who cut their upper teeth first were either killed or given away as slaves. Some of these babies had been rescued and given to non-Christian homes or to other tribes. These women thought the missionaries should provide an orphanage but the missionaries insisted that the babies needed Christian homes and parents rather than an institution. The discussion proved valuable for planning future Bariba women's ministries.

In June, 1963, the McDougalls went to the U.S. for furlough and another Bariba women's conference was not planned until after their return in April, 1965. However, at that conference, five of the women stood with babies on their backs which they said were babies they had rescued and were raising as their own. Meanwhile, in 1964, Annie Van den Brand had begun a very fruitful women's ministry in Bariba towns. At first missionaries taught but, as she persisted, eventually all the speaking was done by Bariba women. By 1966 Annie was living at Amanwignon-Dokparou where she had built a house. There she held two week Bible schools for the women. In time a young elder visited regularly and preached in Ouénou and started a Bariba church there. Later the churches invited Annie to extend her ministry to other language groups. The Lokpas and the Fulanis were the first to make the request. In March of 1965, a Yoruba Women's conference was held which was attended by over fifty women including some from Gurai, Nigeria.

Moira Alexander came to join the work from Switzerland in 1963 and was well suited and equipped to continue the ministry of outreach to the French speaking community in the area since she was fluent in French and experienced in evangelism. She began witnessing immediately to students and government functionaries. She held children's classes, did hospital visitation and made personal contacts. With her energy and enthusiasm the French youth work was flourishing as the number of literate young people increased.

In February, 1964, the mission received an evacuation notice on the rental space they had been using for their book-store in downtown Parakou. The mission had an ideal commercial property to build in the town but no funds for the building. West Africa Field Director, Dr. Davis, came to survey the situation and released funds necessary to start building. The committed funds were sufficient to complete only the main floor for the bookstore and the storeroom. It would take several years to finish the project which eventually housed a reading room and youth center on the second floor. The new store was opened for business June 1, 1965. There was a need and eager-

ness to get literature out to the people. The sale of Bibles had
increased and a greater interest was anticipated after the
upcoming Perrier meetings.

The McDougalls returned from furlough for their sixth
term in November, 1964. The day after their arrival Field
Council Meetings began in Nigeria. In Stewart's final letter to
supporters before leaving New York on November 20 he states,
"As we received letters from the field in this past week, we
were reminded that our task is not going to be easier this
term." He was right. In a letter seeking counsel from their
pastor, Dr. J. Vernon McGee, dated November 25, written from
Jos, Nigeria, he wrote:

> A few weeks ago a Mr. Shaw representing the I.C.C.C.
> was invited by a couple of our disgruntled missionaries
> to speak to a meeting of our church leaders. Our Field
> Director was not aware of the meeting and didn't know
> of it until after it had been held. They assured our
> church leaders that they would not be able to stand
> alone, but if they joined up with them they would be
> able to send them clothes and surplus products. We had
> been cooperating with the I.F.M.A. and E.F.M.A. in
> forming an evangelical fellowship of churches
> throughout Africa. Of course, they said this was an
> unholy alliance and actually printed and circulated
> pamphlets denouncing our mission. We have sought to
> guide our church leaders in a sound evangelical position
> and now they are pulled by both sides and, as you can
> well imagine, are very confused.
>   The situation in Africa today is very touchy and we
> feel that any radical position which could very easily
> lead to criticizing the government would be very
> dangerous. We feel that it is unfortunate that such a
> thing should be introduced into our church at this time
> and would covet your prayers as we seek to guide our
> church leaders.

Another question raised by missionaries had to do with
whether a believer could be demon possessed. This term of
service was going to be different. Stewart was just beginning to
connect the dots between the conflict with the Methodists in

Parakou, the evacuation notice for the bookstore and now the threat of a take-over from the World Council of Churches.

At Stewart's first District Conference meeting of the term, February 23-25, 1965, his authority to make decisions as District Superintendent was called into question by some missionaries who felt that all decisions affecting the field should be brought to them for a vote. They had changed the function of the D.S. by rewriting the "Principles and Practices" of the Dahomey field while he was away on furlough. The missionaries worded the policies so that the D.S. was responsible to represent their interests to the Field Council, etc. but Dr. Bingham, the founder of S.I.M., had set up the mission structure to operate with power to make decisions as close to the situation as possible. One missionary on each station was to be designated "Head of Station" and was responsible in coordination with the D.S. to make decisions for that station. The D.S., along with whatever councils or committees he may set up, made decisions for the field such as: where to assign missionaries, what stations to close and which to build, and was accountable to report field activities to the West Africa Field Council and to carry out mission policy and council decisions on that field. He represented the mission authority structure on the field, whereas the Dahomey missionaries wanted the structure inverted for their field. He was stymied and Mr. Bill Crouch, the West Africa Field Director was called to the meeting by Stewart to help resolve the situation so the D.S. could do his job. As a result Mr. Crouch later formulated the "District Superintendent Job Description" to avoid future stalemates. Not only was the nation changing but so was the mission.

In a letter dated May 16, 1965, Stewart remarked, "If the Lord tarries, I would like to go back to Nikki for a term and just be a missionary and finish the job we started 18 years ago. These past six months have been the most difficult we have ever experienced, and it doesn't seem as though things are going to get any easier. We have had to close our hospital and the past month we have had to close 3 of our mission stations. . . . With the lack of missionary staff we had hoped to use more African staff. The government has been introducing so many new labor laws that missionaries are afraid to hire national staff. I have had to appear three times before the Labor Board through complaints lodged [against] missionaries."

There were many Yorubas to reach in Dahomey, an estimated 500,000. In July, 1965, the Yoruba church in Nigeria sent their secretary and a pastor to visit and report back. They were impressed with the need in Dahomey, mostly to the south of Parakou. They recommended that the Nigerian Church send two pastors right away and Stewart was invited to present the need at two conferences in September. Listen to Stewart's enthusiasm at the prospect from a letter dated August 9, 1965:

> What would this mean to our work? In one of these two churches we have 150 baptized believers but we have never had a trained pastor to give them. There are young men who have asked for Bible teaching but we have not been able to establish a Bible School. The Christians have asked us to start a dispensary, but we don't have a nurse. The representatives of the church saw these possibilities. They are interested in starting a Bible School. They have trained African nurses who could establish and run a dispensary. It would be completely indigenous and be financed wholly by the Yoruba Church and the gifts of the Christians in the area where they will be working.
> We would be very short-sighted if we could see this only in terms of the blessing it would bring to us. I am

> confident that if the Yoruba church catches the vision
> and steps into the gap it will bring rich spiritual
> blessing to the entire church. Do pray that the Holy
> Spirit Himself will guide in their decision.

This had been his dream since coming to Dahomey from the
work in Nigeria.

The Yoruba women had always been responsive to the
McDougalls' appeals. Edna had found them so in Nigeria and
when they came to Dahomey the women had prayed for and
supported financially the pastors who came over to help them.
The Women's Missionary Group of the Yoruba Church in
Nigeria had sent the funds to build the first dispensary to
provide a place in Nikki where Edna could treat simple
ailments. So now in the Sixties the Yoruba women held conferences in the areas where they lived. Women from several
churches would get together for testimonies, teaching, prayer
and singing. In 1966 a group of the Southern Churches held a
conference in Korokoto which was well attended by women
from Parakou, Tchaourou, Kilibo and women's classes were
growing in Tchaourou. In February, 1967, women from four
villages came together in Nikki for mutual encouragement and
prayer.

Having worked for the Billy Graham Crusade in Los
Angeles while on furlough in 1955-56 and again in 1963-64,
Stewart was certain that the cities could be reached by well-
planned crusades. To that end, crusades were planned for
Parakou and Cotonou. Yves Perrier had preached and taught
in French for many years on the S.I.M. mission radio station
ELWA with many regular listeners in Dahomey. Many who
found Christ and a new life at that time had engendered
growth and vigor in all areas of ministry. Stewart poured his
efforts into the 1966 Perrier Evangelistic Campaign in

Parakou. These meetings had been planned long in advance
with much prayer and had been a desire of Stewart's for years.
Now it was becoming reality. Posters were put up all over
town. A car equipped with loudspeakers announced meetings
and invited all to come. Counselors' training classes were being
taught. Ushers were organized and instructed. The Centre
Culturel added extra lights and hymns were played throughout
the day on the public address system.

Opening night came and the Hall was filled. There were
many who listened to ELWA and now men whose voices they
recognized had come from ELWA to speak and sing. The mayor
brought an opening speech of welcome. The Catholic Bishop
came every night and some priests and nuns were present from
time to time. Some girls from Tchaourou Girls' School, dressed
in the colors of the flag, sang the national anthem and were
welcomed with enthusiastic applause. Yves Perrier's messages
were well received and he regularly invited people to accept
Jesus Christ. Over the days, ninety-nine people signed cards
and were followed up. His wife, Françoise, held children's
meetings. Parakou heard the gospel proclaimed clearly and
with power. Many responded and were changed. Among those
who responded was Célestin, the clerk of the Catholic
Bookstore. He was wonderfully saved and through his witness
his wife was saved as well, then two of his teenage sons.

At the close of those meetings on January 30, Yves and
Françoise went on to the capital city, Cotonou, with Al Cross,
Gus Fredlund and Allan Armbruster to prepare for the
meetings there. Stewart attended the Bariba men's conference
in Bori. Forty-three Christians from fourteen villages were
present. The last day three believers from Bori were baptized.
Then on February 4, the McDougalls journeyed to Cotonou to

join the team. On February 11, Stewart and Gus Fredlund
drowned in the accident in the ocean in Cotonou. The drive
back to Parakou with the bodies was a long one for Edna.

Annie Van den Brand, who had remained in Parakou,
wrote:

> The noon the accident took place I represented
> Stewart at a lunch in honor of the Minister of Interior
> who visited Parakou that day. In the afternoon Mary
> Carney and Moira Alexander passed my house and
> dropped in to ask about the lunch. While they were
> there at about 5 o'clock the telephone rang and Al Cross
> told me the crushing news. I went to inform Augustin,
> our Evangelist. He was not home, but after having told
> a few Christians of what happened the news spread in
> no time. Christians and non-Christians alike started
> coming to my house in town and to the Mission station.
> Everybody was deeply moved. The Christians expressed
> their desire to come to the main station and wait with
> us for the arrival of the bodies. At 7 A.M. just after we
> finished prayer meeting where the Lord had spoken to
> our hearts through Revelation 21, the party arrived.
> Edna beaten, but not crushed. The Christian women
> started straightway to come into her room.
> With a voice fraught with emotion, but master of
> herself she told them "God took him." It was awe
> inspiring to witness how the Lord enabled her to say
> with her conduct though not audibly: 'Though the Lord
> slay me yet will I praise Him.' She inspired the
> Christians with the fact that the Lord had taken their
> leader, but now the mantle of responsibility had fallen
> on them. We have ample proof that they understood.
> At 7:30 A.M. Arnold Leuders, Miss Thompson and
> Shirley Hyman were on their way to Kandi to break the
> news to Alice. The day before the missionaries in
> Cotonou had tried to charter a plane from the
> Assemblies of God at Nattitingou, but this had failed.
> An uninterrupted stream of visitors came to salute
> Edna that morning and for days to follow. Most of our
> missionaries were reached with the sad news either by
> telephone or messenger and were able to come on time
> for the funeral of which Gordon Beacham was in charge.
> The party that left for Kandi returned with Alice at
> about 3:30 P.M. Alice was bewildered, it all seemed so
> unreal to her. It was therefore a very hard thing for her

when she was advised not to have the coffin opened to see Gus' body. Alice's testimony all through those days was serene and her trust in the Lord obvious.

Past 4 o'clock we went to the big church in town for the funeral service. The church was packed. The tone of the service was hope. God takes His servants, but His work goes on.

Many recalled in those days how Stewart during the Evangelistic Campaign in Parakou often asked to sing (in French) "For I know whom I have believed." He always paused to stress the I KNOW adding YOU can know too. He also told that singing this hymn in public had been his first testimony after he was saved.

The Christians had lovingly prepared the grave and later provided the tombstones. A short service was held at the grave side. Here like in the church several hymns of victory and comfort were sung in French and in Yoruba.

The following morning Edna went to the Yoruba Sunday service where she spoke encouraging the Christians. Alice attended the Bariba service.

All along Edna was prepared to stay on the field, but bit by bit she began to wonder if that was really the Lord's will for her. A great comfort to her was the telegram that told of Colin, Edna's eldest son, coming to stay for two weeks.

It was a real blow to Edna when we were told, per telephone, by the team in Cotonou that Yves Perrier had collapsed. Its ultimate result was that the meetings were closed before time.

Day after day we waited for someone from Headquarters. It was the 19th when Mr. Crouch arrived and many questions that had arisen could be dealt with. It was decided that both widows go home. Alice felt that the children there needed her. (Victor had come from K.A.[Kent Academy] with Mr. Crouch). Arrangements were made for Edna to return with Colin at least for a period of time.

Edna had felt all along that the Lord wanted her to go to Cotonou to speak with the Perriers so from 22nd - 26th she went. 3 A.M. the 27th Colin arrived here at Parakou.

After Mr. Crouch's visit Alice and Victor had left for Kandi to pack. Also Edna had to pack, but because of the many visitors it was almost impossible so others had to do a lot for her.

Our Missionary Conference was scheduled for the 2nd through the 4th of March to take place in Djougou. Mr. Crouch returned for it with Mrs. and Pastor Holbrook, the speaker. Edna insisted that we all go. She and Colin came the 3rd for the day only.

For the evening of the 4th the Parakou church had planned a farewell meeting for Edna for which Alice and Victor and we three girls that are stationed here returned. After a short but sweet service the Christians brought their food along and we had an informal meal on the compound. The fellowship was very precious to all of us. Saturday morning Edna and Colin left in the mission plane with the others from Nigeria . . . to visit former stations before leaving Africa. Alice and Victor left the 8th for Kano on their way home.
[Parakou Station report, January-March 1966]

Meanwhile life went on for the crippled and distressed missionary staff. Gordon Beacham was elected to finish out the year as District Superintendent driving back and forth between Djougou, where they were stationed, and Parakou which was the business center for the mission work. Since only single women were now living in Parakou, the Crosses were moved

Graveside service for McDougall and Fredlund

from Djougou to provide hospitality and stability for the much coming and going of missionaries. Shirley Spence took over the business office and Mary Carney and her staff began expanding the outreach of the bookstore through colportage. They constructed a wheeled cart that could be loaded with books, pushed to a convenient spot in the market and quickly set up for display. In April, Charles Carpenter was elected to complete Stewart McDougall's term as D. S. and moved to Parakou with his wife, Elaine. A sense of returning order was restored. A few months later, the great Fulani leader, teacher, evangelist, Dogon Yaro, died suddenly in Tchatchou and was buried at the Fulani Bible School. Recovering equilibrium after the staggering loss of leadership in 1966 would require all the collective faith, courage, stamina and focus the church could muster.

A reading room was built above the bookstore called the "Foyer de la Bible" with an entrance on the main street. The activities held there were varied but included Bible studies, children's classes, Sunday prayer meetings and films such as Moody films in French. The outreach to the French speaking community led by Moira Alexander touched many, including prominent towns-people, students and other youth. The French group had meetings every week at Okpara with the young men leading. In the summertime youth camps were held there–both girls' and boys' camps. The Youth Center reached many young people, mostly boys, from the colleges and high schools. Moira had many opportunities. She taught Bible classes in different secondary schools and at the military camp as well as visiting and teaching in all wards of the government hospital.

In 1966, difficulties began with the secessionist move-ment in Biafra as a break-away state from Nigeria, Dahomey's closest neighbor to the east, culminating in an official declaration of independence on May 30, 1967. Unfortunately for the church and mission work in Dahomey, France, in order to obtain the rights to the oil in Biafra, engineered a three country pact involving Dahomey, Ivory Coast and Biafra which naturally antagonized the central government of Nigeria. French troops were brought into Biafra through Cotonou to support the secessionist efforts. The war lasted until January 15, 1970, and during that time many missionaries assigned to Nigeria were denied visas and came into Dahomey to get their language study until the Nigerian visas became available. It was in this period that Don (returning to his childhood home) and Perlene McDougall had been accepted to teach at Igbaja Seminary in Nigeria but were assigned to Parakou and then to Djougou to study Yoruba.

The year 1967 brought new recruits and new life. Dr. and Mrs. Elliot arrived from Australia and the hospital in Bembèrèkè was opened again, bringing relief to many hundreds of hurting people. A missionary couple was stationed in the capital, Cotonou, the scene of the stunning accident of the previous year. Jean and Soula Isch began a very effective work in French among students and young professionals. Charles Carpenter and Oswald Zobrist began the process of writing up a proposed constitution to submit to the African 'Conseil d'Administration' for their approval and to begin to organize the churches that had been planted by the missionary endeavor into a government-recognized national organization of churches.

From 1963 to 1972 Dahomey suffered five coups, nine changes of government and five different constitutions without the assassination of any outgoing president. This uncertainty,

however, exacerbated by the trouble in Nigeria and problems
between Nigeria and Dahomey, made the administration of the
mission in Dahomey very difficult. During this period of
political uncertainty, many of the educated church members
began to question the mission leaders because, in contrast to
the Catholics, Methodists, Muslims and other church
organizations in Dahomey, the mission churches looked
shabby, having been built before cement, corrugated roofing
and factory windows and doors were available. The churches
were mostly native-built, inadequate and unattractive buildings. Pastors and institutional leaders were underpaid and
poorly trained. National church leaders were demanding
change in the relationship between the mission and the
national churches. Massive changes were in the air and the
missionaries were confused as to their role or future in
Dahomey.

Harry and Garnet Wagoner came to Dahomey in 1972
after many years of productive work among the Yorubas in
Nigeria and they impacted the Yoruba churches greatly.
Wagoner took an evangelistic trip together with Yoruba church
leaders to the Savè and Dassa area with the view of establishing an S.I.M. work there. They conducted baptisms in the
Parakou church and in the Tchaourou church. Later they
planned a crash course in the Yoruba Bible and appointed
Augustin Adjaoké to be the teacher. They hosted a spiritual
retreat for Yoruba pastors and evangelists at Ikèmon which
was very successful in renewing the enthusiasm and vigor of
the Yoruba churches.

Augustin withdrew from the Bariba Church and Séko
Damagui was elected President. He came from Nikki to be
pastor of the Sinagourou church in Parakou. Their first church

building had been bulldozed down by the government along
with other buildings during a "straighten the main road"
project. Land had been granted them almost directly across
from the S.I.M. compound and a new church building was
erected.

Moira Alexander planned the first French youth retreat
in 1971 with John Isch speaking, and his wife, Soula, helping
with the music. Some seventy attended and their parting
question was, "When can we have another retreat?" The
French group had been holding meetings Sunday mornings in
the Yoruba church building and in early 1972 they became a
separate church organization but continued meeting there.
They grew in numbers at all services and eventually doubled.

In March, 1972, Roland Pickering was elected District
Superintendent and moved to Parakou, infusing new life and
vigor into the work. Edna returned to Parakou in 1972 and
found God's work was indeed going on and prospering under
Roland Pickering's fine leadership. One of the programs Roland
started was the pastors' retreats with the different language
groups and the missionaries that worked with them. These
were very effective in fostering improved relationships between
missionaries and national pastors. Annie Van den Brand led a
Bible instruction tour (for both men and women) and was
experiencing great success in her ministries to women
which continued to hold well-attended national and regional
conferences especially among the Baribas.

Dahomey endured another military coup on October 26,
1972, by General Matthieu Kérékou which moved the country
toward a Marxist-Leninist ideology and culminated in the
complete change of government on November 30, 1975. This
eventually resulted in the change of its name to the People's

Republic of Benin. It also ushered in a general anti-white sentiment and vigorous youth movement that had serious implications for the mission and the developing church leadership. By 1974 a group of young, aggressive and educated Christian men had taken over the S.I.M.-related churches in the country and were leveling very strong accusations against the missionaries, many of which were accurate, but their spirit was divisive and carnal. One general issue was that national pastors were not being paid minimum wage. Others were mainly ethnic conflicts between various Pila groups, between Pila and Dompago, between Bariba and Yoruba, between Yoruba and Francophone.

In October, 1974, Francophone Field Director, Roland Pickering, was killed in an auto accident on the way to Niger. One month later, Missionary Alan Gibbs was also killed in a train accident and resulting fire, leaving his wife, Ruth, and five young children. And so it was out of this bruised and battle-wearied but determined missionary force and an uncertain church leadership that the UEEB was founded on May 23, 1975, with Reverend Gabriel Doko elected its first president. The missionaries were assured that whatever happened to them, the church they had worked so hard and paid so high a price to plant would go on to become a contributing partner in obeying the command of Jesus Christ to "make disciples of all nations."

Chapter 26: Djougou (1949)

1949	Station officially turned over to S.I.M.
1950	Ed Morrow arrived. Building began.
1951	French Bible School for Evangelist training opened. Gordon and Joyce Beacham arrived. Ted and Addie Emmett arrived.
1952	Dispensary opened by Addie Emmett. Yom Language work begun by Gordon Beachams.
1953	First Yom literacy Primer.
1954	First Yom New Testament Book : Mark.
1955	Pila Bible School begun: Gordon Beacham. Yom translation: Book of Acts completed.
1957	Pila Girls School opened by Elsie Morrow. Yom translation: Book of James completed.
1959	Dispensary closed with marriage and reassignment of Alberta Gibbs.
1961	Part of New Testament printed with Mark, Acts, Ephesians, Philippians, Colossians, I Thessalonians, Titus, James, I John.
1965	Dispensary re-opened by Shirley Spence.
1967	Pila Church took over Bible School.
1968	Linguistic Center started.
1973	Handover church building to Methodists.

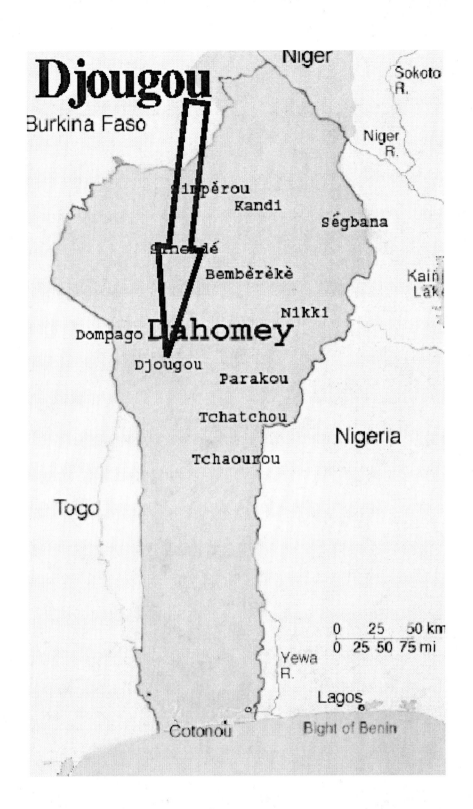

Djougou

Djougou station property was turned over to S.I.M. by
the English Methodists in October of 1949. Earlier in the year
Newton Kapp made a tour of Dahomey about which he
reported:

> One of the purposes of this trip was to visit Djougou
> (89 miles northwest of Parakou) to look into the
> possibility of opening a station there. The population of
> the town is about 6,000 and the district is composed of
> ten tribes with the total population of over 100,000. As
> this is pagan territory it presents marvelous opportuni-
> ties for mission work. Pray that all difficulties will be
> removed and that we may enter this district very soon.
> [The Sudan Witness, January, 1950]

In November 1949 the Methodist Mission representative and an S.I.M. representative met in Djougou for the
formal turning over of the work there. The evangelists were
informed at this time that they would be withdrawn from the
Djougou area and given a new post. Eight young men found
this was an acceptable arrangement but Ogouma Salomon
declined saying, "I am not going to leave just when the
missionaries are coming. If I go away, they will not know
where to find the Christians and all my flock will be scattered."

McDougall, Dudgeon and Morrow arrived on March 14,
1950 and found faithful Salomon there. His expressed joy at
their coming was very touching. He had struggled there for ten
years against strong opposition from both Muslims and
Catholics. He had faithfully evangelized throughout the area,
riding his bicycle on motor roads or bush paths. Many opened
their hearts to the "good news" he brought. The missionaries
found one main church at Djougou and twenty-four churches in

the out-villages. Nineteen of these churches had a building for meetings and housing for the evangelist in eight of them.

Immediately the building of a house for missionaries began with McDougall directing the project. In June, Morrow and Salomon began visiting the villages in a Jeep. Most of these villages were within a radius of twenty miles so they traveled to one each morning and studied language in the afternoon. Morrow reported a variety of spiritual conditions in these churches. Some were in a live, healthy state and were having weekly services on their own. Others were struggling to keep the witness going, and some had discontinued in discouragement in the absence of the evangelists. So the task of beginning a spiritual work and finding true believers as a nucleus was often overwhelming. The need to encourage, exhort, strengthen and also to reprove and rebuke was a daunting challenge.

Stan Dudgeon superintended the building operations, studied language and planted a garden while Morrow and Salomon followed the basic strategy of the village work.

Djougou believers had removed a partition in their church building to make room for people from a Dompago village nearby. Some sixty of these folk walked an hour and stayed for both morning and evening messages, which were given now in three languages. The year closed with the Christmas Conference which was well attended.

Some set-backs were caused by the weather as heavy storms brought much damage, stress and extra expense. Then Salomon's house was struck by lightening and burned completely, however, no one was injured and all the goods were saved. A greater loss came when two evangelists resigned from the work.

Morrow and Salomon found many had the idea that to become Christians meant building a church and meeting regularly. So they had to teach the plan of salvation very simply with careful explanations of how to be born again. Then the same message was repeated week by week until it was grasped. The people were nearly 100% illiterate so they started memory work classes. In September, 1950, Morrow reported in a letter:

> In the village of Soubroukou a definite work of the Spirit is taking place. When the people realized that God had done all that was necessary for their salvation and they had only to accept it as a free gift, a mass movement began in three large sections of the village. When we last visited them over 200 people jam packed the little church with many more crowding around the doors and windows. One of their number has taken on himself the responsibility of the Scripture memory class and either comes personally or sends someone regularly, and when we visited them the whole congregation recited a number of verses quite correctly.

Before the year closed there were other encouragements. A baptismal class was started and taught in Pila, Yoruba and French. Salomon taught a class of eighteen people from teens to elderly. The singing practice on Saturday nights attracted many young people and grew into a regular meeting in the style of "Youth for Christ". A witch doctor was saved in one village and promised to burn fetishes at the next meeting. Chiefs from other villages began asking for visits and preaching. The opportunities were wide open for ministry and the need for a Bible School to train evangelists seemed urgent and immediate.

Missionary Paul Clapp came to Djougou in December of 1950, and January, 1951, was spent turning the village work over to him. In February, Morrow was able to open the prayerfully anticipated Bible School with six students in a small classroom building. The students were temporarily housed in the village until dormitories could be built. Classes were started on February 4 and on March 12 work was started on the Pila Bible School dormitory building. It was completed along with classrooms in May. The teaching was well received with notable growth in the students.

Clapp had made two significant treks: one into the Dompago area west to the Togo border and one south among the Kotocoli and Windji-Windji tribes. There was such a good response among the Dompago people that the Field Council decided to open a mission station among them. This encouraging village work was interrupted when Paul Clapp was taken seriously ill. He had to be evacuated by plane to Jos, Nigeria. This was a terrible set-back to the village outreach bringing it almost to a standstill. Salomon carried on as faithfully as was possible on his bicycle and Morrow occasionally made a Sunday trip.

Encouraged by the promise of reinforcements, Morrow held the fort. The mother church at Djougou needed cleansing and biblical standards of living taught and adhered to before growth could take place. The cleansing started as they dealt with the polygamy issue. The church palavers stirred up by the discipline of polygamists took much time and patience. Confusion about polygamy and church leadership would plague the Djougou church for decades.

Ed Morrow reached out to the children by starting a hostel program in which he had fifteen first grade boys who came in from villages to attend government school. They were housed on the mission compound where they had supervision and an hour of Bible Study each day. Ed wrote to his prayer partners with enthusiasm about some other events:

On December 9 we had our first baptismal service since our arrival in Djougou (and my first baptismal service in my 22 years in Africa). Our whole congregation marched through the town singing hymns, thus making our way to a beautiful little stream outside the town, where there were nine who professed Christ in baptism, including an old man and his aged sister, three young men and four young women. . .

Beginning on Christmas day we conducted a 3-day conference to which Christians from our larger village churches were invited. Attendance (around 70) was better than expected and we believe much blessing ensued. [Ed's previous 20 years had been in the Islamic north without a breakthrough.]

Gordon Beacham and André Boroté

Language work was delayed until a linguist could come. Gordon Beacham and his wife, Joyce, were assigned and were eagerly awaited. They came in 1951 and began the tremendous task of the Yom language. They started with analysis, alphabet, literacy and, in time, began translation and helped others with language learning.

Rev. and Mrs. Ted Emmett joined them later the same year. Addie, an R.N., was prepared to do medical work but the mission's application for the dispensary permit was still pending. Pastor Benignus of the Federation of Protestant Missions for French West Africa came from Dakar, Senegal, on a visit and encouraged them to expect a response soon. The permit finally came through in June when Addie was in Jos for the birth of baby Christine. On October 27 the dispensary was opened in temporary accommodations three times a week. Ted assisted with church work and with the Boys' Home.

There were many other encouragements during 1952. The hostel buildings were built. In the Fall intake, all twenty boys returned along with fifteen new ones. Many of the church members started tithing after clear teaching. Right away the church income increased considerably and the tithers experienced joy in obedience to the Word. Salomon's salary was raised 1000 francs, and they bought him a new bicycle. Later they repaired the church and Salomon's house and planned to raise his salary again. They gave a widow in the congregation 1000 francs and all rejoiced in this new experience of giving. The Yoruba church from Nigeria sent missionaries and three Yoruba pastors for a visit. They were impressed with the need, added Djougou district to their existing Dahomey field, and gave 150 francs to the Evangelist's fund. Then Salomon, along with Andre Boroté and Paul Aboura, accompanied Morrow to the Yoruba Conference in Nigeria to report their progress and plans for the future.

The dispensary was closed in 1959 with no help in sight and remained closed until Shirley Spence came in 1964 and reopened it in 1965. Shirley made plans for a strong follow-up program with church involvement, but in 1966 she was transferred, so the potential for great outreach was always there for this ministry but proved difficult to sustain because of the lack of personnel.

The believers in the Dompago village of Mindjelia received permission for an official outstation. Even at the height of the rains they built a church building. The first two attempts, built up to the roof level, were washed down. They tried again and succeeded and the dedication was on August 5.

The young men of Mindjelia were persecuted in that the fathers of their wives threatened that if the men didn't give up their faith their wives would be taken away. The men stood true and gave up the wives to live single. The chief obstinately opposed them and pursued every pretext to make trouble for them. They continued faithful in prayer, faithful in witnessing and increased their giving.

In the villages the interest held, with fifty-five now in baptismal classes. The first village school was opened in Bariénou. This village had a small church inherited from the Methodists but S.I.M. had no one to occupy it. The Catholics applied to the chief for a school there and he was agreeable. The missionaries were alarmed because if it were granted, the whole area would be given to the Catholics and it included several large villages. A young Dompago man had just completed his schooling in the government school, and Roland Pickering agreed to release him for this project. Morrow and Pickering went to the Chief offering to open the school soon. He didn't refuse as his concern was for a school for his people, not who provided it. The French administrator agreed since S.I.M. already had a church there. Fifty boys and girls were recruited and school began in the church while a classroom built to government speculations was in process. Bible teaching was a part of the curriculum.

The village work continued to spread with a regular ministry now in forty places with evangelists resident in six of them. Ted Emmett found the village work a continuing encouraging factor as he took over the leadership in 1956. In one village some Muslims had responded and pagans had burned their fetishes. Three Muslim converts were suffering considerable persecution for Christ's sake, being beaten and threatened by the town elders but they stood true through it all.

The construction of a proper dispensary building was begun in February of 1953 and completed in June. The staff were caring for as many as two hundred thirty-five patients a day but had a set-back when a consignment of drugs was delayed in shipping and held up at customs for exorbitant duty. The drugs were finally released when the commandant interceded. This event called the dispensary to the attention of

Emmett Family

the Health Services who then gave recognition along with an allocation of government medical supplies to be given twice a year. Mrs. Emmett reopened the dispensary in October with great response, reaching a peak of over two thousand patients a month. The Governor visited the dispensary in December, 1953, and expressed appreciation

for Mrs. Emmett's services. She had to leave for Nigeria for the birth of her second child and from there the family proceeded on furlough. Miss Alberta Gibbs, who was studying in France, was assigned to take over the work in 1954. Its ministry continued to be very encouraging under Miss Gibbs' care. Large numbers continued to come. The church elders appointed a Bible School student to preach daily at the dispensary and visit the in-patients regularly. This resulted in much spiritual response.

In 1954, the Beachams completed and mimeographed the Gospel of Mark and followed this with Bible related booklets: "Way of Salvation", "Showing Children the Way", "Bible Stories", "Parables of the Lord Jesus" and "Miracles of the Lord Jesus".

In 1953 and 1954, the work continued in all its phases (with some special events and some set-backs). The overall picture was one of continued growth. Gordon Beacham continued language work and began a short-term Bible School in Pila. The students studied the newly translated Gospel of Mark and continued for one month with good interest and attendance. The hostel ministry continued to increase reaching fifty-seven students and the third dormitory was completed. Good reports continued to come from the villages about the students' testimony and witnessing during vacation.

There was added blessing when Ed Morrow brought four students of a Bible School in French to graduation who were ready for full-time assignments as evangelists. Also, government permission to hold services in the Djougou prison was given, which gave an added witness each Sunday afternoon.

The missionaries felt a burden to reach the Fulani people in the area. Borori came from Parakou Bible School for two weeks in 1955 and found them very open to the Gospel. He met with very little opposition at the time. Some time later opposition from the Muslims caused some to fall away. However, some started coming to church and a few enrolled in baptismal class. A year later Gus Fredlund came for a three month focused period of evangelization among them and found

that the interest from Borori's visit remained. Some Fulani
came a distance of twenty miles to hear Gus preach the Word.
Thirty-five professed conversions, including the Fulani Chief of
Djougou Circle.

The Pila Bible School continued preparing men for
leadership in the churches under the direction of Gordon
Beacham. New groups of senior students were out preaching on
the week-ends. All were encouraged with the results of this
outreach.

In 1959 Alberta Gibbs left the medical work to be
married to missionary Ed Dubisz and moved with her husband
to Haute Volta.

The Bible School was closed for Beachams' furlough.
The students returned to working their farms but they
continued their village ministries. In 1959 there were seven
graduates from a three-year course. There had been doubts
and struggles as the students changed to a self-support system.
These seven were the first to complete the course under this
new plan, that is: farming some months to support themselves
during the months school was in session and upon graduation
they were to go out with no guaranteed income. These seven
accepted the postings given by the church elders and were
settled in their assigned villages.

By 1961, part of the Yom New Testament was
completed including Mark, Acts, Ephesians, Philippians,
Colossians, I Thessalonians, Titus, James and I John. In
literacy materials there were: Primers 1 and 2; Reader; "God,
the Creator of Everything" and "Old Testament Stories".

Other ethnic groups lived among the Pila peoples and,
though they understood Pila, could be better served in their
own language.

Ouorou Baba from Tchaourou visited in the villages on the N'dali road. Some Fulani churches developed here and on the Parakou road with Jacques, a Pila evangelist, ministering to them. The Ditammari people were reached through the witness in Pila, revealing a need for this group to have their language written and their own indigenous church developed.

In 1960, the Girls' School under the supervision of Elisabeth Gnao was progressing well with several new students. A few married women were admitted for short term Bible training with good results. Funds were provided for enlarging their facilities and building began for new dorms, a classroom and other needs. Elsie Morrow's reassignment to Lagos was a great loss to this ministry and Mrs. Hansen's help and oversight was a welcome relief when she and her husband came in 1966.

The Bible School was closed for several years but it was reported to the Dahomey District Conference in 1965 that it opened again when three students sought out André Siméon in the village where he was preaching. He taught them in his home and the church built huts for living quarters. The students were responsible for all other needs. Others joined this group and it continued under church leadership. They graduated their first class in 1967, but by 1972 it was closed again because of student unrest.

Dr. Beacham and his team persevered in the translation and literature production of the Yom language even while he was involved in several other demanding and time consuming ministries. Among these were evangelism and church development and teaching in the Pila Bible School. He was also required to act as administrator when he took over the duties of Station Manager when Ed and Elsie Morrow left the work in

Djougou in 1964 to fill a need on the staff of "Champion" magazine in Lagos.

Even when he was free to do the linguistic and

Gordon Beacham with linguistic team for Pila translation

translation work that he was trained to do, he assisted others in their language work which took him into other areas. For Monkollé research and evaluation he stayed a year in Kandi. Another year was spent in Ségbana assisting with the Boko language and many other such assignments.

The church met in the former Methodist building but the people kept saving to build a new church. In 1963, the foundation for their new church was laid with high hopes for completing it. However, in 1965 when the Bible Conference of Pila churches was held, this building was still unfinished and without enough money to continue.

The conference was well attended and almost all villages having groups of believers were represented. They enjoyed the mimeographed copies of the recently translated Book of Romans which were distributed and from which messages were drawn. During the conference they expressed some needs: renewal, deepening of spiritual life and greater understanding and application of the Word. They discussed some problems such as fear of witchcraft (revealed when one evangelist consulted a diviner) and immorality. They concluded by making a request for a missionary evangelist to make visits among their churches for teaching and encouragement.

It was encouraging to the church when four Pila evangelists were authorized to officiate for baptisms and marriages.
These were: Ogouma Salomon, Saré Daniel, André Djarra and
André Siméon. Other positive movements were a monthly
church-sponsored Day of Prayer at the Djougou church when
the evangelists met regularly to discuss their work. Also,
during the rainy season, a Bible Reading Conference was held
on a week-end for all the churches of the area.

The need for trained Fulani leadership and continued
teaching remained unfilled for lack of personnel. Charles
Carpenter did visit them in 1965 and in 1968 Shirley Barby
moved to the Djougou area for several months to work among
them. She found openness and willingness to hear as she
visited in the camps and held Bible classes.

After the close of the year of 1966, Djougou Girls' School
did not reopen but a number of the girls went to Tchaourou
Girls' School to continue their education. The Boys' Home
closed also and some boys were sent to Sinendé Boys' School.
The village schools had met a great need and had flourished.
With Independence and a change in administration, the
government was short of funds for education and the government grants for newly opened classes ceased. This curtailed the
educational work in some of the schools.

In 1966 Al Cross left Djougou to help with the Perrier
Meetings in Parakou and Cotonou. On February 12, with the
news of the deaths of Stewart McDougall and Gus Fredlund,
the entire staff went to Parakou and Beachams stayed on to
assist. Gordon was appointed Acting District Superintendent, a
responsibility that required frequent and often prolonged visits
to Parakou. In March the District Conference was held in
Djougou. Dr. Holbrook was the speaker and Bill Crouch, West

Africa Field Director, was also present. One missionary
reported that it was "a helpful, healing time, when we were
particularly aware of the loss of our D.S."

The Bookstore in a rented facility in the middle of town
had good sales with a colporter working out from this center.
Then in 1966 a new shop was opened on the edge of the
Mission compound. This facility was roomier, lighter and airier
and business remained good. This outreach and Gospel
Recordings in Yom added to the tools for reaching people.

In 1968 Gordon and Joyce returned from furlough.
Gordon had completed his work on his Ph.D. in linguistics. He
opened the Linguistic Center at the Girls' School site at
Saabari to concentrate on language and translation work. In
1969 when Gordon held the first workshop at the linguistic
center all the linguists and translators in Benin attended. A
second workshop for linguistic workers was held in conjunction
with a Wycliffe/S.I.M. meeting to discuss orthography, etc.
relating to the Boko and Boussa tribal languages.

This center continued to provide valuable service for the
linguistic needs of the missionaries until it was moved to
Tchaourou in 1974.

In 1968 the All Church Conference was held in Djougou
with twelve missionaries and one hundred nine delegates
attending from forty-four churches. The new church building
had been interrupted by "Methodist" group actions which led to
the complete take-over of the existing church building in 1970
and the suspending of all services. This group was made up of
former Methodist church members who refused to accept
instruction and disciplinary measures passed by Djougou
church elders. This defiance led to a long period of conflict and
resulted in the rebellious members declaring themselves to be

Methodists and no longer S.I.M. related. This conflict was
prolonged until it involved the National Methodist Church and
was taken to government officials. Finally, the matters
concerning the church property were taken to court. The court
decided that the church building must be returned to the
Methodists which seemed unjust to the church leaders. The
matter was finally resolved when S.I.M., in the interest of
peace, turned the building back to the Methodists and received
some compensation for it. The Mission continued to maintain
the station property and held Bible studies and church services
in the Linguistic Center.

      This split affected a number of Yom members and some
village churches in which a spirit of animosity continued for
many years. Two other splits followed, continuing the confusion
and hard feelings. One of these involved an S.I.M. missionary
translator from Switzerland, Annie Zehnder, who refused to
comply with an order from the D.S. in 1974 to move from
Djougou to Partago and sided with a splinter group. It was
mission policy that no single women be stationed alone. These
situations caused set-backs in the S.I.M./UEEB work in the
Djougou area. Satan was indeed alive and well, showing his
power to disrupt and confuse.

      In the outlying villages some went with the Methodists
but there remained nuclei of new groups prepared to start over.
S.I.M. pushed out into the villages where there was still great
need and continued to sow the seed. The Linguistic Center
continued double duty until it was moved to Tchaourou in
1974, but the faithful believers continued meeting without a
church building for ten years.

      What proved true on other stations, but was most
clearly observable in Djougou, is the long term confusion

resulting from unclarified and unresolved doctrinal and church leadership issues. Even though mission policy on polygamy was clearly understood, disagreements about how to handle the issue presented obstacles to S.I.M.'s efforts at planting a unified and reproductive church body. This robbed missionary and national church leaders alike of valuable resources and energy.

Champion being printed

Champion being read

Chapter 27: Sinendé (1951)

1951	Opened in January with Earl and Jean Playfair. By end of year small groups were meeting.
1953	Government permission for Boys' School granted.
1954	Sinendé Boys' School opened with 40 boys by Jean Soutar.
1955	Medical work opened by Jane Dudgeon; Carried on and expanded by Louise Foster.
1958	Dispensary in Yarra started by Shirley Barby.
1960	Bariba Bible School moved from Parakou to Sinendé under direction of Russ Draper.
1962	Bariba Bible School closed (Reopened in Bembèrèkè in 1966). French Bible College (Second Year) under Gordon Beacham and Jonathan Maxwell.
1963	French Bible College (Third Year) moved to N'dali, after which it was closed, later reopened in Burkina Faso.
1964	Medical work expanded–ten in-patient huts built.
1974	Bariba Boys' School closed.

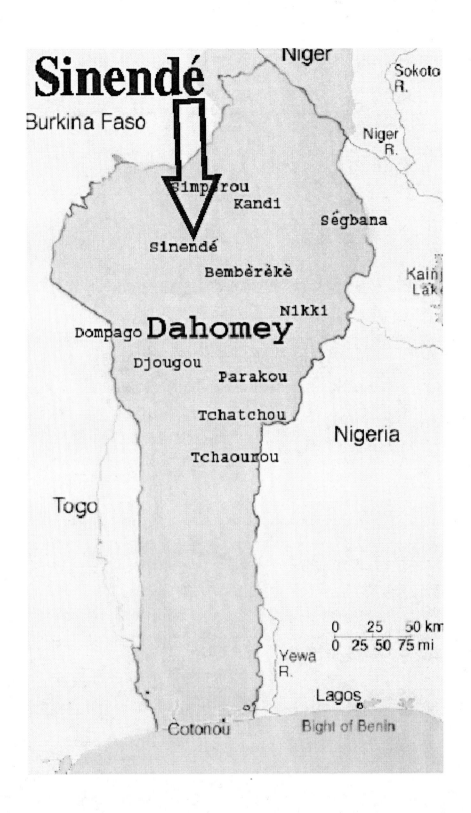

Sinendé

In 1947, McDougall had visited Bembèrèkè and consulted with the commandant about opening a station there. He was encouraged, and it seemed a great possibility since it was on the motor road and there were an estimated 32,000 Baribas, Gandos and Fulanis in the subdivision without a gospel witness. The commandant suggested a site at the foot of a hill with a spring behind it, and tentative plans were made. However, upon a more thorough study of the area, Sinendé proved to be the preferable site. It was the largest village and the center of population of the area between Bembèrèkè and Kouandé. So they proceeded to choose the site and make proper applications.

As early as 1950 the missionaries saw a great need for a training school for boys. A small group of boys were in residence at Nikki station being taught reading and writing along with lessons from the Scriptures by Elisha Olu and David Ekundayo from Nigeria. Parents seemed willing to give their boys to the missionaries to train indicating a need and Sinendé was chosen as the site for such a school.

Earl Playfair family

Earl and Jean Playfair had been chosen to open up this area. After Earl's introduction to the work in Kandi, he went home on furlough, during which time he and Jean were married. They spent study time in France before coming on to Dahomey. In 1951, after nearly a year at Nikki studying Bariba, they, with their first child, Grace, were eager for their assignment.

In January they moved into the government rest house in Sinendé. McDougall had sent in sawyers early in 1950, so the lumber was dried and ready and they were able to make bricks and start building their home.

The Sinendé people were friendly and welcomed on the compound. The people responded well to them when they trekked out to the villages. A young man, Sabiyo Abdoulaye, assisted them in their studies and was very helpful in the preaching.

Elsie McCulloch came in August of 1951 with the assignment to start such a school. After studying Bariba she taught the local boys along with the boys transferred from Nikki until her furlough in 1953. The Playfairs had the care of the boys' home life.

Toward the end of the year Earl wrote, "Our hearts have greatly rejoiced at the evidence of a work of the Spirit in the earnest profession of several people, including older men, women and boys. We have heard that some of these are now witnessing to others. Meetings were begun in our little church building with a steady growth in attendance."

Serving and meeting needs of the people has always been the pattern used for spreading the Word and building Christ's church. So, along with studying Bariba, trekking and preaching, Earl had five students in residence that he was teaching.

Jean Soutar was completing a fifteen month intensive course in France when she received her assignment and wrote to her prayer partners: "I just received some details regarding my school at Sinendé. It is to be all taught in French. (I will have to learn Bariba on the side.) Equipment is as follows: one map of Africa, a blackboard, no cupboards, some benches and desks which aren't so good. Imagine the difference between this and home schools! But think also of these boys who prayed for a teacher to replace theirs and are now thanking the Lord for the answer. . . . I can hardly wait."

When she arrived in August, 1953, she found that Sabiyo Abdoulaye was available to teach the ten boys while she supervised. The Playfairs were in charge of the dorms so this gave her time to acclimate and study Bariba. At this time, application was made for an authorized school and permission was granted with promise of funds for buildings. Plans and preparations were immediately underway since they expected a 100% increase for the new term.

Nurse Janey Younker came in 1953 to open up a dispensary after studying the language. She suffered a heart attack but recovered nicely and was ready to open in June of 1955. Jane had a Chevrolet Carryall and took medicines once a week to the villages. Later two in-patient huts were built and a dispensary chapel. All was going well until a 50% tax was levied on drugs brought into the country making the cost beyond their means and for a time she was doing only occasional treatments.

In the fall of 1954, forty boys came. Sabiyo and Jean Soutar shared the teaching load using the church building and the garage as classrooms. Pastor Timothée Ogouchina and his wife, Marie, were a great help in the care of the boys. Jean Soutar wrote about them: "The Pastor, a graduate of Parakou Bible School, has a real burden for the people. He preaches twice each morning to those who come to the dispensary and goes to a village with Jane on medical trips, preaches Sunday

morning here and in another village in the afternoon, and is
father to the boys in his "spare" time. His wife prepares the
food for the hungry mob while their two-year old twins,
Deborah and David toddle around and visit school sometimes."

There were problems, tensions and struggles but real
progress too, as the team learned to work together. Providing
for the students on a tight budget became a heavy burden and
a constant matter of concern. But when they evaluated at
term's end, they were pleased with the spiritual growth of
many of the students and the Lord had supplied their financial
needs. Prayer was made for increased enrollment.

Playfairs went on furlough in 1954 and, upon return,
were assigned to Tchaourou in 1955 to replace the furloughing
Thamers. Shortly after that Earl, very ill, was flown out to Jos,
Nigeria and died on September 18, 1955, leaving Jean with
three small children. Jean returned to Tchaourou and later to
Parakou before coming back to Sinendé.

The next school year (1955) there were changes.
Barthélémy Sossafey joined the staff and Sabiyo opened a
satellite school at Yarra. There he had twenty-seven day pupils
and a hundred adults in the evening for preaching and literacy
classes. There were times when three hundred gathered on a
Sunday afternoon. At Christmas the two schools celebrated
together with great joy as the sixty-five boys sitting in three
concentric circles sang carols.

Jean Soutar was needed in Tchaourou Girls' School the
following school year and Charles Carpenter came to the Boys'
School for a year. The government grant had come; the
buildings were completed; and the school was moved to the
new compound at Soudé.

Howard and Louise Foster came to Sinendé in 1957 and Louise reopened the dispensary since Janey had left to be married. It took a while for the work to build, but the people were greatly helped when they called on her for difficult deliveries, poison cases and open wounds and the word of her success spread. When the flu epidemic hit, she was flooded with patients which gradually leveled off to about eighty a day. Many came from distant villages and were hearing the gospel for the first time.

There was no evangelist at the time so Howard sharpened his Bariba as he prepared messages for the dispensary services. They were very pleased when Borori came and took over this preaching ministry as he presented the Word clearly and was well received by the people.

So the witness continued in the schools and the dispensary with strong emphasis on the village work by both missionaries and students in the Sinendé district. In 1957 they had their first baptismal service with the Lord's supper following. The church was organized with fourteen members. Borori was there for the opening of a Fulani school and became the pastor of this newly formed body of believers. The first Christian marriage was celebrated when Barthélémy was married to Maria, a student from Tchaourou Girls' School.

Late in 1957, Jean Playfair was able to return to renew contacts with people she had carried in her heart since leaving them in 1954. She went out regularly to Niaro, Guéssébani and Kossia. The struggles of the beginnings of the Boys' School were smoothing out some when Jonathan Maxwell came in 1957. He was well equipped and would add strength and stability by remaining for the most part of two terms. Winston

Adams came to help him that first year and he had good
teachers in Chabi 'Loiye, Barthélémy Esse and Paul Yai.

When the Fosters went on furlough in 1958, permission
was given to open a dispensary in Niaro once a week in an
unused government building. Shirley Barby was now doing the
medical work both in Sinendé and Niaro. She gave the
messages as well as the treatments. People were grieved when
she also left and the work closed again. People daily came
asking for help. When Dr. and Mrs. Dreisbach came to study
language with Mary Draper in 1960, he treated patients three
days a week and relieved this stressful situation for three
months. The need was always there begging to be met but was
often hindered by lack of personnel.

Jean Playfair's ministry in Sinendé came to a climax for
her at a great Easter gathering in 1959, just before she left to
serve in Niger Republic. Her report about that day included:
the coming of Jonathan Maxwell with the boys from the school
at Soudé; believers attending from many villages including
Fulanis from several places; and the attendance of twenty from
Kpésourou accompanied by the chief. Jean described it this
way: "The Spirit gave freedom as I brought the message.
Bouégui's testimony was precious! Perhaps counting all there
were 175 present. In the afternoon we had praise and prayer.
We rejoiced in the way the Lord led us here. I know Earl would
be rejoicing if he were here . . . those heart cries the two of us
made to God in this little office prayer room have been
answered. The Spirit is moving here and will keep on."

The Bariba Bible School was also part of the Sinendé
testimony. It was moved from Parakou to Sinendé in 1960
when Rosella Entz was freed to go to Nikki for translation
work and was under the direction of Russ Draper. The school

opened in September with four students. Two others joined them later.

At this transition time the policy of student self-support was to be strongly adhered to, so Russ spent considerable time visiting Bariba churches to explain the new policy and the ramifications. Sometimes during the first term it seemed as though some would need to leave for lack of finances. However, God undertook for each one and it was great to watch the students' faith increase as they continued to look to the Lord for daily provision. Every week-end found them in the villages preaching, teaching and holding reading classes.

The missionaries who cared for the home part of the Boys' School were vital to success with the boys. The Fosters returned in 1960 and were great "parents" and role models. Louise had a large medical ministry that included people from villages as well as the school. Howard did building and maintenance besides his preaching and care of the churches. The report about them during these years was: "They were a good team, hardworking and very much into all aspects of the work."

Howard designed and built a chapel on the school compound. The students helped assemble the material. In fact, all the work was done by staff men, missionaries, and school boys. They were pleased with their beautiful place of worship and enjoyed meeting in the chapel.

In 1961, they also built four dorm rooms and a class-room for the Bible School and were ready to receive a new class

of fifteen fellows, six of whom brought their wives. As the year
ended in 1962, the thrilling testimonies of how the Lord met
their needs proved their decision for self-support was right.

During the Draper furlough the Bariba Bible School was
moved temporarily to Nikki in 1962. Jim Cail was in charge
until the Drapers returned for the 1964 school year.

Jonathan Maxwell was married to Rosalyn Bettinga in
1960 and they served the Lord together at the Boys' School
until 1962. Looking back on those days from his later fruitful
ministries, Jonathan rejoiced over students who went on to be
leaders in the church such as Bio Saka Salomon and Pierre
Barassounon. Jean Soutar returned for six months and, following her, Shirley Hyman became Directress of the Boys' School
until 1965.

Early in 1964, there was student unrest in the Bariba
Bible School and their objections led to the need for counsel
with Mr. Thamer and Mr. Zobrist along with a local pastor and
elder. They came to an agreement and finished out the school
year. At the annual missionary conference it was decided not to
open the school for one year to better determine the spirit and
desire of the students and then make a decision about the
future of the school.

In 1966, the Bariba Bible School was reopened in
Bembèrèkè. Mary and Russ Draper had spent years building
into the lives of young men at the school. When Mary visited in
1975 she wrote, "The week-end I spent in Sinendé was one of
the happiest of my life. Bio Paul, Sidi Jacque and others were a
delight to be with and their depth of love for the Lord was a
fulfillment of Russ' prediction, 'the Holy Spirit will do His work
in their lives.' I was aware time and again of His working in
their lives.

Some had fallen but gotten up and become strong as they drew nearer to Him."

The medical outreach was an effective arm of the work in Sinendé even though it was difficult to keep it operational. There was a thriving ministry later in the sixties when they were treating two hundred patients a day and built ten in-patient huts which were full most of the time. This gave opportunity for evening services with patients, and follow-up work with discharged patients in the villages with help from the local churches.

These ministries were all pursued with the anticipation that God would draw to Himself a people for His name and a strong church would be established. The purpose in each was to so present Christ and His message that men would believe and follow on to live for Him, kept by the Holy Spirit's indwelling power.

During the period between Independence and the take-over of both Sinendé and Soudé compounds by the Revolutionary government, there was much encouraging church planting in the villages. The Bible School students, under the leadership of Russ Draper and Howard Foster, were a vital part of this growth, especially in the area of Sinendé and along the road to Guessou-Sud. Along with the Bible School ministry, the Drapers held short-term Bible training for church leaders and refresher courses for pastors. In a report in 1965, Russ wrote:

> Never before has the outlook for the Sinendé area looked more promising. The elders from the five churches had met and made plans for the future with a wonderful spirit of oneness and willingness to work hard to achieve their goals. Some of these goals were:
> 1. Nikki school for girls no longer accepted the younger girls so plans were made for teaching them to read at home on their own. Mary would help three mornings a week.

  2. More instruction classes for elders. There was an
     expressed need for instruction in personal
     evangelism.
  3. Medical work was thriving with Millie Davis in
     charge. Plans for better follow-up on patients
     who came to the Dispensary and to in-patients.
     There are 10 grass huts which are always more
     than full.

The plan:
  1. Russ teach the elders how to effectively follow-up.
  2. Nurse (Millie Davis) keep file on spiritual response
     of patient when patient discharged—card to church.
  3. Pastor Lafia take card to the church in patient's
     area.
  4. Elders to contact and disciple the patient and family.

So the church grew with new believers being added to
the body continually. The Drapers had contributed much to
help this growth with short-term Bible School for church
leaders, refresher courses for pastors along with the Bible
School ministry.

Kay Lane began classes with the women and the
response was great. She soon had groups in five villages. Later
when she had a two month Bible School session for them,
fifteen attended.

Alan and Ruth Gibbs came to the Boys' School in 1966
at a very difficult period. Three boys and one staff member died
of small-pox, sobering them all. There was a food shortage in
the North while merchants were shipping food out of the
country. This created a shortage in Dahomey, making food for
eighty boys extremely expensive.

During the years of 1960 to 1972 there were times when
the Maxwells and Gibbs were on the station together with
their children and other times when the Gibbs family were the
only missionaries. Ruth Gibbs remembers, "During the time at

Gibbs Family

Sinendé we found that it was a financial struggle to meet the costs of running the school. . . . We always seemed to have a struggle with that part of the work. Actually we finally closed because we were not able to find it financially feasible to keep open. Although at the time we felt very badly that this had to be, it actually was a blessing that we did not realize until after it happened. The following year the government became Marxist-Leninist."

The hinderer was busy discouraging God's servants, causing teachers to fall, requiring dismissal and heart break.

But God's Spirit was in all and over all, breathing health, new courage, freshness and a spirit of perseverance. Rehearsing the struggles and later, after seeing the results in lives, missionaries and churches together sang, "To God be the glory, great things He hath done."

The Bariba Bible School was closed for a time and reopened in 1966 at Bembèrèkè under Jim Cail's direction. Jim requested that a Bariba man be seconded to the work to learn to do the teaching. Ouorou Sidi Jean accepted this assignment and proved especially gifted for that ministry. About this period the Cails wrote: "At first we did the teaching then gradually we wrote what I would call a teaching commentary that Ouorou Sidi could use. . . . A copy was given to the students and Ouorou Sidi used it to teach from. By the time we had to leave in 1970 we had three years of material to leave to help him continue to teach the Bible School by himself. The classes were held in the Operating Room which had plenty of windows. The blackboard was two sheets of masonite painted black. We used this until Dr. Elliott came to reopen the hospital."

The school was then moved to a grass mat enclosure where they taught for two years after which it was relocated to a permanent school site three miles from the Bembèrèkè Hospital. The Cail family went to the U.S. on extended leave but Ouorou Sidi Jean continued on until 1975 when the school was moved to Soudé where the Boys' School had been. The Boys' School was closed in October of 1973 due to lack of operating funds.

The constant juggling act required to keep these schools operating reflects the commitment and persistence of the field leadership to the stated educational objectives to train a strong church leadership. It is also reflective of the administrative nightmare of mission leadership attempting to maintain operational effectiveness and quality with inadequate personnel and financing. The successes of the church leaders trained by these endeavors is due to the faithfulness of God and the determination and stamina of many missionaries and national leaders working together over a long and very uncertain time. In the end, the burden of maintaining these institutions would have been a load too heavy for the national church to bear.

Chapter 28: Dompago (1952)

1952   June: Station opened with the arrival of Roland Pickering.

1954   Church grown to 75 in attendance.
Translation of the Book of Acts completed.

1955   Training course for church leaders and preacher training courses begun.

1957   Bible School started.

1960   Beginning of Farm Settlement movement:
first at Komté; second at Kangoulouga.

1961   Two settlements at Biguina and Tèprèdjèrissi.

1962   Kpele Ele settlement in Togo.

1963   Yérimbè in Togo.

1964   Timpaa.

1965   By now 10 Dompago churches: 200-300 believers.

1969   Kassikitè in Togo.

1972   Rowland Pickering elected District Superintendent and moved to Parakou.

1973   Chris and Helen Cowie came to administer the agricultural work.

1974   October: Roland Pickering lost his life in a car accident.

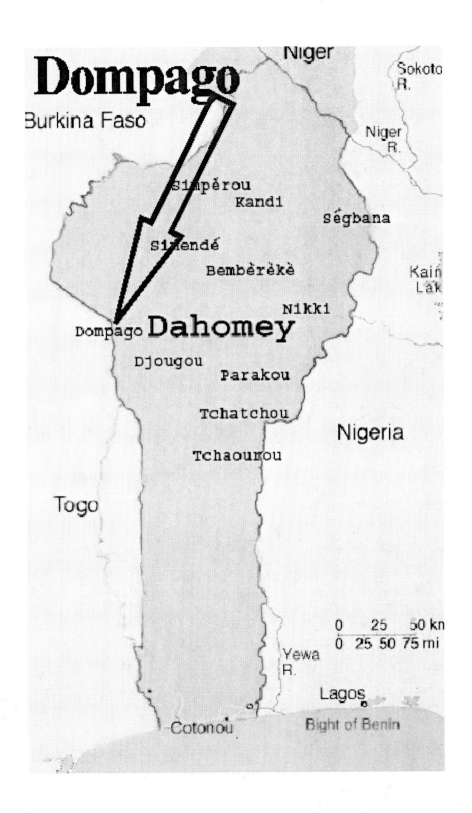

Dompago

Even before a station was opened among the Dompago people there was an evident working of God's Spirit among them. The following story was part of a report from Gordon Beacham.

> Two Dompago Christians were waiting for leprosy treatment at the government hospital at Djougou. While waiting they witnessed to two young men from Mendjenaga, a Dompago village six kilometers north-west of Djougou. They told them that they could learn more if they came to the Protestant mission church in Djougou on Sunday. They came and at the end of the service stood up and said they wanted to "follow this way." The next Sunday they returned with 3 others, the second Sunday with 15 and then the next with 25. Gordon and Pastor Solomon visited them. There was no road so they went on foot across a stream and found a large crowd gathered, waiting for them. Both Gordon and Solomon spoke to them and the message was well received. The Sunday following 40 walked in to attend the "Pila" worship service. The Dompago men for the most part heard Pila. But as each Sunday more and more came and many of them women, they decided to have a separate service in Dompago following the Pila service.

When André Boroté finished his course at the French Bible School he was assigned to this village and they built their own church in Mendjenaga.

There was also an interest in the gospel in the town of Dompago. This was evidenced earlier when an evangelist of the Methodist Mission stationed in Djougou visited there regularly. A small group had built a little mud chapel where they met. Then in the Fall of 1949, when S.I.M. moved to Djougou, missionaries from Djougou continued to minister there as part of the village outreach. Paul Clapp made a trek in 1951 to several Dompago villages and found an enthusiastic response.

The S.I.M. work in Dompago station was opened on
June 16, 1952, with the coming of Roland Pickering. Roland
wrote in a letter in April, 1952:

> I expect to be stationed in
> Dompago, center of a farming
> district. The opportunity is very
> great. When missionary Paul
> Clapp was in the area not long
> ago, he found many proofs of
> eagerness to hear the gospel. At
> one spot he used a mile-and-a-
> quarter road that Dompago had
> built in their village seven years
> earlier, when they heard that a
> missionary was going to visit
> them. At another place, the chief
> ordered the village market to
> stop, and made everyone listen to
> the message.

Young Jonathan Maxwell
was a teenager in Prairie High
School and recalls the impact of a
letter from Roland describing his
beginning days in Dompago.

> I was really moved by his letter. He wrote what it
> felt like to be taken to his first assignment, west of
> Djougou. Ed Morrow loaded up first-termer Roland and
> his duffle bag. Roland knew nothing of the language. He
> had no friend in Dompago. He was granted a hut in
> which to put his duffle bag. Ed left Roland by the side of
> the road.
>   Roland, alone, among strangers whose language he
> did not understand, looked up the road. There went Ed
> Morrow's jeep, disappearing in a cloud of dust. And with
> that departure, Roland felt even more cut off from all
> communication, from civilization, from English-speaking
> friends. The people of Dompago at that time were not
> sitting under a palm tree inviting the missionary with
> his pith helmet to come to them and preach. They were
> openly indifferent, not to say, hostile.
>   Only later, Roland wrote, when the grass roof of his
> hut caught fire, did the neighbors run to his rescue, and,

rallying to help him, tried to put out the fire. From then on, some became his first real friends.

In September, 1952, Roland described his first impressions this way:

> I remember that first day well. The people who had milled noisily around me since my arrival had drifted to their huts to eat. The Jeep that had brought me had disappeared along the path.
> I stood in front of the house (mud and thatch) looking toward the fading sun. Although I had been in Africa since April, this seemed to be the first time I actually felt I was here, and here to stay.
> A few steps to my right stood the little mud church, dark and empty, a grass mat across the doorway to keep the goats out.
> To the left the first walls of the village began. Behind them stretched a mass of little peaks, each one the roof of another tiny, smoky hut, someone's home. It was then that Africa began to settle in around me. There was no 'civilization' to turn back to; no clean, airy mission house to flee to. I wasn't looking at slides anymore!

From his mud hut Roland began to study the Dompago language and reach out in friendship to the people. He drew up an alphabet, prepared literacy material, and in July, 1953, he began teaching sessions four nights a week in the little church where boys and young men studied reading and writing. As the first group showed success in learning to read, many more came to learn. Roland always pressed upon them the claims of Christ and wrote, "Sometimes . . . I will see a glimmer of light peak across the faces of two or three." As the teaching continued, the young men responded and they came in twos and threes inquiring how to become Christians. Soon there were nineteen converts.

By the close of 1953, Roland had completed a rough draft of Mark's Gospel, a wonderful help in instructing the new believers. Growth always brings opposition and in Dompago it

came through the annual pagan celebration in honor of young
men. This was a very binding tradition in which the young men
were required to take part in certain dances. They drank,
slashed one another and offered sacrifices to family fetishes.

The believers agreed that as Christians they could not
participate in the ceremonies, but the parents of the young
men protested vehemently. Parents declared if the young men
would not participate, they could no longer live at home. So the
faith of the new converts was sorely tested and, when a few
boldly refused to participate, their witness revealed the
strength of their faith. However, many young men broke under
the pressure. Roland wrote, "It is a serious business preaching
a gospel that creates issues so great."

The year 1954 opened with some set-backs but ended
with many victories. The opposition of the pagans was stiffer
after the young men's show of separation and church
attendance declined. Some villages showed less interest. In one
village a Catholic school was built.

A four week Bible study with eight young men started
in February, 1954. They were taught reading, writing, Bible
lessons, hymns, memory work and a little French. The growth
of these young men brought new life to the whole church.
Many began to see for the first time that the Word of God had
a personal message for them.

A Sunday School was organized and each of the young
men took a group of children to teach. Women showed
increased interest in the Word and eight enrolled in the new
inquirers' class. There was to be a struggle, however, before
women could come freely since some parents forbade their
young women to come.

By August, Roland had completed a primer and mimeographed two hundred fifty copies. In several villages there were little groups meeting. Those in the first classes were teaching others which generated a great boost in the growth of the work. The first translation of the Gospel of Mark had been mimeographed and was ready to be distributed to these new readers.

In November, 1954, one of the young men from the Bible Study, Barthélémy, brought an encouraging report. He had been going to a village regularly to hold Sunday morning services. They begged him to come Saturday evening as well to teach them the Word. On his last week-end visit his little flock were waiting for him. One among them was an aging Muslim who professed to follow Jesus. Others were inquiring and joining the group. They even took up a collection and talked about building a prayer hut. A nearby village suggested they build halfway between them so they could meet together.

The church rejoiced over the increased number of young men who stood firm for their faith during their annual pagan festival. So the work grew steadily.

As the year closed, prayer was being made for young men to come for training at a Bible School and plans were well under way for its opening. Simple doctrinal studies for a Bible course were being prepared. A neighbor had given permission for them to use a portion of his land. The plan was that students would farm to produce their own food.

Prayer was answered as eight young men enrolled in the training course for church leaders in February of 1955. Classes were held from 8:30 to 12:30. They worked on the farms in the afternoons and studied at night. During the farming season the students went to the fields during the day but continued some studies in the evening. Usually the fields were prepared by mid-September and school reopened. There were some adjustments as these new converts learned to study and apply themselves, but the Spirit had begun a good work in them and Roland's hopes were high as he asked his friends to pray "that they will give themselves whole-heartedly to Christ."

Roland used the break from regular classes to concentrate on language study, working mostly on dictionary files and tone analysis. He was also translating the catechism and Gospel of John with some work on the "Life of Moses", Philippians and the Book of Acts. When Acts was completed and mimeographed, they had special classes every morning to help church people get acquainted with the new book. In a letter, he wrote, "The sitting and dining rooms of my house are filled with these groups of young and old studying together."

Many years later Roland would write about this to his supporters. Calling it "A Golden Week", he recalled:

Not long ago some Dompagos who were among the first group to become Christians spent an evening visiting. The conversation went back to the early years of the work. "Do you remember the time you made the first translation of Acts in our language?" —"Yes, I do. We cut the stencils by hand because we had no typewriter for the job then." —"Well, you gathered us all together for one week between Christmas and New Years— men, women, children, everybody and we read the whole book through." —"I seem to have forgotten that part." —"You explained it section by section as we went along. And that was when the church was born in our area!"

–"Really! What do you mean?"
–"What we mean is it was while we were studying the book of Acts that it dawned on us that it is God who makes people Christians. We hadn't realized that before. But from that time on we knew that was what had happened to us too. Somehow all the good things that have happened to us since then trace back to that week."

Roland went on to say:

Golden week! The two men [Moïse and Sylvain] who led in that conversation are striking examples of lives that God has touched. They have left their work with the government for one year to help us finish up the revisions of the Dompago New Testament. Their determination and dedication at the job are higher than anything I ever dreamed I would see here. What they say about that week between Christmas and New Years rings true somehow.

In December, Roland was ill and was away in Djougou for treatment for a month. He was able to pursue language work, however, and the local church proved themselves in his absence. They carried on all services except the inquirers' classes.

As the Word took root in the hearts of believers and their spiritual strength increased, so did the opposition. At times the pain was very great and they cried out for deliverance. Roland recorded one story of a young woman whose desire to be obedient to the gospel brought her head-on against the social system and customs. She came one evening at the close of the rainy season to the home of one of the believers carrying her few belongings in a calabash on her head. She was a Christian, well known and loved by the Christian community. She was twenty-two, small with a beautiful smile and a happy laugh. One of the young men in the church wanted to marry her so she had run away from her family and had sought refuge with the other believers.

In the tribal system she had no right to have a desire of her own. She had been sold for several head-loads of guinea corn when she was just a little girl. Now she was grown and the system demanded she must go to her owner/husband.

He found where she was and messengers began coming from the local chief demanding that she appear before him. Understanding well what would happen, the Christians refused and refused and refused. In the end they were forced to give in to the chief's incessant pressure and they led her away to the "palaver hut" where three men were waiting. The chief asked the men if she was the girl they had paid for. When they replied, "Yes"; he said coldly, "Take her." She wept and screamed for help as they dragged her out of the hut. One man put her on his shoulder and they hurried away.

Roland made complaint to the area head chief, who agreed to send guards to search for her and bring her back for reconsideration. Of course, she could not be found since they had forced her into a truck with her owner and taken her to Gold Coast [Ghana].

The whole church prayed and God mercifully answered. Word got to the local administrator. He made a series of moves that resulted in her being found, returned home and granted her freedom. The local people were astonished and the believers were overjoyed. Nothing like this had ever been seen in Dompago country! She returned to the believers and the church. Each evening she came with the other young women to repeat her memory work and continue her writing lessons.

So the newly planted church struggled as it grew; each victory won gave them strength to reach out further as Roland left for furlough and linguistic studies. Before leaving, he finished the first draft of John's Gospel with them and they copied it.

Most of the Bible School students found it too difficult to farm for a living, support parents and still carry their studies. Only three of them persevered and went in to Djougou to study during Roland's absence.

The church was running smoothly, but Roland was still concerned for these new believers during his absence. However, upon returning, he wrote, "I arrived back on a Friday evening just as the Christians were gathering for their weekly prayer meeting. I was impressed with the earnestness and vigor of their prayers. Sunday all day I sat back like a visitor and watched how they had been managing during my absence. Periodically, an elder would speak up and say, 'We have started such and such a thing since you left.'"

As far as possible, responsibility for the local church program, village evangelism and Bible School was given to the three church elders. As the Bible School opened again with nine students in a new classroom, Roland was eager that the whole thing should be their vision. The local church was responsible for the total program: the selection and support of the students, supervision of the students and the maintenance of the classroom. The elder in charge was very efficient and made it clear to the students that it was their own work.

This was a great step ahead as Roland worked with these elders not as a leader but as a helper, desiring them to be all that Christ called them to be in shepherding the flock of God. As he concentrated on translation and wrote rough draft translations of Ephesians, I John and I Timothy, the elders were included in every aspect of it.

So the team pressed on together and, in 1959, cut stencils for the "Life of David", I Corinthians, I Peter and mimeographed two hundred copies of Genesis and translated new hymns. The goal of the Bible School to train new leaders and evangelists who would spread out into the villages and be examples of true followers of Christ was near realization. The Church was now dividing their collection into four equal parts: a new church building, operating expenses, an extension program and establishing churches in other villages. Part of the funds helped the first graduate of the Dompago Bible School go into the well-populated area of Alitokomtè. The believers there were building a prayer hut and living quarters for his family. The spirit of the believers was enthusiastic even though they were just a small group. After a few months most of them were in reading classes and some were preparing for baptism. Within a year they had seven baptized believers.

Roland was always concerned for the people struggling to feed their families. He saw the futility of farming the worn out soil close to the villages. Some of the men accepted ideas of crop rotation, leaving some land fallow. With his encourage-ment, five families decided to improve their living and moved to the outskirts. They built a complete Christian community with a church, bigger buildings with larger courts, and houses well spaced for healthier living.

Some of the more enterprising young people considered settlements in the virgin bush. They discussed the great advantages of settling on good new land. Enthusiasm grew as they considered the possibility of richer crops and better food for their children. The plan of a general break away from the local over-populated area and its over-farmed sterile soil challenged them. So 1960 saw the beginning of the farm settle-

ment movement that would change the future growth in the
Dompago church completely. Thus the Dompago church was
mission-minded with a church planting strategy from
inception.

There was a constant urgency to produce more translation so the team pursued their goal with diligence. The first
draft of the Dompago New Testament was finished in
September, 1960, ready for the checking of the manuscript and
circulation among the consultants. Some translation was done
at this time on the Old Testament also: "Life of Solomon", "Life
of Samson" and a few Psalms. The first shipment of Dompago
hymn books arrived and were selling rapidly. The preparation
of literature materials was progressing as they translated a
Church History and "Everyday Life in the Times of Jesus."
Then in December, 1960, the new Dompago "Primers I and II"
and a "Reader" arrived. The growing church now had a
continual supply of material to support them. Roland was their
pastor, their agricultural advisor, professor, translator and
literacy director.

The Dompago Bible School opened with all students
returning and a few new ones from the local church, making
twenty in all.

New works continued to be opened in the villages, and
the Farm Movement now had four settlements with the
opening of Biguina and Tèprèdjèrissi.

Roland returned from a furlough and study leave in
1963 and was encouraged in every area of the work. About the
Bible School he wrote, "The spirit of the students is encouraging. They have a genuine desire to know how to serve Christ in
this tribe."

Gospel Recordings had produced records in the language and these were well received in the villages, providing another avenue of evangelism.

A simple study aid to the Gospel of Mark was completed and many were following the course of study.

The Dompago Church Conference was held every six months. In the conference of October, 1964, Abougousam Fidèle was licensed to give communion, adding to the three previously licensed. The February, 1965, conference was held in Tèprèdjèrissi which was the fastest growing church in the area adding thirty-five to forty members in one year which brought the average attendance to one hundred seventy-five. When they met in October, 1967, ten churches sent thirty-three delegates. Some brought questions for discussion and some brought problems seeking decisions. Some decisions reached were concerning such matters as female circumcision, oversight of weak Christians and drunkenness.

An extension of the Bible School was opened in the Biguina settlement where they prepared a house for Roland to stay during school sessions. The local Christians and the students built the walls and pounded the floors for the new two-roomed school building. The villages were enthusiastically supportive of the students. A number of homes were opened offering board and room for the students.

A graduate helped with the teaching and, at year's end, expressed a desire to stay on and help with language work. This was very promising since the need was very great, demanding tremendous time and concentration. Ouorou Madougou proved to be a great asset and remained with the language team.

There was continued blessing in the villages like Gaouga and others. An elder visited the group in Togo and found the believers carrying on faithfully. He reported that the whole group were reading fluently in the gospels and epistles.

John Herring joined Roland in 1969, studied the language and assisted in the translation program.

By this time, there was a local Church Council for the Dompago churches functioning. This Council handled all church business and sent delegates to the National Church Council. A national overseer visited the churches regularly and reported on all phases of the work.

The Council made decisions regarding the placement of evangelists to new villages as well as in such matters as marriage disputes. So when Roland was asked to serve as the mission's District Superintendent in March of 1972 and moved to Parakou, the church was strong and in good hands. Roland was able to continue with the translation revisions project with the assistance of a team of men.

In an article in <u>Africa Now</u>, February 1975, Roland is quoted concerning the settlements: "We didn't plan it that way, but the farm settlements are one of the most effective means of evangelism we have." Peter Batchelor, a consultant from Rurcon in England, confirmed this when he visited six of the nine settlements in the company of Roland and Ouorou Madougou. Here are some quotes from his detailed report:

We visited last the original settlement, which was started in 1962 and now has over 100 families, with an average congregation of 270 on Sundays.

The exciting thing about the farm settlements is that they are part of a church movement.

Because the settlements are part of what is almost a spontaneous movement, they are sound and stable. Moreover, they are, for the most part, growing in several ways. Not only are people moving in to enlarge many of the groups, but the church in each settlement is expanding rapidly.

And in summary he states:

The settlement movement of the churches in Dahomey is achieving three basic things:

1. Young people are kept on the land instead of drifting and seeking (often unattainable) salaried employment.
2. Food surpluses are produced with consequently greater cash flow which is reflected in higher church giving and in helping others (especially newcomers to get established).
3. The settlements have proved to be a tremendous means of Christian witness leading to rapid church growth in many of them. One settlement reports 65 conversions (adult and children) over the past year.

Chris Cowie, an agriculturist missionary from New Zealand came with his wife, Helen, to the Dompago work in 1973.

Roland was killed in a car crash in Niger Republic in October, 1974, at the age of 48. He and his leadership team had completed the revision of the New Testament and the team led by Ouorou Madougou and Moïse saw it through to completion. The four thousand believers that worshiped in twenty-two Dompago congregations mourned the loss of their beloved leader who had brought them the gospel and planted the church among hem. They were ably shepherded by the leadership of Sylvain Nassam. The very successful agricultural work was continued by Chris Cowie. Roland Pickering's work was finished but he had discipled an experienced leadership team to tend the flock of God among them.

Moïse

Chapter 29: Tchaourou (1952)

1952   Opened by Mr. and Mrs. Orville Thamer.

1954   Girls' School opened by Sarah Buller.

1955   Dispensary opened briefly by Louise Marcotte.

1957   Dispensary reopened: nurse Shirley Barby.

1960   Pastor Elijah in Tchaourou Church.
Carpenters arrived: Charles for Fulani work; Nurse Elaine in Dispensary.
Church in Guinirou progressing well under leadership of Waarando.

1961   Tchaourou Church burned down and new church built. Three villages built churches: Ogamarou, Guinirou, Gokanna. Patricia Irwin came as Principal of Tchaourou Girls' School.

1965   Girls' School became Tchaourou Primary School.

1971   School became co-educational.

1974   Linguistic center moved to Tchaourou from Djougou.

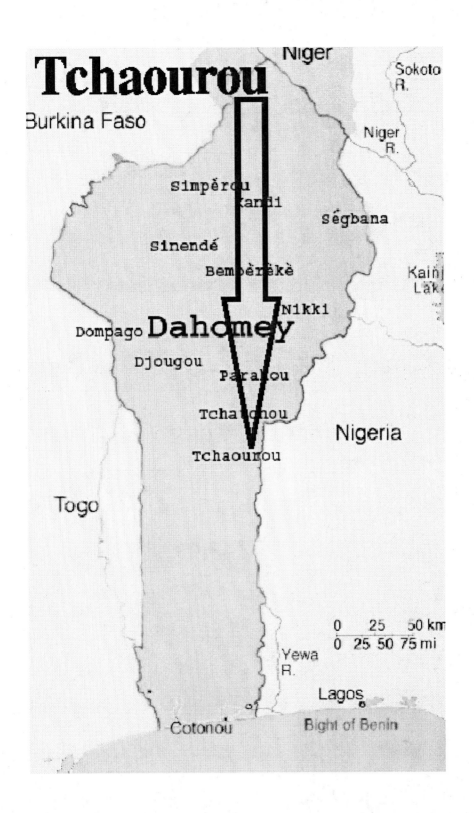

Tchaourou

Orville and Ethel Thamer had served with the McDougalls in Nigeria and, when Stewart put out a call for helpers for Dahomey, they responded. Stewart assured them that their knowledge of the Yoruba language and people would give them an immediate opening. It was evident from the beginning that God had prepared them uniquely for the assignment of opening Tchaourou.

The opportunity came just when national leadership had developed in the Nigerian church where the need for missionaries had shifted and Thamers felt free to leave. They were assigned to go to Dahomey upon completion of their furlough. J.B. Williams had found as he witnessed from his base in Parakou that the most encouraging response in the villages was in the south where both Yoruba and Bariba were spoken. This underscored the earlier research and Tchaourou was chosen as the station site. All were hopeful that this lighthouse would be opened before the end of 1950 when the Thamers were due to arrive. However, the first site application was refused on the grounds that it was too close to a school.

In December, 1950, the Thamers with their two younger children, Gerrie Lou and Orville Jr., proceeded to Nikki, where

they started studying Bariba and Orville brushed up on his
French.

The necessary permissions were long in coming. In July
of 1951 they were still searching for a site suitable to the
mission and acceptable to the government. About the final
decision, Orville reported that the old chief proved to be kindly
disposed toward them and gave them the piece of land they
wanted just outside the town. It was considered enchanted
ground for it was the base of the gin-bottle cult, a shrine which
had been set up by the young men. They had cemented a place,
put two gin bottles in front of it and worshiped there.

In 1952, after the Thamers had built their first small
place and were living there, Orville decided to do something
about the shrine. It should not be allowed to remain now that
the land belonged to the Mission, he reasoned. Lest there
would be trouble he didn't allow any of his workers to assist
him. He took his pick-axe and went out to dig up the shrine.
While he was digging, an old Bariba man came along who said,
"Do you want me to help?" Orville responded, "Would you help
me dig this thing up?" As the man worked, he remarked, "This
thing has caused me more trouble!" It seems the young men
had set it up and the older men did not like it.

A couple days later the witch doctor came, dug deeper
and picked up some small earthen pots. He said, "These are
mine, I put them there. They are powerful medicine." He
carried them away and that was the end of the gin-bottle
shrine.

The Thamers had often wondered why the chief would
have given them this particular place so willingly. Several
years passed before they were told that the people thought the
"white ones" would die if they lived on that ground. Orville was

Ethel Thamer

glad then that early on he had gone down and slept by the shrine and greeted the folks as they passed by on their way to farms in the early morning.

It was quite a challenge for them to turn the snake infested, unwanted property into a beautiful park-like place but they were grateful for the privilege to begin. Later Orville wrote: "The compound which was a fetish place filled with weedy bush is now blossoming like a rose and producing vegetables. We are praying that the whole area will also blossom as we continue to plant the seed of the Word."

Getting the land was important but making friends was even more so. The children were the first to come. They played with the Thamer children and loved the football. When Orville shot a partridge and gave them most of the meat, friendship was underway. The physical needs of the people cried out for help so Ethel treated those who came with sore eyes, coughs and ulcers. There was no building so she put up her table under the mango trees. Remarkable results from this outreach of love and concern showed up in the outlying villages, for now when they went to witness they were received gladly. Grateful patients opened their doors and walls of resistance were breaking down following a turn-around in attitude.

Sarah Buller came to join the Thamers in Tchaourou. She, too, brought a background of a long and fruitful ministry with the Yoruba people in Nigeria. Her fluency in the language gave her ready acceptance and enabled her to teach in the villages while she waited for government permissions on the school site.

Sarah first heard of the needs in Dahomey in 1945. The Lord spoke to her clearly then, after which she made several efforts to leave her work in Nigeria for what she saw as a greater need. S.I.M. felt they needed her where she was and couldn't release her. She worked at fulfilling her assignment to start a women's college for teachers. The call to Dahomey persisted however. She covenanted with the Lord to follow that leading when He released her and then quietly waited.

It was in April of 1951, when an invitation came from the McDougalls to join them in Dahomey. Permission was finally granted so, after a short furlough, she took some French studies in Paris, and in March, 1953, her calling was finally realized when she arrived in Tchaourou. Her assignment was to open a school for girls as soon as possible. Stewart could see that since girls were bought for marriage as infants, if there were ever to be wives suitable for the men they were training in their Bible schools, the missionaries would have to take responsibility for girls' training also. The school site had been applied for but it was a year before permission was granted. In the meantime Sarah lived on site in two small rooms with three Yoruba girls and all her belongings.

The year of waiting was joy-filled as she was able to witness to people who had never heard the message of God's love—people who listened and responded.

However, she was ready when permission for the school came on March 6, 1954. By the end of the month, building was underway on the dormitory for girls and her own house. Soon she was teaching with eleven girls in attendance. The work was very demanding as she continued to build and teach.

Believers continued to send their girls and after one year the
school had grown to twenty-nine. God gave first-fruits of the
work as the year closed when twelve of these were baptized.

The second year opened with forty-seven girls, all
boarders. Josephine, a national teacher qualified to teach the
beginning class, and Dora, who had worked with Sarah before
in Nigeria, taught the vernacular classes and lightened the
teaching load.

Sarah recorded that God's supply of food and other
essentials was a daily miracle. The immediate need for a
kitchen, dining room and two classrooms to adequately care for
the growing student body was strong affirmation and proof of
the Lord's blessing. They trusted that God, who supplied their
food would supply the buildings also.

Earl and Jean Playfair with their three children, Grace,
Samuel and Faith, came to Tchaourou in March,1955, when
Thamers left for furlough. Earl had been in Dahomey ever
since it first opened. He, like his father, had a long-time burden
for Dahomey. Before ever coming to Africa in 1944, he was sure
God wanted him there. He was assigned to Upper Volta until
Dahomey opened and he moved to Kandi. Earl was married to
Jean on his first furlough. They spent a year studying in
France and a year learning Bariba before starting Sinendé
station. Now a term and furlough later they were assigned to
Tchaourou.

The mission physicians had approved Earl's return with
some reservations, but he seemed well enough. He entered into
the ministries with enthusiasm and the Lord used him mighti-
ly in the church and outstations. He could speak to the people
directly in Bariba and his witness brought decisions for Christ.

In one village they burned their idols. But his ministry was not
to be very long. After only a few months he took ill with
phlebitis and had to be taken to Jos, Nigeria for hospitaliza-
tion. At one point he seemed better and was allowed to return
but it was a false hope. Jean stayed on at the station with the
children when he was returned to the hospital. Later she was
called to come to Jos where she found Earl in a coma. On
September 18, 1955, God took him to Himself. He is remembered with love and appreciation for his clear sense of God's
direction for his life and his obedience in fulfilling that call.
Earl allowed nothing to deter him. His love for the Baribas was
evidenced in his dedicated effort to win them for Christ right to
his final days.

Some years later a fellow missionary wrote in tribute:

One day Earl said to his wife Jean, "These people
need to have a hymn of reverence and worship: one that
will awe them with the holiness of their creator. We
haven't anything like that translated." With that he
began to translate.

Years later I sat in a little Bariba Church and
listened as the Baribas sang "Holy, holy, holy is the
Lord God Almighty." A lump came in my throat that
morning and I felt heaven was listening and rejoicing. I
felt Earl was there too among the angels listening and
rejoicing. He had been with the heavenly host for 6
years now but the Baribas and Fulanis were singing his
song.

Jean Playfair and her three children stayed on in
Tchaourou for a time, then moved to Parakou and finally to
Sinendé where she had started her life with Earl and where
she desired to be.

Sarah's furlough was due so Jean Soutar came to
replace her in time to prepare for opening the 1956-57 school
year. Jean found it hard to pull up roots in Sinendé Boys'
School but there was plenty to challenge her as she began the

year with fifty-six girls ranging in age from six to sixteen. They came from six different tribes and half of them couldn't converse with her without an interpreter. Dora as matron was very efficient in the supervision of the girls' food, dorm life and work assignments. Josephine taught one class in French but even so there were many problems to solve every day.

The dispensary ministry contributed much toward this growth even though it was difficult at first to keep it open consistently. It had started with Ethel Thamer under the mango tree, then Louise Marcotte carried on a medical ministry for a few months in 1955. In 1956, Nurse Shirley Barby came from Australia and was studying Bariba in preparation for opening the medical work. She cared for all the girls' ills and was a real prayer warrior which meant so much to Jean Soutar as she completed the year. The local people asked continually for medical help so it was a happy day in November, 1957, when Shirley Barby was able to reopen the work. The needed funds had come in for the new building and, for the first time, medicines were supplied by the French government.

After six months they were well established and the patient load increased daily. This was a place where Muslims, pagans and Christians were together and shared in the loving care. The patients came from at least five language groups: Yoruba, Bariba, Fulani, Fon (while some communicated in French) and a few spoke Housa. Wâarado, Shirley's aid, spoke both Yoruba and Bariba, loved the Lord and gladly shared the Word of God with the people. The story of Jesus was new to many, and some found it difficult to remember His name.

Sarah described her arrival back in Tchaourou in1957: "It was getting dark as the train rounded the corner and I

stuck my head out of the window to see if there would be a
missionary to meet me. The train stopped, and our 60 girls
from the school along with Dora and Josephine rushed to the
train to greet me. I was so glad to see them that tears came to
my eyes, and I was speechless. I had not expected such a
welcome. Three missionary ladies were there also, as well as
the church leaders and some Christians from out villages."

Sarah and Jean spelled each other off for furlough and
worked together until the middle of 1959. When together, they
shared responsibilities: Sarah doing building, upkeep and care
of the girls while Jean covered the academics. They shared the
spiritual ministries also and prayed together for the salvation
of each girl.

Maintaining institutions has a demanding way of
occupying personnel even to the extent of sometimes hindering
the achievement of their main objectives. Jean needed to be
free to work on "The Bible for the Baribas". She was working
as time permitted on foundational material such as: 1) a dictionary as the basis for consistent spelling; 2) material for
helping missionaries learn Bariba; and 3) putting the lessons
for baptismal classes in usable form.

Mary Louise Schneider took over as directress of the
Girls' School for the school year of 1960-61. This released Jean
and, in September, 1960, after a two year delay, she was able
to move to Parakou to work with Rosella Entz on the language
project. The final months of the school year had given Jean
much satisfaction as the older girls had shown real interest in
Bible Study. Four more girls were married to Christian young
men, making six new Christian homes.

At the close of 1961, the first school board meeting with
three African Christians, met and together with the mission-

aries they shared together in planning for the future. One decision made was to offer courses in Bariba and Yoruba as well as in French in order to encourage churches to send their children.

Later, in 1961, Pat Irwin came from France, where she had been studying, to take over the direction of the school. Along with Annie Van den Brand and the teachers, the entire staff was new as the school year opened. The school had a good relationship with the church. Pastor Elijah taught eight school girls the Sunday School lesson on Saturday and they then taught classes at churches on Sunday. In the afternoon, groups of girls went to different villages to witness. The older girls attended prayer meeting at church along with Pat. They had evangelistic services quarterly and there were always first-time decisions.

Meanwhile, the work on the main station had its forward spurts and also some set-backs. Where there is blessing, growth and release from bondage, one may be sure the enemy will strike to hinder.

The testimony and outreach to the villages continued strong at Tchaourou. Elijah, the evangelist, faithfully served the church and town. Thamers returned from furlough in 1956, and Anita Conrad was doing visitation full-time. Several new groups of believers were meeting regularly and some had put up prayer huts. Groups from the Girls' School effectively witnessed on the week-ends. During school breaks, boys who were home from the Sinendé Boys' School continued this testimony, holding meetings in both Bariba and Fulani villages. In villages where evangelists were stationed, they had baptismal and reading classes.

One of the evidences of growth in the Tchaourou church was the faithful attendance of some new young men, among whom was Samuel Carpenter. They regularly came to the services, prayer meetings and Bible Studies and were a great encouragement.

Along with growth came tensions, especially when scriptural teaching crossed traditional tribal practices. The teaching that a Christian girl should not be forced to marry against her will (even though promised earlier), for example, brought a fire storm. The first time this was affirmed in the settlement of a marriage palaver affecting families within the church, tensions mounted. There were mixed reactions whenever discipline by church authority was administered, whether by national or missionary, as when an evangelist was disciplined openly and dismissed after confessing to immoral behavior.

The reactions were typical in Goro village, where a student from the Bariba Bible School witnessed to large groups of children as well as older people. Goro was a strong pagan town whose people tried to drive out the believing Fulanis. At a meeting one Sunday the town people threatened to beat all who came, even the missionaries. Thamer was able to inter-cede and peace was restored. At this time, the believers were meeting in a prayer hut. Tensions were greatly relieved when they decided to build their more permanent meeting place back off the road nearer the center of the Fulani population.

The Tchaourou Church continued its forward thrust in spite of opposing forces. Elijah faithfully continued shepherding the church.

The evangelists also were faithful in the villages. There were churches in eight of them. One church was in a Fulani

village, one in Bariba and the rest in Yoruba villages. The
lighthouse in the Bariba church in Guinerou shone especially
bright. Wâarado led the services, conducted Sunday School as
well as the reading and baptismal classes. They built a church
building and attendance grew.

Wâarado's entire family was Christian, a praying
family, burdened for the people of Guinerou and the surrounding area. Their faith and work kept the witness bright.

The "ministry of healing" brought physical blessing to
many and, to those who believed, spiritual healing as well. It
was sad to close the dispensary near the end of 1958 because of
shortage of nurses, but during the next few months, nurse
Millie Davis made regular visits from Parakou. Many came for
treatment and her visits were greatly appreciated and
continued until the Dudgeons came to Tchaourou in July of
1959. Janey Dudgeon was able to keep the dispensary open
until Elaine Carpenter came in September of 1961.

In 1965, the Girls' School became Tchaourou Primary
School with housing for girls and a day school for boys. Its
enrollment increased each year and in 1972 there were one
hundred sixteen in attendance: eighty-three girls and thirty-
three boys. But it wasn't until 1973 that CI (fourth class)
officially opened with teacher Timothée Baboni, former
Sinendé teacher.

In 1970, Oswald and Irene Zobrist came to cover
furloughing staff and Irene kept the medical work going until
Shirley Barby's return in 1972. Over the years the medical
ministry was faithfully maintained through nurses Louise
Marcotte, Tommy Thompson, Elaine Carpenter, Janey
Dudgeon, Irène Sossauer and Shirley Barby and the message
was heard twice daily in Yoruba, Fulani and Bariba. In 1973,

Mary Stobbe joined Shirley Barby, attending to the many who came every day plus those who filled the in-patient rooms.

Orville Thamer, later remembering that they had not planned on doing medical work when they opened in Tchaourou, wrote in a letter:

> The condition of the people changed all that. They were so needy health-wise . . . so we started out under the mango trees treating eyes, coughs, ulcers, anything else that came along. The remarkable result in out-lying towns from this meager work, was the ability to visit and speak openly in towns where they earlier had told us to 'get out.' We have no doubt that the compassionate and careful use of what little medicines we could dispense, had a great effect on many who came to the Lord at that time.

For three years, there had been only women missionaries at Tchaourou which seemed unwise, so in 1974, the linguistic center, under the direction of Gordon Beacham, moved to Tchaourou from Djougou. The cooperative and friendly atmosphere, initiated and nurtured by the manners and personality of Orville Thamer, welcomed another ministry branch into the family of church work, village outreach, children's education and medical care.

Chapter 30: Tchatchou (1952)

1952 Dogon Yaro's first visit.

1955 Dogon Yaro's second visit.

1956 Church built and dedicated.
     Amos Ayorinde of EMS in residence.

1961 Dogon Yaro and wife Jumai came for 3 years.

1964 Dogon Yaro returned to Nigeria.

1972 School reopened by Samuel Yero.

1975 Tchatchou became an official station.
     Mr. and Mrs. Radlingmayr.

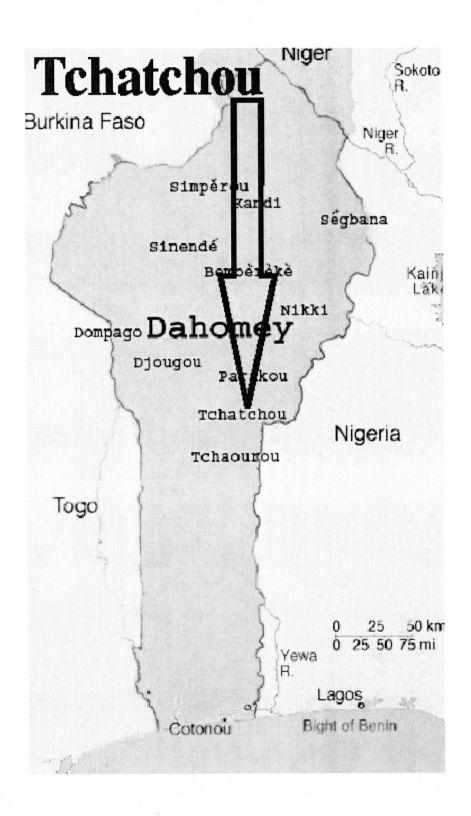

Tchatchou

The beginnings in Tchatchou are all rooted in the story
of the Fulani people and their response to the gospel. These
people are distinctive in their physical appearance as well as in
their mode of living. They are herdsmen whose way of life
centers around their cattle, a pastoral people who move from
place to place to find new grazing land. Their dwellings are
simple shelters quickly made and easily moved. Their daily
lives are filled with tasks related to the cattle. The women keep
busy with milking and churning butter, walking to market to
sell their goods, preparing meals and minding the children.

The daily tending of the herd is the responsibility of
teen-age boys. They find new grazing ground and lead the
cattle to water. A very important event in the life of a young
Fulani man is "Goja", the customary Fulani beating. He must
show his valor and give evidence of his manhood by enduring
the ordeal of receiving many strokes of the whip without
flinching or showing the least sign of pain.

S.I.M. missionary van Gerpen described this ceremony
in The Sudan Witness, May, 1961.

> . . . Scenes of young men gather in the market places,
> stripped to the waist and chewing cola nuts. Charms
> and ornaments are draped around their necks. Drums
> beat wildly as hundreds gather around, including finely
> dressed marriageable girls. A young man calls out his
> challenge before the admiring girls to contenders
> waving green, supple withes standing ready to whip his
> chest, in an effort to make him flinch. Almost
> nonchalantly, and partially drugged by the cola nut, the
> young man on trial stands at ease, resting his arms on a
> pole braced over his shoulders, pretending not to care.
> The crowd gives room, the roaring drums silence a
> moment and a stinging stripe is lashed into his ribs
> with all the fury the contender can muster. The cheers

are barely over when the blood trickles and a huge welt arises. Repeated several times that day, he does not flinch–at least not outwardly–to show his bravery.

Some of this tribe are Muslim and follow the teachings of the Koran. Others are purely pagan, trusting in their charms, and going to the witch doctor to seek favor or deliverance from some evil spirits. For a long time missionaries tried to reach the Fulani people, especially in Chad, the Sudan, Nigeria and the Cameroons but with little success. The Fulani in this area of Dahomey were pagan and quite settled. They were ready for the gospel message, listened eagerly and responded with sincerity. Fredlund had found it so in the Kandi area, Williams in Parakou from the beginning and Thamer reported the same in Tchaourou.

These peaceful herdsman lived among the Baribas and Yorubas, accommodating themselves easily to them but kept their families to themselves, living for the most part in easily movable temporary shelters. It was Tchatchou, where Bible School students had been going for practical outreach ministry since 1949, that became the center for the Fulani believers. As early as 1952 they had built a small grass-roofed mud church and Augustin Adjaoké continued to go there each week for preaching services. A head of household would attend and bring his whole family.

It was because of this response that the plan to bring Dogon Yaro for a visit was conceived. He was a Fulani preacher and evangelist, highly regarded by S.I.M. fellow-workers in Nigeria. His tape-recorded messages could be heard over ELWA radio station.

Stewart and Edna McDougall first met Dogon Yaro and his wife, Jumai, when they were living in Kano, Nigeria. This great walled city with its many gates was impressive. A huge mosque dominated the scene and worshipers crowded its courtyard where they slipped off their sandals before entering the building. Once inside they would prostrate themselves and invoke the blessing of Allah.

Dogon Yaro and Jumai with infant son, Musa, were living inside this walled city. They were the only Christian family surrounded by this darkness. At that time it was reported that 90,000 people lived there, all openly hostile to the gospel. This family lived there in obedience to the call of God

and complete trust in Him was their only weapon as they faced
this darkness and opposition daily.

The McDougalls remembered this missionary in the
heart of Kano city when they found the Holy Spirit clearly
moving among the Fulanis in Dahomey. When Stewart invited
him, Dogon Yaro accepted gladly and came to Dahomey early
in 1953. He traveled with Gus Fredlund throughout the whole
area wherever Fulani people were found. Believers were
greatly strengthened as the Spirit blessed the preaching and
testimony of this man of God. He was one of their own, lived in
their homes, put his arm around them, letting the love of
Christ flow through him. Surely they loved him in return, this
tall man with long arms waving, robes flowing, preaching and
teaching with warm enthusiasm. They never seemed to tire of
hearing him tell the story of his walk with God. In a report of
these weeks of witnessing in the villages, Gus Fredlund
summarized his testimony this way.

> That evening Bariba and Fulani filled the church while
> Dogon Yaro gave his testimony of how the Lord saved
> him in 1932. Here in short is what he said:
> "I was at that time headman of a railway gang. I
> had a good job and good pay. I had two wives but still
> had no children.
> Mr. Tanis and Mr. Archibald often passed by our
> crew while we were at work. They always stopped and
> preached to us. Also I saw boys from their school in
> Kagoro reading. My heart told me that it would be nice
> if I could read and also I liked to hear the preaching. I
> pretended that all I wanted to do was to learn to read
> but my wives both opposed me strongly saying, 'If you
> learn to read you will leave off doing your Moslem
> prayers and we won't stay with you.'
> Conviction deepened as I attended the services. Mr.
> Tanis was preaching 'the wages of sin is death . . . death
> . . . death' and I was afraid to die. I spent a miserable
> week in darkness of soul. Next Sunday I went forward
> when the invitation was given. 'Does Jesus want a

Fulani?' I asked. And when assured that His love and pardon were for all men I said 'Here am I.'

My heart was full of joy as I walked out of church that day until one of the Bible School boys asked what I was doing with all the charms hanging all over me. When he told me that I could not trust in Jesus and in the charms at the same time I refused to listen and went home with my heart full of darkness again. I later prayed to Jesus to show me whether He or charms would keep me in health. I took off my charms and lay down to sleep fully expecting to wake with a splitting headache if not worse. But to my great surprise I slept well and awoke next morning feeling better than ever. So when I went to work I left my charms at home.

Sometime later my first wife was horrified to discover them. "He has forgotten his charms! Something terrible will happen" she said to herself as she picked them up and ran to where I worked. Arriving puffing and tired she scolded me for being so careless. But when I told her the Lord Jesus was taking care of me and that I no longer needed any charms she was angry. "I'll not stay another night under your roof, infidel!" and she marched off, gathered up her things, and left. Sometime later the other wife could stand it no longer and she likewise left.

. . . I decided to go to school and for that purpose got six months leave of absence from my job. The six months were soon up and when they refused to give me more leave I gave up my job knowing that from now on my job was to preach Christ.

Many years later, after I had graduated from Bible school and preached the gospel in many places, God gave me a fine Christian wife, daughter of the chief of Kagoro. The Lord has blessed our home with four lovely children. What blessing can be greater than that?"

From these wonderful times together with Dogon Yaro, a freshness came to the Fulani believers. His message found a place in their hearts and, during his visit, several hundred believed and scores more were interested. One believer, Borori, rededicated his life to the Lord, desiring to follow Him wholly. He had spent much time with Dogon Yaro and had a new understanding of the demands of the gospel. He witnessed fearlessly in his village and led several to know Christ. After a

preaching tour of some villages with Borori, Stewart wrote
about his testimony in a letter.

> Borori spoke in each village where we went and I
> wish you could have heard him. He had the people
> keyed up to hear everything he said. He used very
> homely illustrations that really brought the message
> home to the people. . . .
> Elisha preached and I preached but neither of us
> could come anywhere near Borori. He so simply
> presented the gospel in language and illustration that
> they all understood. The Lord really blessed his
> testimony. It surely thrilled me and made me pray as
> never before for him and the other Fulanis that the
> Lord would keep them from falling and make them real
> witnesses among their own people.

The people didn't want Dogon Yaro to leave, but he had
to return to his family and his work in Kano. The missionaries,
too, wished he could stay and prayed that it would please God
to direct His servant to Dahomey.

After two years
he did return for a visit,
bringing his wife,
Jumai, with him. They
found a warm welcome,
many new groups of
believers that had
formed and some new
churches. The need for a
Bible school for Fulanis
was laid on their hearts
as they returned home.

As the witness
continued, there was
response among the
Fulanis in Kandi,

Djougou, Simpérou and Bembèrèkè. Charles and Elaine
Carpenter were in Tchaourou close by. Charles' knowledge of
the Fulani language and love for the people made him a great
encourager for these believers. As many as two hundred would
gather for worship in Tchatchou and, when the church was
dedicated in 1956, they had three hundred twenty-five Fulanis
and Baribas present. Pastor Amos Ayorinde, a missionary from
E.M.S., was resident there. Nurse Millie Davis came from
Parakou on regular visits to treat patients, and the believers
had put up a grass shelter as a treatment center.

However, the need for a Bible School to train Fulani
leaders had not yet been filled. When Parakou Bible School
opened in 1956 they had seven men and their wives, mostly
Fulani, which emphasized this need. So McDougall went to
Dogon Yaro one more time. This time Stewart found him in
Kagoro. He was just finishing a pastor's refresher course at
Kagoro Bible School. He seemed delighted to see the
McDougalls and, when Stewart presented the need and invited
him and Jumai to join them in Dahomey to work with the
Fulani, he responded, believing this was God's leading.

It was a happy day for all when, in 1961, Dogon Yaros
moved to Tchatchou but especially so for the Fulani people.
Dogon Yaro excuded peace and fulfillment. On one visit the
McDougalls found him reclining with his children in his arms
and the people gathered around him. The missionaries were
used to seeing him with arms waving and voice uplifted
preaching the word. This glimpse spoke of contentment.

Jumai seemed happy too. Their older children were at
home in Kagoro in school. Only their daughter Ruth was with
her. God gave them another child while they were there in
Tchatchou. Jumai conducted the women's section of the Bible

School. Along with Bible subjects, she taught them to read and write and other practical subjects. One would often find her teaching with the new baby tied to her back and her toddler by her side. She was a true helper and role model as wife, mother, and faithful servant of the Lord.

It was cause for great rejoicing when the long-awaited Fulani Bible School became a reality and thrived with this shepherd/teacher living right with his students. Mission leaders were thrilled as they watched God doing something very significant in the lives of these young men and their wives. The years passed quickly and it was nearing time for Dogon Yaro and Jumai to return to their family. They had brought twenty-eight young men through to completion of a three year course and to graduation. Those receiving diplomas had come from all areas of Dahomey and most of them would be returning to those areas.

When Dogon Yaro took his family home for a "leave" in 1964, it was in full anticipation of returning. However, they were hindered when the time came because Jumai had the responsibility of her aged mother. God spoke to him afresh when he heard the Fulani Bible School would close without him. Dogon Yaro decided to return alone.

Jumai hated to see him go alone since he had not been well, but she did not hinder him because he so clearly sensed the Lord's directing.

Sadly for the church in Dahomey, it was only a short time after his return in 1967 that he became very ill. Before Jumai could get to him he had gone on to his Heavenly home. This was a difficult time for the struggling church. In February, 1966, "Missionary to the Fulanis", Gus Fredlund, had died and now, in 1967, their beloved teacher had also been taken from them. But they carried on. Charles Carpenter who was there to help, understood them and their language. Shirley Barby lived among them at Tchatchou and had a great ministry with the Fulani women and children.

There were difficulties with the language because the New Testament they were using was written in the Cameroon dialect and the differences were considerable. Dr. Leslie Stennes, a linguist, came to advise. He concluded that it would be difficult for a Dahomey Fulani, knowing only the local dialects, to comprehend the radio broadcasts from Radio Voice of the Gospel (ELWA) or to understand scriptures if read to him from this translation. The Fulani believers had been reached with the present literature but the witness and growth would be much more effective if adjustments were made. His visit was very helpful in establishing the need for further study of different dialects of Fulani. These studies were pursued by linguistic experts and plans for the Bible School and refresher courses were made by fellow-workers. In 1972 a short-term Bible School was held with Samuel Yero, who had been trained at the French Bible School in Mahadaga, Haute Volta.

The witness continued as God called others to lead the way, but the church remembers with gratitude the ministry and sacrifice of those who planned and planted, laying a foundation on the Rock.

In 1972 Irène Sossauer reported that Dahomey was the only country where S.I.M. had Fulani churches. There were seven Fulani churches and other mixed congregations. Most of these churches had a pastor taught by Dogon Yaro. In 1975, S.I.M. and UEEB designated Tchatchou an official station and Mr. and Mrs. Fritz Radlingmayr were assigned to carry on the work.

Chapter 31: Ségbana (1954)

1954	McDougall took Bob Blaschke to station November 17, 1954. Language and Literacy emphasis.
1956	First Primer completed. Villages welcomed Blaschke's visits. Fredlund visited villages and Fulanis responded.
1957	Beachams work on analysis of Boko language.
1958	Beacham completed assignment and returned to Djougou. Charles and Elaine Carpenter arrived, studied Fulani.
1959	Carpenters evangelized among Fulani villages.
1961	Blaschkes with Bobby arrived in June.
1963	Ségbana church built.
1965	Blaschkes left for Cotonou, then furlough. Station closed through September, 1966.
1967	Church sent first three boys to Sinendé.
1969	First Baptisms: eleven men. Bobéna church built. Ross Jones arrived.
1970	Sérékibé Church built.
1971	Lay Bible School started by Jones.
1972	Blaschkes returned. Joneses to Bobéna. Kamboura & Gbarana Churches built. Pastors' Training course held: Nine from 5 villages.
1973	Salonzi Church built.
1974	Boko Church rejoiced in over 100 baptized believers.

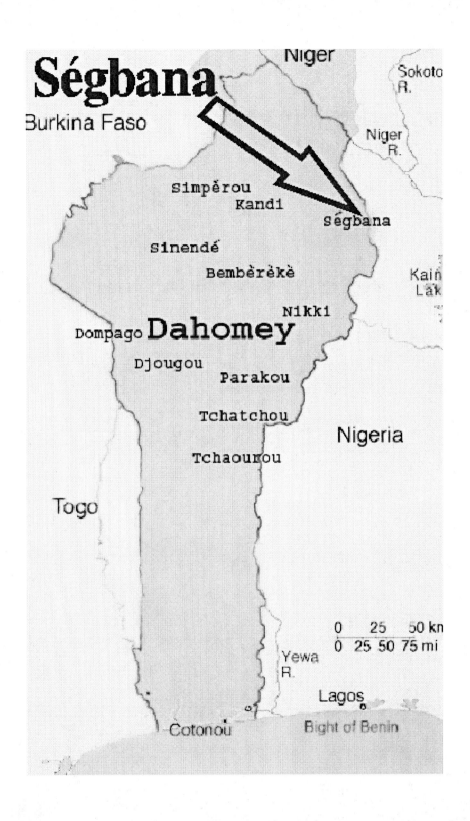

<u>Ségbana</u>

Soon after Gus Fredlund went to Kandi in 1947, he started trekking out to Ségbana about sixty-two miles to the East. He always found the Boussa people receptive and prayed much that God would protect them and keep them from Muslim infiltration until a resident missionary could come. In 1947, in Nikki, the first believer was a Boussa, bringing this tribe to the attention of mission leadership. Numbering about 25,000, their center of population was Ségbana about one hundred twenty-five miles away.

Fredlund continued to reach out to this center whenever he was visiting the Fulanis in the area. In 1952 he and evangelist David Olusiyi visited Ségbana. They were welcomed by the chief who requested that a missionary or evangelist come and live among his people. His son and heir had become a believer with his father's consent. Now the father was saying, "Come and we will build a church."

In the beginning days in Ségbana there were barriers to the preaching of the gospel among them. The Boko were an isolated people geographically and had a reputation for being fierce. The mercenaries or any white man who came was feared. When one would appear the women and children would run into the bush saying such things as, "The white man is coming to eat you or take you to school."

To announce a meeting, a drummer would drum and call out the announcement. Whenever the drummer announced a meeting, no one would come because the last white man who came to town for taxes had beat the people. Consequently, a white person was not welcome. This made it difficult for the

missionary to explain he had come in peace with a message of
love.

The invitation from the Chief of Ségbana to the
missionary to come and his friendly and hospitable reception
from the beginning, explains the entrance and acceptance they
experienced.

The Boko isolation as well as their nature made them a
determined, aggressive people. When they received the gospel
they were stalwart believers and showed initiative in going out
aggressively to other Boko villages to witness.

There was no missionary ready to answer this call. The
door was kept open since the governor granted permission for a
catechism class there and visits were made from time to time.
Fredlund showed his continued deep concern saying, "Now is
the hour or the Muslims will swallow up yet another tribe."
Later when there was no one to enter, he and Alice were
prepared to leave Kandi and move to Ségbana but this was not
to be.

Approval of this site was given by the Mission and the
call went out for a hardy pioneer to respond to this call to a
place which could be isolated six months out of the year, and
the first task would be to put the language into writing.
Stewart wrote in 1953: "I feel that the need in Ségbana is
really pressing. The government has granted the site and if we
do not occupy within a year we will need to make application
all over again."

So, when Bob Blaschke arrived in Dahomey in November of 1954 the missionaries rejoiced for he had been much
prayed for and long awaited. After a brief stay in Parakou, he
and Stewart left for Ségbana, arriving safely over the rough
roads and flimsy bridges. On November 23rd they were warmly

welcomed with greetings, gifts and the loan of a three room
house for as long as he needed it. By the time Stewart left the

next day, Bob, with his Bariba
helper, Boni, were settling in.
They had fixed up an outdoor
shower and were rejoicing in a
good beginning.

Already on the 25th he
records having an informant and
starting his study of the Boussa
language. Part of his learning took place in the evening as he
interacted with the audience that gathered daily to watch him
eat. It was an encouragement for Bob when Chuck Forster
came in January, 1955, for a six months' stay.

In mid-1956, Bob complained that, "Language progress
is altogether too slow. Most of the witness is done in French."
However his perseverance was bringing results and he brought
his first message in Boussa to a gathering in town. A year
later, in May, 1957, the Beachams came and really changed
life at this lonely outpost. Joyce took over the kitchen and
Gordon gave assistance in the language, bringing light to many
problem areas. He wrote an analysis of the grammar as well as
a pedagogical grammar for teaching missionaries to speak
Boussa. His informant wrote stories, folklore, customs, etc. in
Boussa, contributing much to the understanding of the
language and culture of the people.

The fellowship had been sweet, so they were much
appreciated and sorely missed when they returned to Djougou
early in 1958. In May, 1958, Charles and Elaine Carpenter
came to study Fulani and to evangelize and follow-up on
Fredlund's faithful witness to Fulanis in the area. Charles had

Sunday services in French for French speaking nationals with
some interest and he cycled to most of the Fulani villages
around Ségbana.

In an article in <u>The Sudan Witness</u> for January/
February of 1959, Charles Carpenter wrote:

> Nowhere have we sensed spiritual darkness greater
> than here in Ségbana. Some of the people are moslem
> with all of its profound ritualism, most however are
> pagan, fetish-worshiping.
> Usually a year after the death of a person there is a
> feast held. There is lots of native beer, a chicken is
> sacrificed over the grave, and the people wait until the
> spirit of the dead person passes to someone among
> them. . . .
> Recently on his death bed, the head butcher in town
> confessed having murdered several people by black
> magic. He had steeped certain leaves in water, then
> bathed in the water while cursing a particular
> individual. Each of these people had died.
> Bob Blaschke is our only missionary working among
> the Boussa people, from whom not one as far as known
> has been delivered from these awful bonds of darkness
> by faith in Christ. Will you pray for the Boussas?

Bob left for furlough in December, 1958, and could look
back over four years with gratitude for having started a
lighthouse among the Boussas. He had completed some
buildings and an airstrip; removed barriers and fears,
establishing good relations and open doors for the gospel; made
good progress in language; completed primers 1 and 2 and held
a literacy campaign. He also had a good response among the
many villages out of Ségbana that he visited just before
leaving.

Bob married while on furlough, so when he returned in
June of 1961 he had his wife, Carol Lee, and son, Bobby, with
him. It took some time to get everything up and going again.
The airstrip needed repair and clean up, and he had to brush
up on his language knowledge before feeling confident to teach

and preach again. Carol Lee was a nurse and, even though
they had no official permission to do medical work, she was
called on by the government nurse to assist her with difficult
cases. Bob had regular meetings in three Boko villages: Kolawi,
where they had built a chapel; Gifambara where people had
shown great interest; and the village of Kamboura where one
hundred fifty or more attended meetings out under the trees
and were preparing to build a church. But the village of
Kolawi, so promising in 1962, dropped down to nothing in 1963
as the pagans and believers struggled against each other.

The family had reason to be grateful for the airstrip at
this time. On March 29, Carol Lee gave birth to a baby girl,
there on Ségbana station. Mother and baby were safe, but
everyone was relieved when they were airlifted out to Jos to be
checked and nurtured for a while. Later, Bob had an attack of
acute appendicitis so the plane returned to take him out for
hospital care.

When Bob returned, he found the Ségbana believers
had built a very nice mud-block church. What joy to see them
rejoicing in their meeting place and acting with such
responsibility.

Other encouragements were:
1) the return of Gordon Beacham for further language
   work.
2) reading classes meeting four nights a week with
   twenty students in each class.
3) a Bible class for believers.
4) the second primer rewritten.
5) women learning to read.
6) completion of the two books of Lanback's "Story of
   Jesus"(helpful transitional readers in preparation for
   reading scriptures).
7) believers witnessing and finding joy in the response.

These encouragements strengthened Blaschkes as they
prepared to leave these new believers in the summer of 1965

for a year on home assignment when the station would be closed.

Blaschkes returned in 1966 and progress continued in reading classes and translating the Gospel of Mark, but in late 1967, Bob wrote in his report, "If we only had the Scriptures in Boko, how these Christians could grow."

The church continued to grow and it was a special highlight for them when the first three young boys were enrolled in the Sinendé Boys' School in 1967. The church honored the boys with a "send-off", giving them gifts to encourage a feeling of mutual responsibility between the boys and the local church. They explained that even though the boys were going off to seek a French education, they had a certain grassroots responsibility to the local church and its authority over them. The church reserved the right to withdraw them from school if they did not make a serious effort or were not willing to help with work on their parents' farms when at home on vacation. Strong principles were laid down which would strengthen both the church and the students.

The highlight of the year, 1969, was the first baptismal service in Ségbana. It was a day of celebration as eleven men took this important step. However, it also created great consternation and debate among the missionaries because it included two polygamists. After all the division, pain and stress that this issue had caused the Mission and churches in Parakou in 1963 and Djougou in 1968, many wondered how Bob Blaschke could even consider such action. Blaschke's explanation was that he could find no written policy forbidding the baptism of polygamists although he understood that it was a long-observed one in the mission. But he had two very practical problems. His leading Christian witness, song-writer and worship leader had two wives. The tribal reaction was, "If Davidi can't be baptized as a Christian, who can?" The other practical problem was that the scripture says that God hates divorce and he could find no biblical basis for denying baptism. He did, however, advise the men that they could not qualify for the position of deacon, elder or pastor in church leadership. From that experience, he developed a thesis that first generation pagans should be treated differently than a believer who takes a second wife. His decision apparently caused no long-term harm to the church.

Ross Jones joined the Blaschkes in the summer of 1969 and was soon into the language learning and outreach to the villages. Shortly after his arrival, Blaschkes were moved to Cotonou where they managed the guest house until leaving for furlough in the summer of 1970.

The people of Bobèna had responded well and believers were growing as Bob ministered there twice a month, and it was to Bobèna that Ross moved in 1970. The village (Christians, pagans and Muslims) built a house for him at their own expense. Bobèna was his base but he worked much with believers in nearby Sérékibé, teaching reading, writing and Bible. He also held a baptismal class of fifteen candidates. He was in the process of translating selections of both Old and New Testaments.

Ross went on home assignment at the end of 1971 and, while there, married Joy. They returned in 1972 and lived at Bobèna where he continued translation and ran an unofficial dispensary (he was a pharmacist) while Joy was studying the language.

Ross started the first formal Pastors' Training Course in July, 1972, at Bobèna. Training leadership was always a priority since the churches had been started but this training was a new and important step forward. The students were all farmers and found it difficult to be away from their farms for long periods. In the beginning they came only one day a week, then two days a week.

In early 1973, Ross was evacuated to Bembèrèkè and then to London with what was diagnosed as Guillain Barré syndrome. He recovered and returned to his post.

In June of 1973, the Boko Bible School was opened. Bob visited ten villages to encourage Christians in their faith and in holding reading classes. Baptisms were held at the end of 1973 after concentrated teaching lessons. At Gbarana, Ross taught and baptized seventeen and a church was organized. At Salonzi, Blaschkes taught and Bob baptized twenty-three and a church was organized. The Salonzi church conducted reading classes on their own, sent leaders to the training school, and started an outreach to another village.

After fifteen months of training, church leaders and elders were taking responsibility for training others and exercising church discipline. By the end of 1975, the revised books of Mark and Acts had been distributed, the books of Luke, Romans, I Corinthians, I Peter and II Peter had been translated and work on Genesis, Exodus, Galatians and Ephesians was nearing completion. A survey of Boko villages in Nigeria showed a population of 10,000 that had no Christian witness but could be reached through their efforts. The Boko church in Dahomey now numbered over a hundred baptized believers and was gaining depth as well as breadth. More work was required but there was a sound basis for hope.

Chapter 32: Simpérou (1959)

1959   Station officially opened in October by Oswald and
        Irene Zobrist.
        People meeting together for services desired to build
        church.
        Medical work started by Irene.
        Dispensary built.

1962   First baptismal service.
        Beginning of fellowship meetings of churches.
        Inpatient huts built.

1965   Built new Church and evangelist's house.

1967   Simpérou hosted All Church Conference.

1968   Dispensary closed.

1972   Bariba women's conference hosted.
        Dispensary reopened with nurse Greta Jackson.

1975   New Church built.

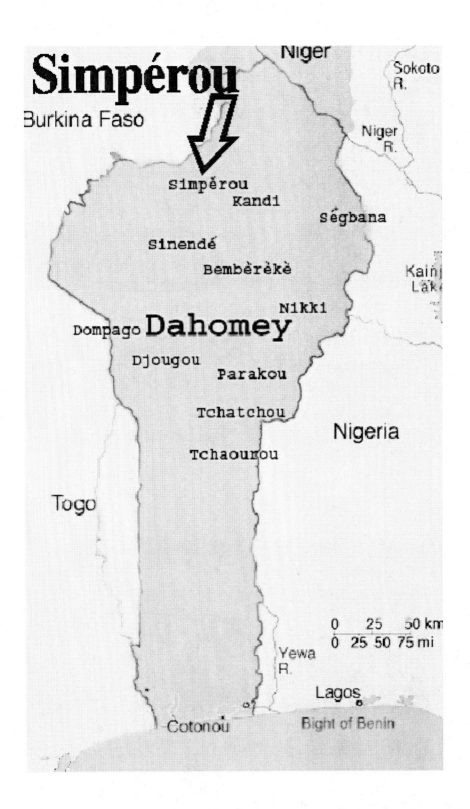

Simpérou

Missionaries stationed in Kandi had always felt concern for the peoples in the Banikoara area. Ed Morrow made a five day trip late in 1949 visiting and preaching in eight villages where he found sincere interest in most of them even though this was their first time to hear the gospel.

At their conference in 1951, the missionaries were in agreement that the Kandi area could not be reached from the one station and plans were made to open two other stations, one at Banikoara and one at Ségbana. With this in mind a team of men, two African young men with Zobrist, Dudgeon and Fredlund trekked the area. In all the seven villages visited there was good response to the preaching and their suggestion for a site was Toura.

Other visits were made by missionaries. Dudgeon visited over fifty villages in the Banikoara and Sonsoro areas in 1953. Fredlund spent a week in 1956 visiting forty Fulani camps with encouraging response. In May of 1958, Zobrist and Dudgeon made a trip and Zobrist stayed in the Rest House in Gomparou to thoroughly scout out the area. After all this research, Emmett, Thamer and Zobrist chose the site at Simpérou on July 18, 1958.

For eight years this area had been on the list of needy fields. As early as February of 1952, Oswald and Irene Zobrist had expressed a desire to be involved in a new pioneering thrust out from Kandi. Now in November 1958, missionaries, together with the Commandant, the Paramount Chief and chiefs from two nearby towns met at the site to make sure that no objections existed to the mission plans for building there.

Zobrist family

By faith they had gathered stones for the foundation of the first small building. Then, when full clearance came, they completed this building by December 11, 1958. Oswald spent January and February of 1959 at the station and by March had completed the garage/storehouse building. This provided a place for Irene and the children to join him there in April.

In May, Irene had already begun reaching to the people with her medical skills. They started in a little round grass hut which soon proved inadequate. In June, Zobrist started work on a permanent dispensary building and was able to complete it in July despite the rains. The people came for help in increasing numbers.

It was a happy day in August, 1959, when Lafia David with his wife Léah and four children came to join them. Lafia had spent three years at Parakou Bible School, so the ministry was greatly expanded with his preaching in the dispensary and the villages. In Kokè, several young men showed great interest, especially when Kuré Suna, who had said Muslim prayers for ten years, responded and wanted to know how to pray to God in Jesus' Name.

In Simpérou itself the services continued to be well attended and those who came wanted to build a church so a site was chosen. All the services were in Bariba. A group of Protestant Yoruba traders met separately since they did not know Bariba or French. Zobrist had oversight of this group and helped as needed, but a former Parakou Yoruba church elder, Emmanuel, preached for them regularly since they gathered in his home.

As 1960 opened, the Simpérou ministry continued to experience blessing and encouragement. Responses were encouraging as missionaries continued to trek out to the villages, especially in Keki, Bouhanrou and Tounago where the Muslim influence was strong. In June of 1962 the Church at Simpérou invited the believers from the three outstations for a week-end of fellowship. They came on Saturday afternoon and stayed through the noon meal on Sunday. Some women came and together they celebrated their faith with great joy.

Other activities of the church included a baptismal class which was well attended. Two young men had been baptized and others were preparing. Parents were responding to Zobrist's urging and were sending their children to the mission schools. Bakiu was the first student from Simpérou to go to the Bariba Bible School. Further evidence of progress was the Ecole Catechist in Bouhanrou where Bouraïma taught a class of forty children.

Irene's ministry in the dispensary was greatly extended when funds came in from a church in Germany to build in-patient houses. These were constantly filled from the moment of their completion in 1962. Later they were able to build two additional houses as isolation units for T.B. patients. These met a great need for the people and provided a most effective opportunity for sharing the gospel message each evening.

Two graduates from the Bariba Bible School, Sabi Pierre and Matthieu, had come to share in the ministry, helping greatly in both the medical work and evangelism. They carried the work alone for a time since the Zobrists were

leaving for furlough. Gus Fredlund visited them from Kandi.
Then in 1965 nurse Irène Sossauer and Margaret Bevington
with her school of girls came for a year. Irène came fresh from
a year's experience at Bembèrèkè Hospital and ably met the
needs of the many patients at Simpérou. She started a bush
dispensary at Tintémon, a village an hour away by motorbike.
After a couple of months of operation, one hundred sixty
patients were coming to the clinics held twice a week. She also
had women's classes and Sunday School each Sunday.
Matthieu came every Sunday morning to conduct the
preaching service which had about seventy in attendance.

In 1967, the National All Church Conference with
seventy-one delegates from thirty-three churches was hosted
by the Simpérou church.

All Church Conference - 1967

The Zobrists returned to Dahomey after furlough, but,
in 1968, were transferred to fill in at Bembèrèkè and
Tchaourou. Several ladies were stationed at Simpérou to assist
over the next few years. Margaret Bevington returned to
oversee the station and do village visitation. Shirley Hyman
worked on Bariba literature preparation and the outreach in
French which included a Sunday afternoon service. Christa
Moos came as a language student. Annie Van den Brand came

briefly to encourage the Bariba women in the area who were responding well, but there was no trained staff available to reopen the dispensary until September of 1972 when Greta Jackson came on permanent assignment.

In 1972, the Bariba Women's Conference was also hosted by the Simpérou Church. As the witness continued on many fronts, so the church continued to grow and expand.

Chapter 33: Bembèrèkè (1960)

1960   Station first occupied by Dr. and Mrs. Dreisbach.

1961   On July 3, Hospital officially opened.

1965   Hospital closed. Only clinic open.

1966   Bariba Bible School moved to Bembèrèkè: Jim Cail
with Ouorou Sidi Jean in charge.
Clinic closed.

1967   June 1: Hospital reopened with Dr. Ken Elliott.

1970   Dr. and Mrs. Serge Bagdazarianz arrived and the
hospital doors remained open.

1974   Bagdazarianz left due to Cheryl Bagdazarianz'
illness.
Dr. and Mrs. Christian Klopfenstein arrived.

1975   Jim Longworth came as hospital administrator.

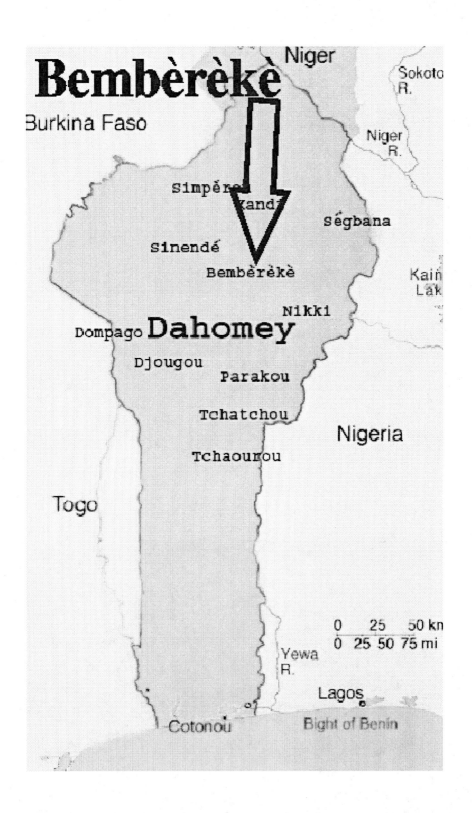

Bembèrèkè

A 1961 Field Report describes the start in Bembèrèkè:

It was a thrilling moment when at Bembèrèkè, in Northern Dahomey, at three o'clock in the afternoon of July 3rd, a great crowd of approximately eight hundred people waited expectantly for the arrival of the President of Dahomey, His Excellency, M. Hubert Maga. Officials and dignitaries of Dahomey, including many Europeans, the American Consul, the British Consul, S.I.M. missionaries and hundreds of Fulani and Bariba people formed a picturesque sight as they lined the circle entrance before the new Evangel Hospital. On one side there was the 36-piece military band. In the centre was a colour guard of soldiers with the beautiful red, green and yellow Dahomey flag. A military Guard of Honor was drawn up on the other side, and as M. Maga and party arrived at the entrance of the hospital, they alighted from their cars and walked into the centre of the circle entrance. Here they were met by Rev. Stewart McDougall, District Superintendent of S.I.M. in Dahomey, and the American Consul. The band played the national anthem as M. Maga and a number of other important personages . . . marched up the steps of the hospital to the microphone.

An address, in the French language, was then read to the large assemblage present, expressing the government's appreciation of the work of the [Sudan Interior] Mission in Northern Dahomey, and particularly of their initiative in building and equipping a hospital in this needy area.

Then followed a tour of the Hospital, as the official party led by Dr. J. A. Dreisbach, who himself had done a great deal of the actual work involved in its planning and erection inspected. . . .

In one of the ward rooms which had been reserved for the official reception, the party of officials was seated, with approximately one hundred personages, including Dahomians and expatriates. In welcoming the President and his party, Mr. McDougall expressed regret that the Minister of Health had been detained by official duties and could not be present as he had desired. Mr. McDougall then introduced Rev. R.J. Davis, Associate General Director of S.I.M. who was officially

to present the Hospital to the Dahomey people through
their elected leader, the President. . . .

Now, as Dr. Dreisbach remarked, the more difficult
work begins, for the accumulating and erecting of stone
and timber, while not an easy task, has not been as
demanding as will be the actual treatment and care of
the many patients whom the hospital will serve. For it
is the desire and prayer of the Mission and of all
associated with the work that this new hospital may be
the door through which many of the people of Dahomey
will be introduced– perhaps for the first time–to the
Lord Jesus Christ, the Saviour of the world. [British
Sudan Witness, October 1961]

This was the crowning day after much prayer, planning
and hard work along with sacrificial giving and living.

During the McDougalls' first year in Nikki, in 1947,
they had visited Bembèrèkè. The French Commandant spoke
to them about S.I.M. opening a station there and he had picked
out a site at the foot of a hill with a spring in the hill behind it.
The whole hill seemed to be covered with springs making it a
beautiful spot.

There were 32,000 people in this division without a
gospel witness so the need was clear. Mr. and Mrs. Williams
were enroute to Dahomey and were coming to Nikki to study
language. They were considered as potential missionaries for
this area.

With more research it was found that the wiser strategy
would be to reach this people by opening a station at the
largest village of the division, Sinendé. Though further from
the main road, it was more centrally located demographically.

Years later, at the Dahomey Conference of 1958, the
decision was made to open a hospital and plans were set in
motion. Dr. Ray Davis and Ted Emmett were to look for a
suitable site. It was required by the government that the
Mission Hospital be at least one hundred kilometers away from
the nearest government hospital. Two possible sites were

chosen, Djougou and Bembèrèkè. The decision was for
Bembèrèkè since it was on the main North-South road and
accessible to more people.

In 1959 Dr. and Mrs. Dreisbach came from Nigeria,
where they were stationed, to visit Dahomey with a view to
starting a medical work. They returned in June of 1960 to
prepare for the work at the hospital by studying Bariba with
Mary Draper at Sinendé.

The medical personnel met to make plans. Stewart
McDougall went to the coast to make the government
applications. After many frustrating months, all the
government permits had been received and building began.

None of the missionary builders was available for the
job so Dr. Dreisbach had to do the bulk of the work: the
planning, hiring of workmen, supervision and then whatever
was needed. The report in the British "Sudan Witness"
describes the situation well: "His skilled hands accustomed to
surgical instruments, took up wrenches, pliers, hammer and
saw. He personally did all the plumbing and wiring and many
other tasks."

The plan for a completed building called for a hundred
beds and an isolation ward. On opening day all rejoiced in the
completion of the first units containing wards with thirty-four
beds, examination and treatment rooms, an operating theater,
laboratory and X-ray rooms and facilities for out-patients.

McDougall, President Maga, French Official & Davis

Opening of dedication

McDougalls and M. Maga

The hospital was soon fully functional with patients coming from far and near. It gained a good reputation with the government as well as the people. The nurses working in village clinics were now able to refer difficult cases to the hospital. This was a welcome relief to the heavy responsibilities they had been carrying.

In addition to Dr. and Betty Dreisbach, the staff included Stan Dudgeon in maintenance, nurses Jane Dudgeon, M.L. Schneider, Greta Jackson, Shirley Barby and Irene Zobrist, six national helpers and four volunteer evangelists. Together they treated 2430 patients in the first six months.

After two years Dr. Dreisbach left and was replaced by Dr. Kuster from Switzerland who ministered ably for nearly two years in spite of poor health. However, after Dr. Kuster's departure at the end of 1964 there was no replacement for three years. The nurses cared for all they could in an out-patient clinic but they had to turn many away who needed surgery. When a doctor had been on staff they averaged five hundred fifty operations annually and 2000-3000 out-patients per month. The nurses treated about 1000 per month.

From its opening in 1961, evangelism was the priority for both the missionaries and the national staff. They had an evangelist, the pastor from the local church, and students from the Bible School who ministered to the spiritual needs of the patients through their preaching, personal visits in wards and follow-up in the villages. Bible studies and film ministry in the evenings were conducted with much prayer and loving kindness.

Many people responded to the outreach and, upon return to their villages, witnessed to others. Then, when someone came to the village to follow-up and instruct further in the Word, a group would gather which sometimes grew into a church.

People who came with common hurts, needs or stresses were united across language barriers, ethnic groups and cultural differences: a microcosm of the peoples of Dahomey. All were ministered to lovingly by staff who also encouraged them in their sufferings.

Millie Davis worked hard in the clinic but when she became ill the clinic had to close. Nurse Jane Dudgeon wrote in 1964 about a crowded hospital and asked for prayer for more wards and then in 1966 she sent out an urgent request for prayer for a doctor and the reopening of the hospital.

Doors are closed and locked. Windows are fastened tight. Medicine on the shelves is covered with dust. Bandages lay in boxes. The surgery table is covered with spider webs. The windows of the ward stare vacantly out into the branches of the near-by trees. The soul of the hospital is dead. The living, moving loving hands—both black and white—have gone. The hands that wrote the admission sheet, the hands that gave the injections, the hands that guided the microscope, the hands that dispensed the medicine, the hands that held the scalpel, the hands that took the pulse, the hands that held the Bible, the hands that held the cup to the feverish lips—are gone! Only the gray shadows of the past are there—only the memories of what once was real and living and eternal.

The blind no longer come to receive their sight in this place of healing by the side of the road. In darkness they grope their way through their long weary days. The weak and the suffering do not come instead they die in pain in some village hut. The mothers do not hurry along the footpaths, instead they weep while their little ones die in their arms. The women in difficult labour do not go into the surgery-room, instead they drink the witch-doctors lethal dose and are laid in shallow graves.

Names were written in the Lambs Book of Life in this haven by the side of the road. Burdens of sin rolled away and peace filled hearts that 'till then had only known fear. But "The Hand" has been stilled for the hospital doors are closed and locked and no one comes

any more. The dust grows thicker and the vines more
tangled.
        A Dr. laid his scalpel down. His gloves and gown
were folded up. He went away. The days and nights, the
weeks and years pass and we wait . . . . Oh, where is
that man of God who will come and again pick up that
scalpel and set into vital life this place by the side of the
road?
["Dust Covered Hospital", November, 1966]

The Mission received an ultimatum from the Minister of
Health that it was mandatory that S.I.M. have a doctor at the
hospital. The Minister of External Affairs stated it this way in
a letter to S.I.M.:

> The Dahomean Government would be very happy if
> you could envisage re-opening the hospital and also
> extending this health service.
>   The re-activation of this hospital would be a
> valuable help to the present undertaking of the
> Dahomean Government in meeting the health needs of
> its people, in particular the people of the rural areas.

And in late 1966 the President himself visited the closed
hospital.

The Bariba Bible School, formerly in Sinendé, with Jim
Cail in charge moved to Bembèrèkè in 1966. Sidi Jean accepted
the assignment to assist Jim and they proved to be a most
effective team.

When the school first opened in Bembèrèkè, the hospital
was closed—and they held the classes in the Operating Room,
which with all the windows proved very suitable. After the
reopening they moved from there to a grass mat enclosure
where they taught for two years. Then a permanent school was
built on a site three miles from the hospital. This proximity
enabled Sidi Jean to minister at the hospital by preaching as
needed and personally witnessing on the wards while
maintaining his busy schedule at the school.

The cries of the people for help, the prayers of God's people, the commitment of the missionaries, and the urging of the government were all satisfied in the coming of Dr. and Mrs. Elliott from Australia. The hospital was reopened on June 1, 1967 without fanfare but with deep gratitude to God for sending His servants. The wards were soon full again and doctor's operating schedule filled.

In anticipation of this happy occasion, Jim Cail wrote in his report: "We praise the Lord that the hospital will soon be reopened. Reopened to treat the many who come for help. Reopened to tell many that God loves them and that Christ died and rose again for their sins' forgiveness. Reopened to show that a doctor has answered a call. Reopened to show in a practical way love's ministry through caring for the physical needs."

From the reopening with Dr. Elliott, the hospital continued to minister daily to patients who came from all over Dahomey and, on occasion, some from Upper Volta, Niger and Nigeria. Dr. and Mrs. Bagdazarianz took over from Dr. Elliott in 1970 and had a very effective spiritual as well as medical ministry until the end of 1974 when Cheryl Bagdazarianz became very ill with cancer and they had to go home. They were replaced by the welcome arrival of Dr. and Mrs. Christian Klopfenstein.

One of the stresses over the years was the difficulty in keeping a full staff of nurses, and there were times when it was necessary to curtail the intake of patients to match their capabilities . The first African Nurse joined the staff in 1971. Martha Adjaoké, daughter of Pastor Augustin Adjaoké of Parakou, was a graduate of the Nurses Training School of Egbe, Nigeria, and her coming, along with short-term doctors, medical technicians plus summer volunteers added the extra

help to keep the hospital going in strength. Jim Longworth
became hospital administrator in 1975. His capable service
made for a smooth-running operation under difficult
circumstances.

As the tempo of the work increased over the years and
staff increased to meet the need, the hospital was a
tremendous power source for the spread of the gospel and
provided credibility with the government and validation with
the people.

Bariba Bible School: Jim Cail teaching

Chapter 34: Cotonou (1967)

1966   Perrier evangelistic campaign and outreach.

1967   Guest House and business office opened by Thamers.

1970   Bob and Carol Lee Blaschke take over for nine months.

1971   September, Mr. and Mrs. Carpenter administer Guest House and business office.
French ministries begun with Jean and Soula Isch.

1972   "Groupe Biblique de Jeunes de Cotonou" formed by Isches.
Edna McDougall arrives in February; reassigned to Niamey in November.

1974   Bob and Carol Lee Blaschke returned to Guest House.
Alan and Ruth Gibbs came to work at Youth Center in June.
Center moved to new location in July.
Name of center is changed to "Foyer Evangelique de la SIM".
Alan Gibbs lost his life in train accident November 6.

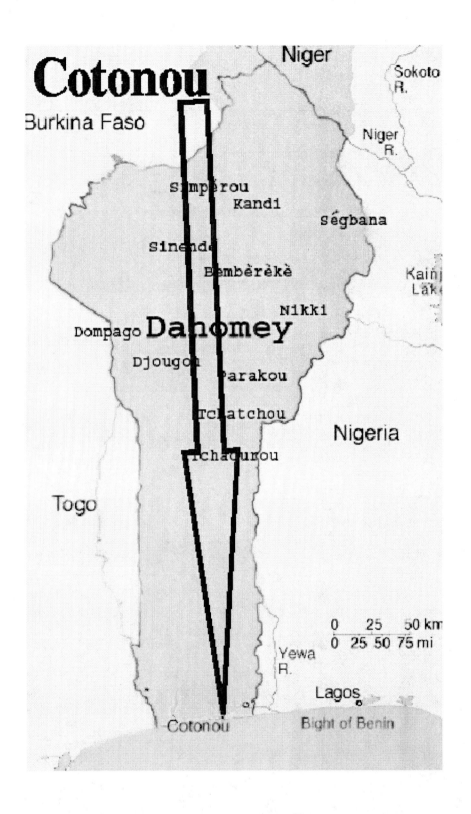

Cotonou

The McDougalls' final assignment in Nigeria was in the port city of Lagos in 1945. They knew that many young people from S.I.M.'s rural churches had moved to the capital city for education or jobs and were living there, so as they met them and moved among them they were impressed repeatedly with the needs in the cities.

Stewart wrote in a letter in November,1965:

> Ever since the beginning of our work in Dahomey we have sought to reach the masses. In the past 18 years our missionaries in Dahomey have reduced four unwritten languages to writing and have prepared primers and readers to train people to read in order that they might read the scriptures. We now have portions of the scriptures in all their languages. As the Lord gave us converts we have sought to teach them and have opened Bible Schools in the vernacular where national pastors have been trained to minister to these small groups of believers.

> We realize that in doing this we have neglected a small, but growing group of educated city people. I believe that this is possibly one failure in much of the work among primitive people. We have felt this for sometime, but have not known how to cope with it. Some months ago we were asked our opinion on the possibility of having a French Evangelist come over and hold meetings aimed at reaching these people. We felt that it was of the Lord and for the past 6 months have been working on plans for this. . . .

> Cotonou is a large port city and the largest city in Dahomey. There are 100,000 people there and, as most of the government offices are there, we will have a large potential audience. There has been a large letter response (from listeners in Cotonou to ELWA radio broadcast) and we feel that many who are regular listeners may, through a personal contact, make a decision for Christ.

> Earlier, under the French administration, the boundaries of our work was defined and Cotonou came under the influence of the Methodist Church. With the

coming of Independence (1960) these boundaries have
been removed and we are allowed to minister wherever
we wish.

The Mayor arranged for the crusade to rent the
Cultural Center for evangelistic meetings each evening from
February 6-20, 1966. The Methodist Mission and the Assembly
of God joined with them for this city-wide campaign. ELWA
Radio had been preparing the hearts of the people for many
years with their French radio broadcasts. Yves Perrier had
been an associate of S.I.M.'s radio station, ELWA, for a long
time and now the listeners would have the opportunity to meet
him personally. The campaign in Parakou was very well
attended with great responses, so the anticipation level of the
missionaries and volunteer workers was very high as they
came to Cotonou on the evening of February 4. Missionaries Al
Cross, Gus Fredlund, Alan Armbruster with the Perriers had
preceded the McDougalls to care for last minute preparations
for the campaign. The Perriers were housed at the Methodist
Mission and the rest of the party, including Arnold Leuders of
ELWA, shared a house with Stewart and Edna (a house lent to
them by the Assemblies of God). This became a precious family
time as missionaries shared together, prayed much and
rejoiced each evening over God's evident blessing.

There was great response during the first meetings.
Yves was not only very gifted but preached from a loving,
tender heart. When Yves and Françoise sang [words of
Psalm 23], everyone loved them. People were buying much
literature, Bibles, New Testaments, etc. About the great
response of these evenings, Arnold Leuders later remembered,
"It was a reliving of the early days of apostolic times." The days
were full and evenings were late after counseling all who
responded. All of them felt pressed for time but did agree they

should have lunch on the beach with a brief time to relax on the 11th. During the morning Stewart and Yves Perrier had an interview with Colonel Soglo, who had recently come into power after a coup. They presented him with a Bible which he graciously accepted. The missionaries enjoyed the beach and after lunch Al Cross and Gus Fredlund enjoyed the water, jumping in the waves. Stewart rolled up his pant legs and joined them. The three of them were about waist deep and letting the waves wash them in. Soon Al realized they had crossed the beaches and were being carried rapidly out to sea. Al had naval training and, taking charge, ordered, "Turn on your back and float and swim." Gus, a bit further out quietly said, "I can't float" and in a few minutes he was gone. Al's last picture of Stewart was of him calmly praying there in the water. Al decided to try to make shore and call for help. It took him about twenty minutes since the waves took him back continually. No one had heard his earlier calls for help. Both men were good swimmers and the missionaries on the beach were unaware of their danger until Al reached shore completely exhausted.

It took forever, it seemed, for help to come. The men had all gone to find some help. Edna was alone on the shore. Some nearby fishermen found a rope in Stewart's car and tied ropes around their waists and went after the bodies. After some time a Coast Guard Cutter came. It took a long time to get Gus' body in but they were able to bring Stewart in with his heart still beating, and missionaries worked over him. The men returned while Al Leuders was doing artificial respiration on Stewart. When it became clear to the men that a doctor was not going to come to the beach, they rushed Stewart to the hospital where they did all they could, but by 5 o'clock it was certain Stewart would not survive.

During the afternoon Gus' body had been found by a swimmer in a life-belt and a canoe brought his body ashore.

The American embassy did everything they could to help and sent their car with the embalmed bodies to Parakou. Alan Armbruster accompanied Edna as they followed after, arriving in Parakou 7:30 A.M. on Saturday, February 12. The missionaries in Cotonou had tried to charter a plane so they could speedily inform Alice Fredlund. Failing this, they proceeded by car to Kandi on their sad mission. Alice returned to Parakou with them.

The missionaries had all come to Parakou and the service for Gus and Stewart was held at 4:30 P.M. on Saturday.

The meetings in Cotonou were not continued because Yves Perrier had collapsed and was unable to carry on. Edna returned to Cotonou and was there when her eldest son, Colin, arrived from the U.S. on emergency leave from BIOLA College where he was teaching.

Previously, in 1965, Messrs. McDougall, Beacham and Cail had gone to Cotonou to locate property for an office and guest house so someone could be stationed there to care for the needs of missionaries coming and going. In 1967, Orville and Ethel Thamer relocated to Cotonou to be in charge. They cared for guests, took care of passports, visas, plane tickets, shipping, etc. until 1970 when they left to retire in Canada. Bob and Carol Lee Blaschke replaced the Thamers in September, 1970.

In fulfilling his many commissions, Bob was in and out of offices and stores most days where he left French scripture portions and a spoken word as opportunity allowed. A chauffeur opened his home for Bible Studies on Sunday mornings. American High School kids came on Monday evenings for supper and stayed for discussions. These were beginnings which would open doors to future outreach in the community.

In 1971, Bill Crouch reported that Jean and Soula Isch who had been serving at ELWA in Monrovia, Liberia, had expressed interest in working in a French speaking republic. They came to Cotonou in the spring and talked with the Blaschkes. Their vision for reaching the elite and students in Cotonou fit well with plans and desires of the mission, and the possibility of their coming was welcomed with enthusiasm. When they searched for and located a suitable property and proceeded to negotiate for it, they found it was only four hundred yards from the French school their children would attend.

The Isch family went on leave and returned to Cotonou to begin their ministry in September, 1971. Within the first week they were meeting with the young Christians who had been praying for a teacher. Within six months thirty-five to forty young people were meeting regularly in their living room for teaching and Sunday worship. The gatherings soon outgrew their home. They were able to move the meetings into rented quarters adequate for Sunday services, study groups, games and lending library. Edna McDougall had been in the U.S. for six years with her children and returned to Dahomey in February, 1972. She was assigned to Cotonou to work with women in the vernacular. When she found that her apartment was located in the same building with Jean and Soula, she was delighted and impressed that Isches had not waited until they had the Youth Center but reached out with open hearts and an open home from the beginning.

Jean first contacted people to measure the interest level by putting a questionnaire in postal boxes. He was encouraged when he received thirty responses. By April, 1972, the "Groupe

Biblique de Jeunes" was born, starting with five and building to twenty-five by June. Once a month an evangelistic rally was held in a hall loaned to them and four hundred attended the June Rally. One emphasis was on the distribution of Gospels and correspondence courses. Jean's stated objective was to "evangelize and train young people to win others to Christ."

Within the year, the Youth Center was functioning as a church. Jean instructed them to shoulder their responsibility explaining, "This is *your* work amongst *your* people—*you* must nurture it."

In 1972, the Carpenters were reassigned to the Guest House and office replacing Blaschkes, and Charles supervised the Cotonou ministries. He also continued having a small Sunday morning gathering in a courtyard near them.

The timing was not right for the women's work, and the strategy for reaching the city was not well enough articulated for her to function as anticipated. In November, 1972, Edna was asked to assist in the development of the newly appointed office of the Field Director for Francophone Africa and was moved to Niamey, Republic of Niger. Missionaries Don Smith and Phil Delsant carried on the Youth Centre ministry.

In 1974, two of the young people, Lucien Awo and Ephraïm Codjoseignon went for training in Centre Biblique de la SIM in Niamey, Niger so they could carry the pastoral responsibilities. Isches returned to France but the weekly Bible Studies continued. The believers witnessed in the civil prisons, and there was a thriving Sunday School and children's meeting with missionary Elisabeth Egloff instructing and overseeing. With missionaries and nationals working together the work continued to grow.

When Alan and Ruth Gibbs came in 1974, they opened the Center at a new location. The programs changed some as students began dropping in, stopping to read and ask questions. The name was changed to "Foyer Evangélique de la SIM". The average attendance per month for July through September of 1974 was eight hundred, but July had a high of 1302. This new location was good and the interest was great, drawing new people.

In November, Alan died in a train wreck on the return trip from meetings in the Centre Biblique in Niger leaving his wife, Ruth, and five children. Pastor Gabriel Doko was immediately assigned to the Youth Center and Ruth stayed to assist in the transition.

After a painful and costly beginning, foundations were being laid for a great future ministry in Cotonou, the capital and largest city in Dahomey.

UEEB Church leaders Bio Saka Solomon, Bio Darius, Gabriel Doko, David Atchadé, Madougou (1975)

Part IV:

Perspective: Thirty Years Later

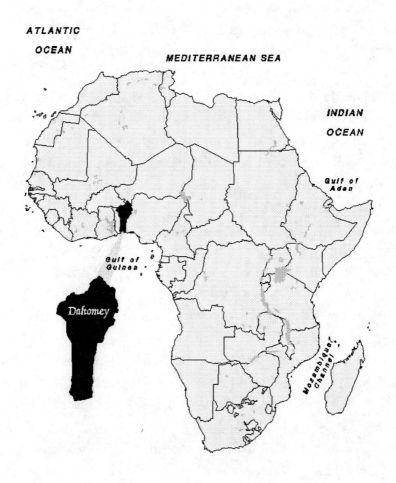

Good Night

In 1993, Edna moved from southern California to Robbinsville, North Carolina, to live with her son, Colin. The church in Benin celebrated its fiftieth anniversary in October, 1996, and invited Edna and other veteran missionaries to attend. She was able to go with the financial support of many friends and her home church, the Church of the Open Door, now in Glendora, California. An excerpt of her letter of thanks follows: "It also meant much to me for you to participate in the expenses of my trip to Benin. COD's interest, prayer, concern and financial support has undergirded me over many long years, beginning in the 1930's and continuing until today. The committee's wise counsel, encouragement and support through all these years gave strength and courage to keep going. The church has nurtured me and my family through three generations and into the fourth. So you are very precious to me though I have moved away. I'm interested in all your activities and pray often for you all." The dedication of the Bariba Bible was planned to coincide with the celebration but its arrival was delayed and was finally presented to the church on December 21, 1996.

Edna returned home to her thousands of letters, quarterly reports, minutes of meetings and documents with a renewed vigor and determination to complete her research and this book.

In March, 1997, Colin took her with him on a ministry trip to Canada so she could visit Stewart's family in British Columbia while he traveled to meet his speaking engagements. On March 2, during a McDougall family dinner in Maple Ridge, Edna suffered a mild stroke and was hospitalized. She

remained under the generous care of Stewart's family while
Colin completed his assignments. When they arrived back in
North Carolina, both of them realized that she could no longer
get the care she needed in the seclusion of the Smoky
Mountains and contacted S.I.M. about moving her to the
mission retirement village in Sebring, Florida.

Edna moved to her duplex apartment on Liberia Street
in Sebring in December, 1997, and worked on the research and
documentation for this project. In this endeavor, Dr. Jean
Soutar came from Canada to assist in organizing the material
for several weeks and Janet did most of the filing of data on
her many visits. On Sunday, September 4, 2003, Edna suffered
a powerful stroke and was airlifted to Tampa General Hospital.
She was returned to Sebring a week later and was admitted to
Kenilworth Care and Rehab Center where she remained until
her death early on Tuesday morning, May 4, 2004 at the age of
ninety. On Monday evening, she told her roommate, Tina
Koning, "Good night, I won't see you in the morning. I'm going
home to Jesus." And she did.

Her primary goal over the last twenty years of her life
was to provide the documentation of the history of the planting
of the church in Benin to the church for its encouragement and
growth. Her greatest fear was that she would die or become
incapacitated before being able to complete the project. Colin
assured her that if she did the research and provided her
perspective on the events in writing, he would write the book.
She did her work well and the book is now complete. However,
her goal was to present the account to the church in Benin
which will require the additional step of translating into and
publishing in French.

The U.E.E.B. in 2004

Although the church planting effort in Dahomey/Benin now has a history of almost sixty years, the church organization has been in existence only since 1975. The official name in translation is the "Union of Evangelical Churches of Benin." They now have over four hundred member churches served by one hundred twenty trained pastors and represented in unreached areas by over a dozen evangelists. In remote areas where there are no schools or government workers, services are conducted in the vernacular languages (about fourteen of them). In major population centers, worship services are conducted in two languages: Bariba/French or Fon/French or Lokpa/French, etc. in order to allow the maximum participation, especially of visitors. Almost every pastor services more than one church and growth in the number of churches continues at a greater rate than the training of pastors.

After independence, when the state threatened to take over all the mission properties, the S.I.M. deeded all properties including mission stations, churches, schools, dispensaries, and the hospital to the UEEB. However, since the mission strategy (and federation assignment) had been to plant churches in tribal areas where the population is engaged primarily in subsistence farming and hunting rather than among the professional classes in the cities, the churches have been unable to afford to maintain the buildings and programs they inherited. The church leaders were even taken to court because their pastors and evangelists were being paid less than minimum wage laws required. They were given waivers to the law because of their clergy status but lack of a financial base continues to hamper growth in the number of trained pastors and places the families of current pastors under enormous stress. Unfortunately, this keeps the church organization dependent upon the continuing assistance of missionaries and fails to fulfill the strategy objectives from the beginning of planting a fully independent, indigenous, mature church, able to send out missionaries itself. It also results in a lack of respect from missionaries and government officials for national church leaders and constant frustration for the leadership.

There are other complex issues at work. The UEEB has the same diversity of missionaries to deal with that mission leaders had: paople from eight or nine different countries, different theological traditions, cultural norms, personalities and professional interests besides having member churches worshiping in fourteen different languages. Attempts to promote unity by using 'French only' for Bible schools, church conferences and business meetings instead of having six or seven translators is opposed, not only by tribalists but also by missionary linguists who wish to preserve tribal and linguistic distinctives. The organization's attempts to finance any increase in the salaries of its pastors or the support of its Bible training schools will be determined by its ability to generate the support by the wealthier, professional member churches of the rural ones.

Public credibility will be more difficult. The UEEB's competition for building permits, schools, etc. is large religious organizations like the Catholics, the Methodists, the Muslims, etc. that get significant support for their operations from outside the country and build much more modern and attractive facilities. The UEEB's strength is its breadth of influence and its ownership of properties the early missionaries developed, however, these are also the areas of greatest challenge. For the church to realize its potential and the strategic objectives of the pioneer missionaries who planted it, the UEEB will need leaders with strong faith, creativity, stamina and a clear vision.

The SIM in Benin 2004

The SIM Prayer Guide for 2005 lists over forty missionaries assigned to Benin: ten to Bembèrèkè hospital and Bible School, the remainder to Theological Education by Extension, Christian Education, translation, language and literacy, radio and television, agricultural development and Fulani church development. The UEEB owns all former mission properties which it is unable to maintain without mission assistance. Since it was the mission's pioneer strategy to plant churches in the tribal areas that caused this imbalance, the mission is expected to keep the church afloat even though the arrangement is unhealthy for both its missionary staff and the leaders of the church organization. It is also mission strategy to see the church plant through to completion which must be measured by the UEEB being self-supporting, self-governing and fully able to evangelize the nation and reach beyond its borders to other nations.

It is difficult for missionaries to submit to the leadership of the UEEB in making decisions or to show them the deference due their offices when their house help (which must receive at least minimum wage) is paid a higher wage than church pastors and leaders. It is also difficult for church leaders to go hat in hand to missionaries living on their property to request copies to be made or to receive and send e-mails because they have no equipment in their offices. Bridging this gap may require more wisdom, patience and statesmanship than most of the previous challenges.

We're back to the question of the Igbaja elders. Where will the mission find the leadership necessary to effect the required changes among the largely professional missionary

staff and a maintenance-based set of operational guidelines?
How will executive action come from a representative
leadership functioning under managerial job descriptions? To
whom can the church turn to break the strategic impasse that
is the key to its future?

Personal Observations

SIM is a first class mission organization which finishes what it starts and cares for its missionaries and their families. I grew up through SIM schools and homes. My parents, siblings and my son have served under SIM. I appreciate all the mission does for its SIMKids but I have learned something valuable in this exercise: the best thing the mission can do for its adult children of missionaries is to validate the work for which they and their parents paid such a high price. Had someone asked me before writing this book, "What has the church plant in Benin cost you?" I would have had difficulty responding, not because I was unaware of the cost, but because every kid has trouble growing up and my childhood difficulties were not comparable to those of the thousands of kids I saw and many who were my friends. I accepted the fact that God is sovereign and also loving, so if He placed me in a missionary family, He would equip me to manage the liabilities and the assets for His glory. This book has helped me to articulate the cost.

I stated in the introduction that one of my prospective audiences I was my family but I have discovered that many of my MK cousins are eager to read the book to find similar resolution to their questions and for validation of their parents' service. In fact, it was after a phone conversation with a Dahomey MK that I arrived at the title, <u>Acceptable Costs</u>. I indeed found it to be so and pray that my MK friends will find it so as well. We needn't minimize the costs to make them acceptable.

I was also surprised by my own emotional involvement with the success of the church in Benin. When I was trying to contact the UEEB to arrange for the coming of Pastor Gabriel Doko and ran into the mission bureaucracy and business-like distance from the affairs of the church organization, I was angry. I asked myself, "What is the mission doing in Benin if its primary objective and occupation is not the church?" Of course, as I became more aware of the complexities, I became more rational about it, but the question remains.

Having served as the missions elder in a local church for many years and as the director of a missions organization, I have engaged in hundreds of discussions about the wisdom of sending financial assistance directly to any national church without appropriate accounting. Placing large sums of money under the control of poorly paid administrators has proven unwise in any context. There are also sound reasons for mission support of the national church with expatriate personnel but minimal financial resources. However, I (and many others) have a large investment in the success of this endeavor and want to see the job finished well. I hope this book will help to move the issue beyond discussion to effective resolution.

Jesus' expression to the Father (John 17:4) is instructive in this regard: "I have glorified You on the earth. I have finished the work which You have given me to do." The costs are acceptable only when the mission is accomplished. To God be the glory.

Finishing the Job

The primary objective of this project was to present the church in Benin with an eye-witness account of its beginnings. Unfortunately, merely completing this work in English will not achieve that objective.

When Edna McDougall died, the board of Eternal Truth Ministries of North Carolina, authorized the setting up of the "Benin Project" fund to facilitate the financing for the writing of this book and authorized my taking the time required to write and publish it. Many contributions were made which enabled the purchasing of the plane fare for Pastor Doko to come for a month. It also enabled the provision of a laptop computer set up to operate in French to enable the translation of the book into French for presentation to the Benin church.

Anyone wishing to participate in this ongoing project may do so by sending contributions made out to:

Eternal Truth Ministries
"Benin Project"
P.O. Box 1240
Robbinsville, North Carolina 28771

Letters of response, reaction and encouragement are also welcome.

Colin S. McDougall
President